The
Coaching at
Work Toolkit

A Complete Guide to
Techniques and Practices

The
Coaching at
Work Toolkit

A Complete Guide to
Techniques and Practices

Perry Zeus &
Suzanne Skiffington

The McGraw-Hill Companies, Inc.

Sydney New York San Francisco Auckland
Bangkok Bogotá Caracas Hong Kong
Kuala Lumpur Lisbon London Madrid
Mexico City Milan New Delhi San Juan
Seoul Singapore Taipei Toronto

McGraw·Hill Australia

A Division of The McGraw·Hill Companies

Reprinted 2005,2006
Text © 2002 Suzanne Skiffington and Perry Zeus
Illustrations and design © 2002 McGraw-Hill Australia Pty Ltd
Additional owners of copyright are acknowledged on the Acknowledgments page.

National Library of Australia Cataloguing-in-Publication data:

Zeus, Perry
 The coaching at work toolkit: a complete guide to techniques and practices

 Bibliography
 Includes index.
 ISBN 0 074 71103 2.

 1.Employees—Training of. 2. Organisational change. 3. Self-actualization (Psychology). I. Skiffington, Suzanne. II. Title.

658.312404

Published in Australia by
McGraw-Hill Australia Pty Ltd
Level2, 82 Waterloo Road, North Ryde NSW 2113
Acquisitions Editor: Javier Dopico
Production Editor: Alice Drew
Editor: Megan Lowe
Proofreader: Tim Learner
Indexer: Shirley Johnston
Internal design: Kimberly Taliai, blue orange
Cover design: Lucy Bal
Illustrator: Alan Laver, Shelley Communications
Typeset in Zurich Light Condensed 10.5/13.5pt by Kimberly Taliai, blue orange
Printed on 80 gsm woodfree by RR Donnelley in China.

About the Authors

Perry Zeus B.A., Fellow VAAR

In the 1980s Perry worked as a project and business development management consultant (both in the United States and Australasia). In the early 1990s, as an executive coach and management mentor, he conducted various specialist coaching clinics with a variety of professional groups including health care professionals and management consultants. In 1995 Perry teamed up with Dr Skiffington to create a coaching practice that spanned six countries. Perry and Dr Skiffington then went on to establish specialist coach training workshops. Perry is also the founder of the 1 to 1 Coaching School. As well as being the course registrar he is a sought after organisational tactical coach, facilitator and lecturer. He has written numerous articles on organisational coaching, co-authored *The Complete Guide to Coaching at Work* and now devotes much of his time to coaching research and development. His varied formal training includes financial accountancy, fine art, business management and workplace counselling.

Dr S. M. Skiffington B.A., MCP, PhD, MAPS, MISH

Dr Suzanne Skiffington has a doctorate in clinical psychology. In the early 1990s she delivered coaching seminars and workshops to hundreds of organisations and professionals. In 1998 she pioneered and published research on 'Towards a validation of multiple features in the assessment of negative emotions' that has stimulated new research and instrument development in this domain by personality and social psychologists. She is the world's leading educator in psychology-based, professional coaching, with a global delivery program from Australia to the United Kingdom, from Canada to Asia and the United States.

Over the last decade, working as an educator with Perry Zeus, she has provided specialist coaching services to clients around the world. She has accredited several hundred professionals involved in therapy, consulting, training and management on her successful personal change methodology and business practice. Her respect for the values of education, personal responsibility and accountability to clients is embedded in the philosophy of the school whose world-class standards attract the best students from around the world and celebrates a growing list of successful and influential alumni.

1 to 1 Coaching School and other coaching services

The 1 to 1 Coaching School provides a rigorous, personalised educational experience for busy professionals with demanding schedules by offering a focused, short-course structure. The one-to-one teaching and customised course format has created its own niche and is unique in the world of professional coach education.

The school is committed to being the world's leading provider of specialist business coaching education. It incorporates proven industry expertise, research facilities, academic and management resources in coach education, and the development of coaching systems, curricula tools and techniques. The 1 to 1 Coaching School has a close working relationship with some of the world's leading educational institutions, various professional coaching bodies and industry and its programs are tailored to meet the specific practice and business needs of each participant and the market/region they operate in.

Through two decades of research and practice, Perry Zeus and Dr Skiffington have created a unique coaching methodology, and the tools and standards of business practice for coaches. These world-class coaching processes are now taught and practised through their global coaching campus. Dr Skiffington's coaching education is unique because there are no classes, only a one-to-one dialogue between herself and the participant.

Global educational coaching services: (all courses can be 'delivered' to you where you live/work)

➤ *4 Day Certified Master Coach Course*   A unique, customised one-to-one or small group professional development program with Dr Skiffington. For: (1) professionals wishing to learn how to establish a successful coaching practice and receive instruction and practice in the relevant psychology-based behavioural change tools; (2) established in-house/external coaches working in an organisational environment who wish to learn how to use proven industry processes/behavioural change tools and business management practices that specifically relate to their working environment; and (3) life skills coaches who wish to learn how to use the latest behavioural tools, techniques and practice management strategies.

➤ *4 Day Internal Organisational Master Coach Course* (one-to-one or group)   For professionals who wish to learn: (1) how to use proven industry processes, behavioural change tools and business management practices that specifically relate to their working environment; and (2) how to design a coaching program and establish a coaching culture. Includes personal backup and support by Dr Skiffington.

➤ *2 Day Manager as Coach Course or 12 hour Comprehensive Leadership Workshop*   A one-to-one or group customised workshop that trains managers, supervisors and/or team leaders to: (1) learn the language of coaching; (2) develop their emotional competencies and interpersonal skills; (3) act as a supportive coach to those they manage in a way that builds relationships and accountability; and (4) learn how to use coaching as a vehicle for change and as a means to enhance personal, group and organisational performance. Includes two months of follow-on personal mentoring/support by Dr Skiffington.

➤ *Mentoring Program* (client management and business practice support)   This important but optional follow-up support service is personally provided by Dr Skiffington upon the completion of any of the above courses. The support can involve multiple levels of agreed upon assistance and guidance. It provides the glue to creating foundational strength and resilience in the mastery and practice of the coaching skills that have been learnt.

➤ *Coaching Clinic* (half day or full day, conducted by Dr Skiffington)   This is an introductory seminar or group workshop explaining the benefits of coaching as it relates to your organisation.

➤ *Specialty coaching workshops*   One and two day interactive, small group workshops to enable practising coaches to develop their coaching skills and techniques. The workshop titles are as follows:
 – Dealing with emotions in the coaching alliance
 – How to challenge and confront a coachee's self-limiting beliefs, emotions and behaviours
 – Dialoguing to engender trust, commitment and action
 – Enhancing self-awareness in the coach and coachee

➤ *Strategic Partnership Licence*   A five-day one-to-one course where a qualified individual, business or organisation is trained and licensed to supply Dr Skiffington's A+ Certified Coaching Course within their organisation or particular country and region. Includes backup and support by Dr Skiffington.

Global business coaching services:

➤ *Assessment* The first step prior to implementing a successful coaching program. On-site. For one or two days Dr Skiffington or a nominated other assesses your organisational coaching needs and recommends a suitable coaching program.

➤ *Evaluation* Are your coaching efforts taking you where you want to go? On-site. For two to four days Dr Skiffington or a nominated other evaluates your organisation's current coaching development processes to develop a 'best practice' gap analysis.

➤ *Online Coach Referral* Dr Skiffington's 1 to 1 Global Coaching Network provides a free search to find the organisational or executive coach best qualified to meet your needs.

➤ *Strategic Partnership Licence* (see above last bullet point in Global educational coaching services section).

For further information on the above, we encourage our readers to visit: **http://www.1to1 coachingschool.com** (for individuals) and **http://www.behavioral-coaching-institute.com** (for organisations).

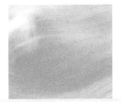

Contents

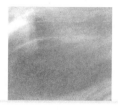

Preface

Coaching is a rapidly expanding business, second only to the IT industry in its growth rate in the United States. The industry comprises a large, disparate group of tens of thousands of service providers. As it develops and evolves, more and more coaching niche areas are opening up and coaches are adopting specialist roles in life skills coaching, executive coaching and business coaching. The profession continues to attract individuals from various backgrounds such as management, counselling, consulting and psychology, to name a few.

This book evolved from our work with coaches, organisations, educational institutions, and input from master coaches around the world. Our own practice also provided a great deal of impetus for the project. It is a coaching resource that provides assessment profiles, tools, and techniques for aspiring, novice and experienced coaches.

The purpose of this book is to firstly discuss coaching today—some of the issues facing the coaching profession as well as some misconceptions about coaching. We examine the challenges created by change in organisations, and provide guidelines to help develop an organisational coaching program. We also discuss the process of coaching, that is, the steps involved in the establishment, development and progression of the coaching partnership.

The main body of the book presents the tools and techniques we have used, some of which we have developed over a decade of working effectively with coaches in the process of coaching. We explore assessment instruments and methods of evaluation, and offer guidelines on how to use techniques such as: dealing with emotions, inducing self-awareness, working with self-limiting beliefs, dialoguing and problem solving. Finally, we explore some of the future trends in coaching, particularly the issues facing the coaching profession such as credentialling.

The corporate coaching profession of today is a vastly different business service provider from its predecessor of five years ago. Client requirements, including advanced coaching education, proven methodologies, and validated tools and techniques, will be even greater over the next five years.

Coaching is both a practice based in psychology and a psychological process involving behavioural change. Regardless of the particular area a coach may be working in, all coaches require training and practice in the use of the assessment instruments, tools and techniques used to facilitate the coachee's learning and change. This book is a resource guide for the use of these psychological tools and techniques which require training, supervision and practice.

PART ONE

Coaching—
the new technology for learning and change

Coaching at work today

Today, coaching is no longer regarded as just a fad, or the latest trend in management. Neither is it seen as a 'feel-good' exercise unrelated to business. Coaching is increasingly recognised as a methodology for creating more effective conversations, for assessing and reformulating values and goals, and reaching solutions. Coaching is also evolving as a natural form of leadership.

A 1999 survey of human resource professionals found that 90 per cent of companies in the United States offer some form of coaching to their key executives. Some of the areas in which coaching was employed include:

➤ leadership development

➤ retention of top staff

➤ management succession planning

➤ ensuring success after promotions or new hires.

The increasing popularity of coaching is partly related to the perceived need for companies to develop opportunities for promotion in order to retain top talent who can drive and expand the business. Coaching aids staff retention and staff retention is a function of good management and good leadership skills. Yet poor communication skills are the number one problem of senior executives. As discussed in Chapter 2, retention of key staff is one of the greatest challenges facing companies today. The costs of staff recruitment and training have increased dramatically over the past few years. In a climate where the quality of a company's products and services are seen as reflecting the company's interpersonal skills between its employees, coaching can turn some companies around.

Today, public organisations are also subjected to massive and unprecedented change. Because, historically, these companies have been quite stable, with only incremental change, they have a limited capacity to create and manage rapid change. Coaches assist public organisations to communicate and relate in a way that engenders commitment, responsibility and accountability.

Coaching has also moved beyond the territory of Fortune 500 companies. Entrepreneurs, manufacturing industries, small businesses and public organisations are adopting coaching as a means to develop and drive business. Entrepreneurs, especially in the high-tech area, are working with coaches to develop feedback systems, to communicate ideas and to delegate responsibility and manage staff.

Some general benefits of coaching

In our previous book, *The Complete Guide to Coaching at Work*, we noted the scarcity of empirical research on the effectiveness of coaching. While the need for further studies into all aspects of coaching still remains, there is more statistical data available now than ever before. For instance, Manchester Consulting Inc. conducted what is believed to be the first major research project to quantify the business impact of executive coaching. In a study of 100 executives who had completed a coaching program between 1996 and 2000, they found that the estimated return on investment (ROI) was 5.7 times the initial investment outlay. And because the business market is now better informed and more sophisticated, business is demanding that coaching show a return on investment. Other less tangible business impacts of coaching included:

➤ improved teamwork

➤ improved relationships with peers

➤ improved job satisfaction

➤ reduced conflict.

A study by Gegner explored the outcomes of the coaching process from an interpersonal and intrapersonal perspective. As a result of coaching, executives reported that they had become more aware of self and others and that they assumed more responsibility for their actions. They all reported positive changes in performance.

Management generally is aware of the benefits of coaching. It is increasingly recognised that individuals and groups perform better with coaching and that this performance translates into business results. Some of the specific ways in which coaching is beneficial include the following:

➤ Coaching for leadership increases productivity, improves communications, increases staff commitment and loyalty, and decreases levels of stress and tension within companies.

➤ Coaching assists individuals to remain loyal and committed to the company in the face of demanding global business hours, language barriers, differing work ethics and economic fluctuations.

➤ Coaching can help prevent executive derailment. Some studies suggest this can be as high as 33 per cent for senior executives.

➤ Coaching helps managers to develop better interpersonal skills. Some common reasons for interpersonal conflict include executives that are too abrasive, too controlling and too isolated. Coaches work with executives to explore these behaviours, and to recognise and modify their self-defeating beliefs, assumptions and actions.

➤ Coaching helps leaders to think and plan more strategically, to manage risk more effectively and to create and communicate vision and mission.

➤ Coaching aids in developing a culture of trust and personal responsibility within the organisation, and with clients and customers.

➤ Coaching enables executives or managers to use their personal power more effectively.

➤ Coaching can develop those leadership qualities that have been empirically proven to be associated with success. These include cognitive capacity, social capacities, personality style, motivation, knowledge and expertise.

On a more specific level, coaching provides an answer to some of the new challenges facing today's leaders. It allows leaders to:

➤ recognise any new competencies they should be learning

➤ reflect on the leaders of tomorrow and prepare them for the challenge

➤ align their personal commitments and actions

➤ sustain momentum—both theirs and that of others in the organisation

➤ align team members with the goals and visions of their organisation

➤ develop team unity and team spirit and enrol others in new possibilities and breakthroughs

➤ help others expand their levels of responsibility and increase their levels of initiative and creativity

➤ recognise weak links in the organisational system and develop strategies to strengthen these

➤ review the organisation's goals—can the leader aim higher and be more successful?

Large-scale coaching interventions today generally use the remedial, performance coaching/ workplace counselling model, for example coaching in sales and customer satisfaction. This model remains essentially a training one although it includes follow-up and is therefore called coaching. Executive and business coaches are often employed to first work in a remedial capacity before they are invited or contracted to prove their sensitivity and skills with senior managers and at a broad organisational level.

Most coaches cannot expect to be invited to work with senior executives as their first introduction to an organisation. Trust has to be established. The private conversation that is coaching still goes against the grain of many organisations where open discussions are the rule, or at least the espoused theory. Although the privacy of coaching is one of its major attractions and one of the reasons for its effectiveness, some organisations still view coaching with mistrust. They are afraid they may lose confidential information about the organisation, or lose the coachee. Therefore, it is wise for a coach to adopt an incremental approach when introducing coaching into an organisation. It has to prove itself to all responsive stakeholders. It takes time before the coach is able to work with senior managers and CEOs to develop their strengths and explore their weaknesses.

Some misconceptions about coaching

1 Workplace counselling is coaching

Many organisations and HR personnel report that they utilise coaching when in fact what they are employing is an outdated, traditional counselling model. Research (and our experience) shows the following similarities and differences between the two models.

➤ Both involve a client–practitioner model that focuses on the performance and functioning of the individual.

➤ Both build rapport and use advanced listening, questioning and reflecting skills.

➤ Both use goal setting and action planning.

However, the differences between the two approaches are significant. These include:

➤ The counselling model generally follows a remedial approach that emphasises deficits and the problems involved with not meeting a set, required standard of conduct. Coaching emphasises empowerment, strengths and achievements and how the coachee can use these effectively to grow and develop.

➤ There is a greater power differential in counselling. The employee has the problem and the manager/counsellor is an expert who will 'fix' him or her. Coaches are not experts, but guides and resource providers.

➤ Counselling focuses on exploring reactive behaviours and changing these. Coaching is proactive—it aims to recognise and solve problems before they arise.

➤ Counselling is needs based and occasional, coaching involves ongoing development.

2 The coach is a business expert

Coaches are not experts in all areas of business. Of course some coaches who work in organisational settings may be experts in business but this is not generally the case. The coach is an expert in the use of behavioural change tools and techniques. Coaches are resource people rather than experts or gurus. They assess the individual's or the organisation's needs. Then, drawing from their extensive coaching toolkit, and research, they provide clients with the necessary resources to enable them to meet their stated goals.

3 Coaching doesn't require specialist training

Coaching involves bringing about profound changes in thinking and behaviour. It is not something that can be just an 'add on' to any practitioner's existing services. Although coaches may have received initial training when acquiring coaching skills, they need to continuously update and develop these skills in order for them to be truly effective. Coaching is a profession, and like all established professions it requires extensive training and supervision. Coaches, especially, require one-on-one supervised training by a clinician in the instruction and practice of using tools and techniques to produce sustained behavioural change. Our coach training and specialty workshops grew out of the recognised need for coaches to have individualised training and practice in working with various psychology-based coaching techniques such as dialoguing, working with emotions, self-awareness, and challenging and confronting self-limiting beliefs and behaviours.

The history of coaching

The word 'coach' first occurred in English in the 1500s. It referred to a particular kind of carriage that transported people from one place to another. Of course today the idea of coaches 'carrying' individuals is diametrically opposed to the underlying philosophy of coaching which is based on an active, collaborative partnership. In the 1850s the word coach was used in English universities to refer to a tutor or person who helped students prepare for examinations. However, the notion of a passive passenger can be seen again in the 1930s and 1940s in the form of an individual who was assisted by a mentor in becoming all that the mentor thought they should be.

Coaching as an aspect of business management was first introduced into management literature in the 1950s as a management skill. Life skills coaching began as an educational program for disadvantaged individuals in New York in the 1960s. The program, with the addition of problem-solving skills, was transported to Canada. Here, life skills coaching and business coaching fused. For the first time, coaching was acknowledged as a profession with widespread training and credentials for coaches. Indeed, in many respects Canada continues to lead the way in life skills coaching. However, until the 1980s, coaching did not receive much attention in business literature or in the business world. In the 1980s, as an outgrowth of leadership programs, the concept of 'executive coaching' began to emerge as a new and powerful discipline.

Coaching today derives many of its principles, even practices, from sports psychology. Some of the specific applications of sports psychology to business, executive and life skills coaching include:

➤ examining values—those of the individual and team members

➤ developing vision

➤ goal setting

➤ visualisation or mental rehearsal before an important event

➤ centring and maintaining focus

➤ working with and managing negative or self-limiting beliefs.

There are several reasons behind the rise in the popularity of coaching. First, the business world is characterised by increasing turbulence and massive changes. These changes have resulted in a recognised need for leadership and guidance from professionals who can support, encourage and help individuals and organisations to master changes and succeed in an increasingly competitive and challenging world. Second, the managed care revolution of the 1980s brought about a decline in income for therapists, many of whom are now applying their skills in the corporate arena. Third, the rise in a sports consciousness, and the recognition of the sports coaches' contribution to sporting success, has also fuelled the boom in business coaching and life skills coaching.

Finally, and importantly, more and more organisations are recognising that the training and learning cycle is incomplete. Learning is not sustained unless individualised follow-up is incorporated into a training program. For example, recent studies suggest that without follow-on coaching 87 per cent of new skills learned will be lost. Typically, and this is common across many organisations, individuals revert to old ways when the new skills prove too difficult or awkward to use. It is now widely recognised that coaching can prevent this slippage.

Today, business organisations and educational institutions, such as the Harvard School of Business, recognise the relationship between coaching and leader effectiveness. Furthermore, as discussed in more detail in the following chapter, the relationship between managerial coaching skills and employee retention is gaining increasing recognition.

The literature on coaching continues to proliferate and emphasise niche coaching areas such as coaching for leadership, executive coaching, coaching for change and coaching as a management skill. Some of the leading authors/experts who have contributed to the current wealth of knowledge on coaching today include: Laura Divine, James Flaherty, Marshall Goldsmith, Richard Kilburg, Mary Beth O'Neill, David Petersen, Jim Selman, Robert Witherspoon and publications from The Center for Creative Leadership and The Hudson Institute.

The philosophical underpinnings of coaching today

While, from a practical point of view, coaching has historically been influenced by adult learning and sports psychology, psychological and philosophical theories have also played a part. In our coach training workshops, we explore the following theoretical influences on coaching.

Humanism

Coaching ascribes to the humanist notion that man is the measure of all things. The dignity and value of the individual is uppermost and human needs assume priority over material things. Abraham Maslow and Carl Rogers are associated with the humanist approach to therapy and coaching adopts many of their principles. For instance, coaching is about 'self-actualisation' and the individual's need for self-fulfilment, the realisation of full potential, self-expression, accomplishment and growth.

We believe that although coaching does subscribe to Rogers' notion of a 'client-centred approach' and 'unconditional acceptance' of the coachee, this should not produce a passive acceptance of the coachee's experiences. The coach does not simply listen and reflect back. The coach's role is to challenge and confront a coachee when necessary. Interestingly, in our coach training programs with therapists, we have found the issue of challenging and confronting the coachee to be difficult for many.

Existentialism

Coaching also derives several of its fundamental premises from existential traditions in philosophy and psychology. A central idea of existentialism, as Sartre proposed, is that we are essentially free and responsible for finding out who we are and what to do with our lives. Our behaviour is always a choice and we can always resolve to change. The concepts of choice and responsibility are central to coaching. The coaching alliance will not prosper if the coachee does not make a commitment to change his or her world views, self-limiting beliefs or self-defeating actions. Furthermore, unless the coachee is willing to assume responsibility for his or her choices and actions, no real sustainable changes will be made.

The ontological model of coaching derives in part from existentialist tenets. It emphasises making the coachee's 'structure of interpretation', or the way he or she views the world, explicit and accessible. According to this approach, it is the way we view the world that determines our actions at any one time. The coach uses language, in the form of listening and questioning, so that the coachee can make new observations and new interpretations. When these occur, new actions can follow.

Some models, such as that proposed by Divine and Flaherty (1998) attempt to understand the coachee's structure of interpretation in three domains. These are the 'I' domain (the internal world), the 'we' domain (the interpersonal world) and the 'it' domain or external world. Each domain requires particular leadership qualities and skills, and coaching focuses on building and developing these competencies.

Eastern influences

Various aspects of coaching are influenced by Eastern philosophy. Management and coaching books, for example, employ the samurai metaphor for the relationship between the coach and the coachee. The notion of living in 'the now' or 'the continuous present' manifests in the coach's emphasis on 'what is happening now' for the coachee. Other fundamental concepts of coaching which reflect Eastern philosophy, particularly Zen thought, include the belief that all individuals are in possession of what they need to know. Coaching is also seen as a means of clearing out or helping the coachee discard old beliefs, reactions and behaviours that are blocking clarity and progress. When the coach and coachee focus on the present, with their minds uncluttered by problems or solutions, they are able to dialogue, plan and act in a more spontaneous, effective manner.

Constructionism

Constructionism, or the idea that there is no single, true interpreter or interpretation of reality, underscores some of the fundamental principles and practices of coaching. According to this approach, meaning is only known through our social interactions and through negotiation with each other and the world. Knowledge is created or 'constructed' out of conversations and we have no other direct access to reality other than through language.

Coaching, as we maintain throughout our books, is a dialogue. It is a process whereby the coach and coachee construct the problem and the solution using language. Coaching recognises that there are always alternative ways of viewing the world and that the coachee is not limited through his or her history from adopting new and more useful interpretations of self and the 'problem'. Coaching deals with the individual coachee's experiences and highlights the importance of co-creating (with the coach) a new and more empowering reality.

Coaching in relation to other professions

In our first book we distinguished between coaching and other, related professions such as training, consulting, mentoring and therapy. Here, we shall briefly discuss coaching in terms of its similarities to consulting, therapy and mentoring, with an emphasis on how coaching draws from these disciplines. To a certain extent, we believe coaching is a synthesis of the best these professions have to offer. Coaching however is a profession with a difference, and it is critical that it does not lose its distinctiveness by becoming synonymous with these other disciplines.

Coaching and consulting

It is sometimes difficult to distinguish between consulting and coaching. For instance, coaches may work with leaders in organisations on strategic issues and changes to systems and processes. These technical or operational mastery skills have historically been the domain of consultants. The competencies necessary for these tasks include a recognition and understanding of systems functioning, project management, aligning stakeholders, advocacy and visioning. Some coaches consider these roles to belong solely to consultants. Other coaches appear to move freely from consulting to coaching, depending on the client's needs.

More and more consultants are adopting a coaching role in organisations. We have noticed a definite global trend in the past few years in which increasing numbers of consultants are enrolling in our coach training programs. Consequently, there will be future issues that coaches will need to address regarding coaching as a stand-alone discipline and the question of credentials. We shall return to these matters in the final chapter where we discuss future trends in coaching.

Coaching and therapy

Coaching, like therapy, is clearly a psychological process. When a coach is dealing with the inner psychological world of the coachee, he or she is functioning within the realm of therapy. Trained psychologists and therapists may feel comfortable in this arena. However, if trained psychologists and therapists wish to explore the coachee's inner world, it is important that they clarify with the coachee that they are in fact moving into a therapeutic role. In our experience, it requires considerable skill to move in and out of a therapy framework. Boundaries and limits have to be redefined, and the emotional intensity of the interaction is heightened. It can prove confusing to the coachee. In most cases, it is wiser to refer the coachee to an external therapist.

Coaches who are not trained psychologists or therapists are duty bound to refer out a coachee who has recognisable psychological and emotional issues. The coach's major challenge is to recognise when the coachee would benefit from therapy. Suggesting that a coachee seek therapy can damage the coaching relationship, especially if the coachee feels this is unwarranted. Of course, the repercussions for not referring the individual to a therapist have to be considered. We suggest that it is crucial that all coaches align themselves with a clinical psychologist or a trained psychotherapist with whom they can discuss a coachee's need or suitability for therapy.

We shall now briefly describe some of the shared aspects between coaching and one type of therapy model, solution-focused therapy (SFT)—which is perhaps the therapy most closely aligned to coaching.

➤ Both recognise the critical role of trust and commitment in the partnership. Techniques are important but likely to prove ineffective in the absence of a genuine, trusting, caring relationship.

➤ Both are focused on building upon the client's own strengths, competencies and resources. It is assumed that the client has the answers within himself or herself. Answers or solutions will emerge from the client's own repertoire of skills through the language of questioning, listening, guidance, support and mutual problem solving.

➤ Both recognise that all clients have the potential for growth and self-discovery.

➤ There is always an expectancy of change.

➤ The partnership can require the therapist or coach to be supportive, directive, challenging and confronting when necessary.

➤ The client's definition of the problem or issue provides the agenda for problem solving.

➤ The focus of both disciplines is clear, attainable goals.

➤ Both assume that we often understand the past by reflecting on the present and the future rather than by a direct and lengthy historical investigation.

➤ Both underscore the importance of the client's choice and responsibility regarding change.

➤ Both view resistance as something that can be worked with.

Coaching then is similar in many respects to solution-focused therapy. We do not believe that all coaches have to be psychologists. However, as we reiterate throughout this book, coaching is change and change is a psychological process. The coach has to understand the psychological aspects of coaching and be confident and competent to deal with these. To do so requires training and supervision by a clinician.

Coaching and mentoring

The terms 'mentoring' and 'coaching' are sometimes used interchangeably. In some organisations, mentoring is being relabelled as coaching although the old style of passing on knowledge, skills and experience remains unchanged. Today, many organisations seek outside mentors—experienced individuals who can work with newly appointed leaders or leaders in transition to help develop and guide their careers. A mentor is an advisor, a guide who can assist an individual to learn faster and more effectively than he or she might do alone. To do this successfully mentors employ a range of coaching skills. Creating a trusting, committed partnership is as crucial to mentoring as it is to coaching. Furthermore mentoring, like coaching, involves continuous and long-term learning within a supportive environment.

As we discussed in our first book mentors, like coaches, work with the coachee's agenda in the context of the organisation's agenda. They employ honest and authentic dialogue to clarify issues and seek solutions. Although they may give more advice and be more directive than a coach, successful mentors couch their language in such a way that the individual receives the advice in the form of a suggestion or a possibility. Mentoring is a partnership where both individuals work together to develop and enhance the full potential of the client.

A coach who has worked with a coachee for a considerable period of time may adopt a mentoring role once the formal coaching program has ended. The coach no longer adheres to the coaching process of setting goals and action plans but acts more as an advisor to the coachee. In this role the coach supports and encourages the coachee and offers professional and tactical advice as the need arises.

Who can coach?

Coaching is the number one home-based profession according to the American magazine *Start-ups*. Although it is still a growing discipline, coaching has emerged as a legitimate profession. However, while there is certainly a broad consensus on the benefits of coaching there is little agreement as to who can coach. There are no worldwide standards and criteria against which to judge a coach's competencies. There are numerous coaching schools and associations but none that are recognised and joined by all coaches. Of course standardisation and the establishment of credentials is difficult in a profession which attracts practitioners from such varied disciplines as consulting, psychology, therapy, training, education and business. Individuals bring their own competencies and ethics from their own professional backgrounds. We shall return to this topic in the final chapter.

As coach educators, we are frequently asked to nominate the attributes of a successful coach. We consider the following to be a useful guideline.

Checklist

- ☐ If the coach is working within an organisational environment, he or she requires experience in organisational and individual problem solving, planning and evaluation.

- ☐ Working in organisations also requires a broad knowledge of theory and practice in organisational systems and behaviour, and group processes.

- ☐ All coaches require training in the knowledge, skills and abilities necessary to perform their job properly.

- ☐ All coaches require a working model of change and the change process.

- ☐ Regardless of which area the coach works in, he or she requires excellent communication skills, such as dialoguing, listening and questioning with the intent to understand rather than be directive or impose solutions.

- ☐ All coaches should have an understanding of human development.

- ☐ All coaches require an understanding of adult learning principles.

- ☐ Self-awareness and recognition of one's strengths and limitations are essential for all coaches.

- ☐ The ability to establish and build an open, empathic, trusting and committed partnership is at the core of every coaching alliance.

- ☐ Coaches require the ability to make commitments, persevere, and follow through on them.

- ☐ Coaches have to understand that transition is a process that takes time and requires patience and empathy on the part of both the coach and coachee.

- ☐ Coaches require knowledge of the appropriate assessment, measurement and feedback instruments.

- ☐ Coaches have to have the knowledge, skills and ability to challenge the coachee's self-limiting beliefs, feelings and behaviours.

Coaching practice niche areas

Our experience shows that as coaching becomes recognised as a legitimate profession, there is a growing move towards specialisation within the field. In the early days of coaching there was a greater emphasis on the actual process of coaching. Indeed, it was once thought that a skilled coach could apply this process in any coaching area, be it life skills coaching, executive coaching or business coaching.

Despite moves towards specialisation, there is still no real consensus when it comes to defining the various types of coaching, their areas of application or the requisite coaching competencies. For instance, some coaches call themselves business coaches and work solely with executives and leaders. Other business coaches work solely with entrepreneurs and small business owners. Some coaches classify themselves as executive coaches and only work on a one-to-one basis with executives and leaders while others work within the broader organisational realm. Discussed below are the three major areas of coaching as we see them today.

Executive coaching

Executive coaching is an individualised, one-to-one relationship designed to assist executives in developing and enhancing their professional effectiveness and on-the-job performance. The executive receives comprehensive feedback from a multitude of sources and the coach and executive work together to develop strategies, alternatives and options to deal with nominated issues. The following is a list of some of the major intervention areas of executive coaching:

➤ helping the individual executive who requires new skills for a new position due to a change in organisational structure

➤ working with the manager being groomed for promotion

➤ coaching high performing executives whose personality style impacts negatively on their relationship with peers, staff and clients

➤ working with executives wishing to develop their career paths and prospects

➤ coaching as a follow-on from 360-degree performance appraisals

➤ increasing the executive's capacity to manage an organisation—planning, organising, controlling, visioning, developing others, etc.

➤ increasing the executive's psychological and personal mastery skills such as self-awareness, recognition of 'blind spots', defences and limiting thoughts, and emotional effectiveness

- improving the executive's balance between work and life demands

- improving the executive's leadership, management and team-building skills

- coaching an executive to work more effectively within a changing organisational structure

- working with a leader to coach others in transition.

Some coaching tools, techniques and interventions for executive coaching

Assessment techniques

- Personality style, job profile, leadership competencies, managerial competencies, self-awareness, values and learning styles (see Chapter 4 for assessment profiles)

- Coaching needs analysis—for organisational assessment

Interventions

- Communication skills training and practice

- Skill development—rehearsal, practice and feedback

- Conflict management

- Delegation

- Negotiation

- Group or team coaching

- Self-regulation of emotions

- Challenging and confronting beliefs, behaviours and response patterns that are limiting the individual's growth

- Clarification of goals, vision and the individual's communication of these

- Exploring and developing more effective interpersonal relationships

Tools to use

- Brainstorming and problem solution generation

- Self-monitoring

- Journalling

- Benchmarking and evaluation of coaching interventions

- Direct observation

- Shadowing

Executive coaches may be in-house or external. As noted in our first book, we have found Witherspoon's typology of executive coaching to be comprehensive. He classifies four types of executive coaching:

1   *Coaching for skills*   In coaching for skills the executive learns specific skills, abilities and perspectives over a period of several weeks or months. The skills to be learned are usually clear at the outset and are typically associated with an executive assuming new or different responsibilities.

2   *Coaching for performance*   This type of coaching focuses on the executive's effectiveness in his or her current position. Frequently it involves coaching for one or more management or leadership competencies, such as communicating vision, team building or delegation.

3   *Coaching for development*   Coaching interventions that explore and enhance the executive's competencies and characteristics in order to develop them for a future job or role come under this type of coaching. It can be associated with outplacements, restructuring and re-engineering in the organisation.

4   *Coaching for the executive's agenda*   This type of coaching generally entails working with an executive on any personal or organisational concerns he or she may have. It can focus on issues surrounding the executive, such as change and company downsizing. Personal issues are more likely to arise in this type of coaching.

Business coaching

The boundaries between executive and business coaching remain unclear. Some classifications even nominate a separate category for organisational coaches. Business coaches may be in-house or external, although they usually function as an external service provider. Generally, business coaches tend to work on issues of operational mastery such as:

➤   organisational restructuring

➤   establishing a coaching culture, for example managing a pilot coaching program

➤   strategic planning

➤   performance management appraisals

➤   developing change initiatives

➤   establishing approaches to deal with resistance to change

➤   business rejuvenation and growth

➤   succession planning

➤ identifying critical issues in the organisation

➤ improving the work climate and morale of groups

➤ working with individuals and groups in transition.

Business coaches sometimes work on a one-to-one basis with managers and leaders on personal mastery skills and adopting a coaching style of management. Some of these areas of expertise include leadership support while a new team is being assembled, effective delegation, conflict mediation, and managing workload stress during transition. It appears that the extent to which a coach is engaged in business or executive coaching is often a function of the breadth of the coaching assignment.

Business coaches also work with entrepreneurs, with start-up businesses, family businesses and small- to medium-sized businesses to grow and expand their services. When working in these arenas there is frequently not a great deal of separation between the business and the person. The owner/manager is the business. In this role the business coach specialises in some of the following areas:

➤ establishing business and marketing plans

➤ sales coaching

➤ clarifying the future direction of the business

➤ prioritising goals and developing strategies to achieve these within a nominated time frame

➤ working with difficult employees

➤ encouraging, developing and retaining top employees

➤ dealing with conflict—with staff and with customers

➤ enhancing customer satisfaction

➤ streamlining business processes and systems

➤ networking

➤ identifying new target markets

➤ negotiating skills—with internal staff, external clients and customers

➤ time management

➤ balancing life and work issues

➤ working with the dynamics of family-owned businesses.

Personal or life skills coaching

Today life skills or personal coaching is widespread and focuses primarily on personal growth and development issues outside of an organisational context. The life coach works with individuals who want to change and grow, to restructure or improve their lives, to work through transitions and to find fulfilment and balance.

Life skills coaching emphasises the role of continuous learning in the individual's life. Coaches assist individuals to learn new skills, to learn about themselves and others and to adopt strategies that allow them to live the life they choose with purpose and joy. Life skills coaching is a collaborative relationship between the coach and coachee that promotes the coachee's overall wellbeing and enjoyment of life.

Clients frequently approach life skills coaches when they are in the midst of a transition. Coaches work with individuals through the various transition stages to accept life change as an ongoing process, a journey that has no end until death. Some areas of life transition include early adolescence, the adult years, middle age, pre-retirement, retirement, and coaching for the final transition.

In some respects, life skills coaches can work with individuals on any aspect of their lives. However, the following is a broad summary of the specific areas in which life skills coaches operate. These include:

➤ clarifying vision and life purpose

➤ establishing life goals—both short- and long-term

➤ enhancing health, for example developing and maintaining an exercise program, practising relaxation and other stress reduction techniques

➤ developing self-awareness and insight which can be fostered through creativity, journalling, reading and cultural pursuits

➤ clarifying career choices

➤ working with the coachee to foster curiosity, insight and self-regulation techniques that contribute to emotional growth and more satisfying intrapersonal and interpersonal experiences

➤ clarifying the coachee's spiritual beliefs and values

➤ increasing the amount and quality of leisure activities

➤ enjoying a fulfilling and meaningful retirement

➤ enhancing the quality of the coachee's relationships through the recognition and development of trust and commitment both within and beyond the coaching partnership

➤ setting and reaching life goals

➤ financial planning

➤ pursuing educational goals

➤ exploring and developing techniques to establish and maintain a greater sense of life/work balance.

Part of the coach's role involves working with the coachee to accept that one is not able to maintain a predictable and static life balance. Rather, the coachee develops attitudes and skills to allow flexibility and the ability to adapt to the rapidly changing demands of life.

Coaching models

Coaching encompasses numerous and varying models. Many coaches adopt an eclectic approach to the models and frameworks that underpin their practice. Coaching demands flexibility and not all models are appropriate for all coaching interventions. The following discussion offers a broad overview of some current coaching models employed by life skills or personal coaches, executive coaches and business coaches. We suggest a holistic approach to coaching can incorporate many of the features of these models.

1 *Appreciative inquiry (AI)*   Developed by David Cooperrider, AI is a relatively new approach to coaching. AI's fundamental premise is that coaching should focus on an individual's strengths, resources, competencies and opportunities, rather than on the problem. It emphasises the coachee's ability to reflect on and solve his or her own issues. According to this approach, learning cannot occur in the absence of affirming and reinforcing the individual's strengths and achievements. The coach guides and helps the coachee to accept, manage, reframe and resolve the paradoxes he or she confronts.

2 *Reflective coaching*   This model assumes that the coaching partnership is about helping executives to reflect on their own issues rather than helping fix them. Executives frequently are expected to have all the answers. Reflective coaching allows the executive to have an 'I don't know' mind and to reflect deeply on his or her situation without having to come up with an answer. Coachees already have what they need to resolve their own issues. The coach and coachee engage in a collaborative relationship where the coach may challenge the coachee's basic assumptions and frames of reference.

3 *Observational coaching*   This approach usually involves three phases:
  ➤ Phase one *Observation and data collection*—Observation can involve self-monitoring or direct observation of the coachee's performance. The coach can shadow the coachee while he or she is performing specific work functions. The coach observes the coachee

and gives direct and constructive feedback, either on the spot (live coaching) or immediately after the event. Data can also be gathered from 360-degree performance appraisals or surveys.

➤ Phase two *Analysis*—The data is analysed in such a way as to nominate and clarify pertinent coaching issues.

➤ Phase three *Formulation of strategies and action plans*—Strategies and action plans are constructed and put in place to achieve the goals and desired outcomes established in the second phase. In many respects, most coaching interventions are built upon an observational model.

4   *Business practice coaching*   This refers to the methodology a business coach employs when working with individuals trying to establish and develop a business. It is a particular business practice model applicable to start-up companies, entrepreneurs and other professionals wishing to establish a private practice.

5   *Peer coaching*   This usually occurs within a formal educational setting or a business organisation. It can assume two forms. *Expert* coaching involves one individual with acknowledged expertise giving another person feedback, support, alternatives and suggestions. *Reciprocal* coaching, on the other hand, entails two individuals, often of comparable abilities, observing and giving feedback and support to each other in a mutual learning situation.

6   *Systems coaching*   This model engages key stakeholders, key business units, or departments in a public or private organisation. The fundamental aim of systems coaching is to promote alignment, at all levels, with the organisation's goals and mission. Coaching the executive or manager involves a recognition of his or her place in the system and how changes in the individual impact on the system as a whole.

7   *Group or team coaching*   This involves working with clients in a series of workshop-type sessions over a period of several weeks or months. Group coaching focuses on a group of individuals, such as senior managers across departments, who share a common issue. Team coaches work with individuals who are part of a team, such as a project team or a brand team.

Coaching and learning

Coaching is a vehicle and a platform for learning. As we discussed in our first book, learning involves a relatively persistent change in an individual's possible behaviour due to experience. Coaching enhances the individual's ability to learn and take effective action. Coaching *is* learning.

Learning presents opportunities and challenges. Some individuals and organisations create and encourage fears and anxiety about learning. These fears and anxieties may or may not be voiced. However, coaching promotes learning in a way that can alleviate these potential barriers. Unlike traditional, standard educational methods, coaching is a personalised, self-directed means of learning. It caters to the individual's personal style, agenda and need for control.

Adult learning principles

In order to work successfully with the model of coaching as learning, the coach requires a general understanding of adult learning principles. For instance, research by Argyris (1991) has established that highly successful individuals base their actions on four values. These are:

➤ remain in unilateral control

➤ maximise winning and minimise losing

➤ suppress negative feelings

➤ be as rational as possible.

The coach has to appreciate that these values serve as a defensive screen to protect the individual. They are tactics used to avoid self-analysis and blame others. Learning can be blocked because the individual's energy is diverted into maintaining these defensive behaviours. If these individuals are to learn then coaching has to focus on generating self-awareness that will encourage self-criticism and feedback from others. Otherwise, change is unlikely to occur.

Coaching as learning can be related to Maslow's hierarchy of needs. Coaching seeks to meet the individual's needs for self-actualisation. As mentioned previously, these needs include self-fulfilment, the realisation of one's potential, self-expression, accomplishment and growth. Yet these needs, which occur at the very top of Maslow's hierarchy, can only be met if needs at the lower levels, such as those for security and acceptance by others, are satisfied. Furthermore, learning will only occur in the context of a trusting, accepting relationship that actively contributes to the individual's self-concept and self-esteem.

Learning will only take place if the goals and interventions of the coaching partnership are relevant to the individual's current life situation. The coachee will learn if he or she can translate the new information and skills into the workplace and his or her personal life. Therefore, coaching programs have to target specific skills and behaviours. Vague promises of enhanced performance and increased interpersonal effectiveness will not suffice to attract and align individuals and organisations in a coaching venture.

The coach as teacher

One of the roles of the coach in the learning process is that of teacher. Depending on the particular coaching intervention, the coach can adopt different versions of the teacher role. For example, when coaching for skills, the coach's role is to transmit knowledge, information and skills. If the coach is working with a leader on enhancing interpersonal competencies, he or she may act as an inquirer and catalyst, challenging the executive's basic beliefs and habitual assumptions. When coaching for the executive's agenda, the coach may adopt the role of facilitator and guide. These are all aspects of teaching. Finally, the learner internalises the 'teaching function' of the coach and becomes his or her own teacher.

Models of learning

As discussed in our previous book, there are numerous models of learning that the coach may adopt. Different models may be appropriate for different types of coaching and different coachees. It is important that coaches familiarise themselves with a learning model. It allows them to explain the learning cycle to the coachee so that both partners can revisit the model in order to monitor progress.

Regardless of which model the coach decides to employ, we agree with Divine that coaches have to be aware of:

➤ the underlying assumptions about learning

➤ the type of learning they wish to foster

➤ what the coachee will gain from the coaching/learning intervention.

Coaches can no longer afford to act as motivators or support coachees in a theoretical vacuum. For example, we have to be clear about whether we are coaching for learning, or coaching for performance. Although performance obviously involves learning there are some distinctions. For instance:

➤ Learning tends to focus on what is happening inside the individual, whereas performance has its focus on the outside work environment.

➤ Learning involves an increase in the individual's knowledge, skills and abilities whereas performance is a function of the individual's competencies in the workplace.

➤ Learning is about new information, assumptions, beliefs and feelings that produce changes in the individual's entire way of being in the world. Performance can be measured against external, behavioural standards.

Just as coaching engages the coachee in a program of continuous learning, so too coaches are always learning. We have to be familiar with the latest developments in coaching, with the best tools and techniques available and, importantly, we have to meet the increasing demands on our knowledge, skills and abilities. We are required to develop or adopt models and techniques that are always open to revision and amendment. Today, the coaching profession requires that we continuously update our skills and pursue lifelong learning and development through formal training and continued practice.

Summary

Coaching as we know it today has a long history, with solid foundations in psychology, philosophy and education. Over the past few years, coaching has altered in shape and form. Professional standards, coach specialties and coaching niche areas will further evolve and change as coaching continues to establish itself as a recognised, stand-alone profession.

Change in organisations

Change is the nature of existence. Our bodies are always changing and ageing, and nature is in a constant state of flux. Impermanence underpins existence. Change occurs through birth, death, new jobs, new relationships and new places. These life experiences cause us to examine our values and beliefs, and our purpose and mission in life. Change can require a total reinvention of who we are, what we are doing and where we want to go. Change creates loss—something is ending and there is a void. We are forced to reflect on what we have lost and what we might gain.

Superimposed upon the natural, evolutionary changes we face, we are also subjected to remarkable and sometimes overwhelming changes resulting from technology, information and globalisation. We have to manage the changes we in fact have created. Yet we often fear, resist and even resent change. Staying the same though is not an option. We cannot ignore change. We have to take risks and we cannot be certain that all will be better after a change has been made. However, unless we are prepared to change we may never realise our possibilities. Change involves courage and the ability to accept failure.

To a certain extent, it is not change itself that creates difficulties for us but rather our ability to change situations to suit ourselves. We can aim to get the best we can from imposed changes. We can adopt change as part of our lives and we can plan change in a way that allows us to maintain control.

Coaching and organisational change

Change is at the heart of coaching. Coaching plays a critical role in helping individuals and organisations create, adapt to and accept change as a challenge rather than an obstacle. The process can be a difficult one though.

The coach's role as a change agent in an organisation can assume the following forms:

➤ The in-house or external coach who is introducing a coaching program to an organisation that is working to establish a culture of coaching.

➤ The coach who is working with executives to develop and enhance their leadership skills in areas such as inspiring and leading organisational change.

➤ The coach who is working with leaders or managers to adopt a coaching style, for example, a 'manager as coach' program.

➤ The coach who is working with an executive or leader to enhance his or her personal skills or operational mastery skills within an organisation. Concentrating on business issues such as clarifying values, challenging beliefs, and working on goals and strategies allows the executive to employ these skills with staff and colleagues and thereby play his or her role in creating a learning organisation.

A systems perspective

Many coaches and authors, such as Mary Beth O'Neill and Richard Kilburg, adopt a systems approach to coaching. Essentially this involves viewing an organisation as a system in which executives and managers function interdependently with other people and processes in the organisation. The coach too, forms a part of this system. In fact the relationship between the coach and coachee(s) is possibly a reflection of the individual's relationship with the system as a whole.

Although we emphasise the importance and usefulness of conducting a coaching needs analysis (see Chapter 3), this on its own will not enable the coach to begin working in an organisation. In the same way, neither process knowledge nor proven ability to work with personal mastery skills will equip the coach to work effectively in an organisation. The coach has to be familiar with the various models of organisational change and the model or framework, either explicit or implicit, within which the particular organisation operates.

If a coach chooses to work within an organisational environment it is recommended that he or she adopt a systemic approach, that is, one that recognises, acknowledges and can work with both internal and external factors that impact on the organisation and its individuals. The coach's role may involve:

➤ focusing on human processes in the organisation

➤ implementing an organisational design

➤ developing and enhancing job competencies

➤ coaching individuals through technology changes

➤ developing managers and leaders

➤ instituting a broad coaching change program.

Regardless of which enterprise the coach is engaged in, he or she requires a solid knowledge of the organisation. The coach has to be aware of its climate and culture, the challenges it faces, its current learning and development programs and its people-management programs and philosophy. Every organisation is a living organism. It is a dynamic system with its own unique values, beliefs and processes. Any coaching program has to be tailored to the individual organisation's unique, systemic needs. Generic solutions are no longer feasible or acceptable in the marketplace. In our coaching clinics for managers as coach, we conduct half-day seminars and whole day workshops to establish the specific coaching needs of the organisation as a whole. One cannot approach an organisation with the intention of 'imposing' a model or solution.

A successful coaching change program has to move from theory into practice to help individuals, groups and organisations manage their own transformation and growth. An approach grounded in systems theory entails viewing experience in terms of complex and dynamic patterns found in natural, biological systems; in created, organisational structures and in systems concerning human relationships.

Changes, whether in the form of one-to-one executive coaching, training managers to be coaches, or business coaching, do not occur in a vacuum, and change in any one part of the system impacts on the system as a whole. The coach requires a multidimensional view of the organisation and an understanding of where the changes are impacting and how this will affect the coaching process or program.

Organisations are undergoing massive restructuring, downsizing, and re-engineering and all parts of the ecological system are affected. The coach has to be aware of where coaching can best assist the organisation to meet its needs. A coaching program can involve executives, managers and anyone else affected by the proposed changes.

To be able to nominate the specific areas where coaching is needed and will add most value, a coach has to be cognisant of the organisation's culture. The coach has to speak the language of the organisation and have an idea or working model of organisational dynamics.

Understanding the dynamics of a particular culture and how the system functions is crucial. Leadership development, authentic trusting and committed partnerships are critical for organisations both today and in the future. If the coach is to introduce changes, particularly at a cultural level, he or she must nominate areas where coaching skills such as honesty, authentic feedback, challenging, and building trust will be most effective.

For example, in order to work effectively with an executive in an organisation, the coach has to understand and be able to analyse the organisation in terms of the systems at work, the dynamics of structure and power and the symptoms and causes of organisational ineffectiveness. Assessments, goals and action planning have to be conducted within the framework of a system composed of interdependent units. Personal changes, changes in staff, in technology, structure and strategy will impact on others and the system as a whole.

Systems theory can approach the organisation from two different perspectives. The first method is to focus on the problems inherent in the systems operating within the organisation. It is essentially a conflict model which sees the organisation as a problem to be solved. This approach is an action-oriented one that looks to isolate the problems, the causes, and the solutions and actions necessary to solve these.

Conversely, the appreciative inquiry (AI) model of change emphasises discovering and appreciating what is best in the organisation and the times and circumstances when the organisation was most 'alive'. This in turn leads to envisioning what might be achievable, challenging the status quo and engaging in conversations about possibilities for the future. The organisation is seen as 'a mystery to be embraced'. There is a process of dialoguing about what should be done, what the structure and processes of the organisation will be and the competencies or qualities necessary to reach the vision.

Finally, the AI model focuses on creating ways to deliver the 'images' of the future. Achieving the vision is done through a process of continuous learning, adjustment, improvisation and revision. The coaching change program draws everyone in the system towards the desired changes rather than away from what is unsatisfactory or anxiety provoking. The initiative is one driven by curiosity, courage and innovation. It is a process of working towards possibilities.

External versus in-house coaches

At this point it is appropriate to raise the issue of the advantages and disadvantages of working as an external coach in an organisation. Some of the obvious benefits in providing external coaching services include the following:

➤ Individuals are likely to be more honest and forthcoming about their opinions, perspectives and aspirations.

- Individual coachees do not have to acknowledge their weaknesses to others in the organisation.

- The coach is not seen as being a key player in the organisation's politics and, therefore, is more likely to be trusted.

- The coach can provide an objective, realistic and fresh perspective on issues that may be unclear within the organisation.

- The coach can provide benchmarking criteria.

However, there are certain disadvantages to providing external coaching services. Some of these include:

- The coach is viewed by many as an outsider who does not know the company.

- Management may be mistrustful and reluctant to reveal corporate secrets to an outsider.

- The coach may fall into 'traps' through lack of knowledge of corporate politics.

- It may be difficult to access, and therefore align, all key stakeholders.

Of course whether the advantages of being an external coach outweigh the disadvantages depends to a great extent on the organisation and the skills and experience of the coach. There is however a growing consensus that coaching provided entirely by external suppliers may not contribute to the growth of genuine leadership and development. True leaders wish to replicate the skills they learn and develop. In order to establish a climate where this can be realised, a culture of internalised coaching has to be fostered. The external coach's role may then include coaching others to coach. Otherwise, if the coach has a limited coaching brief, it is likely that the valuable skills acquired in coaching will not be propagated throughout the entire organisation.

The coach's place in the system

The coach is part of the system. In our experience, many coaches working in organisations often feel 'caught in the middle' between the organisational demands as expressed by senior management and those of the individual coachee. Such conflict can occur regardless of whether the coach is working externally or in-house. In these situations it is important to remember who the client is.

We believe that the person receiving the coaching is the client, not the manager or HR professional who refers him or her. Who the client is should be established from the outset along with the limits of confidentiality and the fact that the coachee, not the organisation, is setting the agenda. At times coaching can be used as the final stage in terminating an employee. That is, a decision may have been made to let the employee go, and coaching is used to show that the organisation has done its best to help the employee. In this situation, often unbeknownst to the coach, there is already a sense of collusion and mistrust and the coaching venture is doomed to failure. Typically though management is seeking to develop the individual coachee and there are no hidden agendas or tests with regard to of the limits of confidentiality.

Having said this, coaches can sometimes find themselves colluding with the executive against other forces in the organisation. Such a position benefits no one in the final analysis. O'Neill suggests that the coach has to be 'self-differentiated', that is, he or she has to feel the effects of the system but avoid reacting automatically or getting personally involved.

When a coach is aware of the system's demands, he or she can make certain that the executive is fully aware of this information so he or she can take the appropriate action. The coach is a sounding board, a resource person and a source of support and encouragement, but it is the coachee who owns the problem.

Finally, it is important that everybody in the organisational system knows what coaching is and its benefits. Otherwise, targeted individuals or business units may be seen as having 'special needs', and the remedial metaphor of coaching will become widespread within the organisation. As a result, alignment and commitment will be more difficult. Coaching has to be recognised throughout the system as an integral and critical part of an organisation's learning and development initiatives. It is not a remedial program.

The coach as change agent

Coaching *is* about change. It involves change at various levels—enhancing current skills, learning new skills and transforming values, beliefs and behaviours in the personal and organisational arenas. Today, various professionals are working with change. Words such as 'change management' and 'change agent' are part of everyone's lexicon. In fact, the notion of 'change programs' is now dismissed by many as a fad. Change is everybody's responsibility and cannot be relegated to the human resources department, consultants or coaches.

We rightly claim that coaching means change, but what is the exact nature of change within the coaching process? What theories, models and tools does the coach require to produce sustained behavioural change? We have to develop or adapt models of change that explore how and why change occurs at various stages of the coaching alliance. We need to assess the readiness for change and be able to accurately and reliably evaluate the degree of change that is occurring. Unless coaches become recognised as experts in change, coaching is in danger of losing its momentum and of being coopted by the more established and accredited professions such as training and consulting.

As coaches we need to have some underlying assumptions about how to change behaviour. We need to know what type of learning is being fostered, where the source of change is and what the coachee is left with at the end of the coaching intervention. For example are we, as Divine questions, holding to a model of behavioural change that focuses on information, feedback, emotions and encouragement or to a model of 'change through reflection'? A model of reflection involves looking at the coachee's 'structure of interpretation' or the way the person sees the world at any particular time. It highlights conversations, observations and practices, and employs metaphors, self-observation and self-reflection exercises. As coaches, we should know when it is appropriate to employ a behavioural model or a reflective model and whether we can combine features of both models.

Finally, according to the model suggested by Beckhard & Pritchard (1992), coaches may begin the work of change in any of the following seven areas:

1   change in the kind of work and how it is done

2   change in the roles and relationships between people

3   change in the organisation's identity in the marketplace

4   change in the organisation's relationship with customers and the external world

5   change in the organisation's mission

6   cultural change

7   change in the organisation's processes to deal with change and challenge in the environment.

Coaching competencies

We suggest the following competencies for coaches working within organisations in either an in-house or external role. Coaches should:

➤   have a working knowledge of a model for organisational change

➤   have a clear idea of what changes they are to implement, what will be learned and how the changes will best be learned

➤   understand the organisation's culture

➤   have confidence and experience in delivering seminars and workshops on coaching to members of the organisation

➤   be skilled in the politics of executive alignment

➤ have a clear map of the organisation as a system

➤ have a clear idea of the specific challenges, internal and external, facing the organisation

➤ recognise and competently deal with the forces of resistance in the organisation.

Personal change

Personal change is an individualised process. There is no one model of change that fits all coachees. Change occurs on an intellectual, emotional and behavioural level. It is not a linear process and usually occurs in stages. Despite the claims of some 'self-help' literature, there is no easy '3-step process' for change. It demands time, effort, support and persistence and the amount of effort does not necessarily equal the amount of change. To deny the difficulties associated with change can lead to unrealistic expectations and, eventually, discouragement for the coach and the coachee.

In order to track change throughout the coaching process, it is necessary for the coach to dialogue with the coachee about critical aspects of change. Until this is done the change process is likely to be derailed. The coachee may not be truly committed to change and fears about change may overcome the initial impetus. Any changes made may be lost through lack of organisational support.

The following change readiness assessment is designed for coaches as an appraisal before the coach and coachee embark on effecting behavioural change. The assessment should be completed by the coach before the coaching change process begins.

Exercise ✍️   Rate the following questions on a score from one to ten.

1	2	3	4	5	6	7	8	9	10
Not at all				Somewhat				Absolutely	

1 Can you identify a successful history/track record of the coachee's past personal changes? ....

2 Can you identify the special competencies that have contributed to successful change? ....

3 Can you identify the coachee's level of cooperation and trust? For example, what is the resistance factor? ....

4 Can you identify the personal style, values and attitudes that will produce change? ....

5   Can you identify resilience, adaptability and durability factors? How much change can the coachee handle?   ....

6   Have you identified belief factors? Does the coachee believe this change will benefit him or her?   ....

7   Have you explored the commitment factor? What is the coachee willing to do to achieve the change?   ....

8   Have you identified the status quo? Is the change going to affect other activities or persons?   ....

9   Can you identify the fear factor involved in undertaking the change?   ....

10   Have you established whether the coachee accepts that continual change is a necessity?   ....

11   Have you identified what reward factors are recognised or in place?   ....

12   Have you established the degree of organisational support? Does the organisation support risk taking and change?   ....

The value of this assessment lies in the information it provides the coach. If the scores are low- to mid-range on several items, this should be taken as an indication that the coach and coachee need to engage in further preparatory discussions to highlight key issues before the change process can begin in earnest.

Models of personal change

Once the coach has explored the issues mentioned above and recognised specific factors that will impact on the coachee's propensity for change, he or she can begin the coaching change process. We have found the following three models of personal change to be effective when working with individuals both within and outside of organisations.

1 The four stage model of personal change

This model, built upon a continuous feedback loop, is based on the work of Kurt Lewin. It nominates four stages within the change process and we have adapted various functions and roles for the coach at each of these stages.

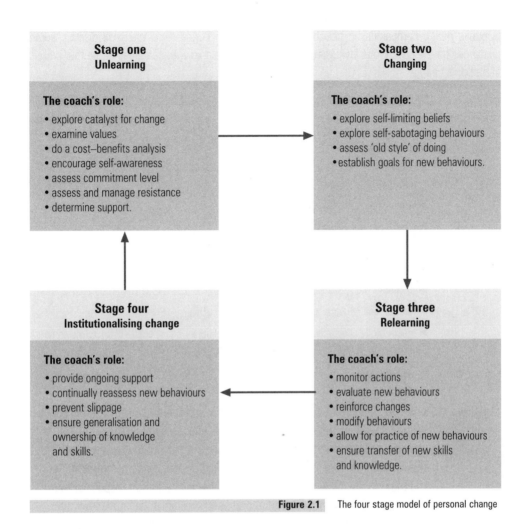

Stage one
Unlearning

The coach's role:
- explore catalyst for change
- examine values
- do a cost–benefits analysis
- encourage self-awareness
- assess commitment level
- assess and manage resistance
- determine support.

Stage two
Changing

The coach's role:
- explore self-limiting beliefs
- explore self-sabotaging behaviours
- assess 'old style' of doing
- establish goals for new behaviours.

Stage four
Institutionalising change

The coach's role:
- provide ongoing support
- continually reassess new behaviours
- prevent slippage
- ensure generalisation and ownership of knowledge and skills.

Stage three
Relearning

The coach's role:
- monitor actions
- evaluate new behaviours
- reinforce changes
- modify behaviours
- allow for practice of new behaviours
- ensure transfer of new skills and knowledge.

Figure 2.1   The four stage model of personal change

2 A motivational model of change

The motivational model of change developed by Prochaska and colleagues in the 1980s is particularly relevant to coaching. It suggests that individuals move through four stages in the change process and that each stage involves a certain period of time and a set of tasks to be mastered before the individual can move on to the next stage.

According to this approach, individuals are at one of the four stages of readiness for change, and specific strategies can be employed to match their state of readiness. The model is widely used in public health campaigns, in health psychology and in counselling. We shall discuss some guidelines for the coach to follow when using this model to deal with coachees at the four stages of personal change.

Table 2.1   The precontemplation stage of change

Precontemplation

➤ The coachee may have been referred by management and does not recognise that there is a problem.

➤ There may be blaming of others.

➤ The coachee is reluctant to be coached.

The coach's role will be to:

➤ develop rapport with the individual

➤ try not to 'sell' coaching

➤ provide the individual with information about coaching

➤ gently probe about management or the referral person's concerns—try to induce some awareness of how the individual's actions may be perceived by others.

Case Study

K. T. is a 27-year-old department head who was referred to an external coach by the general manager. The general manager expressed the need for K. T. to work on his interpersonal skills and facilitate the transition of a new manager. The company, a large national retail organisation, was undergoing restructuring and the new manager was assuming many of K. T.'s former responsibilities. K. T. believed he was qualified and competent to fulfil these duties and felt betrayed and angry with the company. Initially, K. T. was clearly reluctant to be coached. He blamed the company and insisted that reports of his interpersonal 'blow ups' were magnified for political reasons.

The coach did not try to convince K. T. of the benefits of coaching. Rather, she allowed him to vent his frustrations and anger, and gently reinforced the idea that, according to management, his interpersonal behaviours were creating major problems in the workplace. She gave K. T. some information on coaching and asked him to consider what he might personally gain from the sessions.

Table 2.2 The contemplation stage of change

Contemplation

➤ The coachee accepts that there is a problem or issue at stake.

➤ The coachee minimises or denies the seriousness of the problem.

➤ The coachee remains reluctant to be coached.

The coach's role will be to:

➤ encourage the coachee to monitor the behaviour

➤ encourage the coachee to do a costs–benefits analysis of holding on to the old behaviours

➤ discuss the consequences of the coachee persisting with the current behaviours.

After three sessions, K. T. began to acknowledge that there was a problem, although he insisted that management was exaggerating the severity of it. The coach encouraged K. T. to monitor his angry outbursts and his unhelpful behaviour towards the new manager. Together, the coach and K. T. conducted a costs–benefits analysis of his current behaviour. They also explored the ramifications of K. T. continuing to act in the same manner, for example the impact of constantly feeling angry and anxious.

Table 2.3 The action stage of change

Action

➤ The coachee has decided that changes have to be made.

➤ The coachee commits to the coaching alliance.

➤ The coachee is now ready to take action.

The coach's role will be to:

➤ examine values and purpose

➤ establish goals, obstacles and solutions

➤ develop strategies and action plans, and determine evaluation methods.

Case Study

After conducting the costs–benefits analysis, and much reflection, K. T. decided that there was nothing he could do to change the work situation. He realised however that being angry, anxious and withdrawn at work was impacting on his health, was inimical to his professional values and was lowering his self-esteem even further. He committed to changing his behaviour. The coach and K. T. worked together to establish goals and strategies. The strategies included anger management exercises and a process through which K. T. could adopt a mentoring role with the new manager.

Table 2.4 The maintenance stage of change

Maintenance
➤ The coachee will need support to maintain the changes.
The coach's role will be to:
➤ provide follow-up sessions
➤ suggest ongoing exercises and assignments
➤ review and rehearse possible obstacles to maintaining the new behaviours.

Case Study

The coach continued to conduct regular sessions with K. T. while he was instituting the changes. They then identified future potential difficulties and how K. T. might cope with these after the coaching sessions ended. The coach and K. T. also agreed to a series of bimonthly follow-up sessions.

3 A model of change—the individual in the organisation

The following model of change is designed specifically for coaches working with individuals in organisations.

Table 2.5 A model of change—the individual in the organisation

Assess
➤ Assess the individual: administer the relevant profiles as described in Chapter 4. For example, a biographical profile, a work performance profile, a self-assessment competence profile, a competence feedback profile, etc.
➤ Give an individual, confidential debrief of all assessments.
➤ Establish values and the overall objectives of the coaching sessions.

Plan

➤ Establish the specific, desired changes.

➤ Nominate the benefits to the individual.

➤ Nominate the benefits to the organisation.

➤ Explore how these changes will impact on the organisation as a system.

➤ Establish what personal, interpersonal and organisational factors might hinder achievements.

➤ Develop a desired list of changes—an action plan.

➤ Determine the resources that will be needed.

➤ Determine how changes will be measured and in what time frame.

Action

➤ Put new actions in place.

➤ Develop monitoring procedures for the coachee.

➤ Establish how success will be measured and evaluated.

➤ Nominate who else (e.g. a senior manager) will observe and report on these new actions.

➤ Develop a continuous coaching feedback loop.

➤ Review. Reassess. Refine.

The above models of change allow the coach to chart the progress of the coaching sessions and to recognise where the coachee may be 'stuck'. The coach is then able to develop specific strategies to deal with particular stumbling blocks. Furthermore, knowing which stage of change the coachee is at minimises the possibility of the coach becoming frustrated with or blaming the coachee for the rate of change.

Managers and coaching

The manager as coach

There is increasing evidence to suggest a significant causal relationship between people-oriented management and sustained corporate success. For example, studies at the Center for Creative Leadership found that the most critical success factor for leaders was their relationships with subordinates. Conversely, executive derailment was related to insensitivity and an inability to understand the perspectives of others. Furthermore, in a survey of readers of *Fast Company* magazine, 72 per cent selected social skills compared to Internet skills as being more essential to business success in the next five years.

Coaching is not a fashionable substitute for managerial control. Leaders do not have the time or capacity to control anymore. They have to empower and delegate to create a culture of responsibility and self-generated actions. Coaching and managing are, in many ways, synonymous. Both work by using relationships and dialogue to generate possibilities and growth. It is not simply a matter of learning certain techniques. Coaching is not a technique. It involves a way of viewing the world, relationships, and the organisation.

Selman lists some competencies of the leader and coach. Leaders and coaches:

➤ commit to building trusting and authentic relationships

➤ are aware of their own blind spots

➤ allow others freedom, power and choice

➤ generate possibilities for action and achievement

➤ generate new conversations.

➤ allow others to be responsible for their own moods and interpretations

➤ invent the future.

According to the feedback we have received from managers participating in our coaching clinics for managers to become coaches there is an ever increasing dissatisfaction with the current control-oriented type of management. These progressive, success-oriented managers recognise that a culture of coaching is needed to shift the paradigm of management from one of authority and control to one of a committed, responsible partnership. Those leaders who wish to retain top performers and a highly skilled workforce are wise to adopt a coaching role within the organisation.

In some IT companies in the United States, managers are being coached to become more skilled in dealing with, and therefore retaining, highly skilled workers by taking on a coaching role. Organisations are realising that high-tech employees are demanding more than financial gain. They demand appreciation, recognition, open communication and self-actualisation. Management is being forced to adopt a more 'humanistic' model. Internal resources such as courage, intuition, creativity, honesty and integrity are increasingly valued and becoming an integral part of the organisational culture. Self-actualisation is a critical driving force for many employees, and some leaders and managers are learning to explore and develop this aspect of themselves and their employees. Coaching, and aligning the individual's goals with those of the organisation, has become imperative in the race to retain valued staff. Managers have to be aware of what keeps people and what drives them away. The employee's growth has to be stimulated, learning and development opportunities have to be maximised and career paths explored.

Several studies show that job retention rates are more a function of the opportunities provided by management for growth and development than compensation packages. Companies claim they lose employees for financial reasons. However, research suggests that, beyond a certain point, money is not the issue. High performers leave organisations because:

➤ they do not like their manager

➤ they were not challenged

➤ there was a lack of opportunity for cutting-edge learning

➤ they experienced a lack of control over projects and their work life.

In the IT industry especially, individuals are promoted because of their technical expertise and not their people skills. Yet managers require training and coaching to learn to manage more effectively and stop people from leaving. They need to lead a strong, living culture with clear values, clear goals, strong leadership and opportunities for growth and learning.

In some leading IT organisations, employees are called team members, managers are coaches and even the CEO is called the head coach. In fact, anyone with a direct report is a coach. Employee development is the focus and much of the coaching involves dealing with transition. Interestingly, coaching skills are not directly tied to financial compensation but the results of coaching do figure in promotions.

In our work with managers, we emphasise that coaching is not a technique. It is a way of achieving results. We also discuss the following roles of the manager/coach:

➤ Rather than direct and control, the manager/coach empowers others to accomplish results on their own initiative.

➤ Rather than focusing solely on the organisation's goals, they take care to align the individual's goals and commitments with those of the organisation.

➤ Through empowering others, setting goals and collaborating on strategies, the manager/coach taps into the individual's intrinsic motivation.

➤ Power is no longer a function of position but rather of personal force which is manifested in a coaching relationship of mutual commitments.

➤ In the new paradigm, employees are responsible for their own commitments, decisions and actions within the workplace.

➤ Traditional managers focus on what is wrong, and how and why the problem occurred. The manager/coach emphasises development and future possibilities.

➤ Manager/coaches develop their team to lead rather than leading them from the top.

➤ Managers tend to function on a contractual basis whereas the manager/coach develops individuals to see possibilities and choices and work towards their own development and fulfilment.

➤ Managers maintain the existing organisational culture. The manager/coach encourages creative thinking and challenges the status quo.

➤ The manager is essentially results-oriented. The manager/coach is fundamentally people-oriented.

➤ The manager tells. The manager/coach listens, questions, supports and collaborates.

Some common objections to adopting a coaching role

When working with managers to adopt a coaching role, coaches are frequently met with objections or resistance patterns. Research has established that executives typically resist coaching others for the following reasons:

➤ *They are not comfortable with their coaching skills* Managers may feel they lack the competencies to coach and develop others. Indeed, this may be true. Compounding this problem is the fact that some executives may not wish to disclose their weaknesses in this area.

These barriers are not insurmountable. We agree with coaches such as Fred Friend that it is important to establish an objective, acceptable method for assessing the leader's skills in this area. Questions that relate to the executive's skills in developing others can be included in a leadership assessment instrument such as those described in Chapter 4. It is also important to obtain information from other sources. A 360-degree assessment or even a mini 360-degree appraisal (see Chapter 4) could provide data from respondents on their experience of the leader's developmental contributions. When development skills are included in the overall leadership skills profile, the executive is more likely to accept his or her shortcomings in this area. The coach can then train managers in these skills, some of which are: delegation, giving feedback, encouraging open and honest communication and developing staff.

➤ *Development of others is a low priority because of time constraints* It is a common misconception that coaching takes up valuable time. Such an attitude partly stems from wanting a quick fix, an external 'cure' that will alter structures and systems and bypass any need for real personal change.

Leaders and managers are bound by very tight time constraints and, as we know, coaching takes time. Coaching is about change and change involves learning. It takes time to replace old habits and ways of thinking and feeling, and learn and practise new ways of being. However, it should be emphasised to the leader that coaching and developing others actually saves time in the long run. Rather than having to intervene on individual issues, the manager can coach for skills that are transferable within the workplace. Also, coaching for development through goal setting and action planning is likely to generate loyalty and commitment from employees who feel the company appreciates and rewards their efforts.

➤ *They do not value the development of others*   It may be true that executives and managers exist in a highly competitive environment that emphasises their own personal success over that of others in the organisation. Yet, they are ambitious and willing to engage in roles that are highly valued by the organisation. The organisation itself then must value and prioritise coaching and development. Unless executives and managers value coaching it is unlikely that they will give it much time or attention.

➤ *They dislike formal training programs*   One method to offset this objection is to offer one-on-one coaching to executives and leaders. Rather than attending group programs on 'manager as coach', coaching competencies can be explored and developed within the confines of individual coaching sessions. Such an option is likely to prove more attractive to senior executives and managers who do not like to attend formal workshops and who are wary of exposing any inadequacies they may have in this area.

Further to this, research and our work with managers has identified the following concerns that managers have about adopting a coaching role.

➤ *They fear they will be unable to meet the organisation's business goals if they adopt a coaching role.*   Delegation skills and the manager's ability to inspire others and build an environment of trust and commitment where individuals collaborate and share responsibility are at the core of this issue.

➤ *They believe they are unable to communicate the organisation's vision and business goals to coachees.*   Coaching focuses on the manager's ability to articulate the company's vision, and to set standards and measurable outcomes. The coach has to work with the manager to meet and maintain current demands but at the same time introduce new, measurable goals.

➤ *They doubt their ability to align others in the coaching program.*   Many managers lack the ability to give praise, and reinforce and reward employees. However, like most coaching skills, they can be learned. The coach can examine the manager's self-limiting beliefs around the subject and together the coach and manager can nominate specific behaviours to be praised and role-play these in the safety of the coaching sessions.

The coach's role when working with managers as coaches

The role of the coach when working with managers training to become coaches is to build self-awareness and flexibility. This will enable the manager as coach to influence and motivate a wider group of individuals. Some specific areas the coach may address include:

➤ exploring the manager's issues, strengths and challenges through individual, confidential assessments

➤ generating and maintaining effective relationships

➤ understanding organisational and interpersonal dynamics

➤ communicating vision and aligning others

➤ developing trust

➤ developing high-performing, cross-functional teams

➤ developing assertiveness

➤ working with conflict

➤ matching the style of others, and awareness of interpersonal style

➤ giving feedback

➤ delegating.

The impacts of introducing a coaching culture

The benefits and advantages of coaching are now fairly well established in the corporate world. Yet, generally speaking, many managers still resist the change that coaching represents. It is true that some organisations have adopted a coaching culture, where all managers are called coaches. Many organisations fail however to answer the call for coaching, and the concept of a consultative, supportive and participatory work environment remains in the realm of rhetoric.

Most of us express hesitancy in the face of change. As well as this natural tendency, managers may not fully comprehend the changes coaching will bring and how they will positively affect business results. Some coaches may lack the ability to explain to 'hard-nosed' businesspeople just how coaching can impact on the bottom line. There are several other possible explanations for the reluctance to adopt coaching. For instance, as suggested by Evered and Selman (1989), managers may already believe they know how to manage, they may be more committed to control and authority than to results, and management may not actually feel responsible for their teams' results.

Some managers may fear that coaching entails a loss of power and position. Yet, managers are not outmoded. A shift in the paradigm simply means that managers derive their power base from a different source. Changes in the global economy, markets, technology and employee attitudes mean that management cannot control everything from the top. Members of an organisation cannot simply be told to deal with the astonishing rates of change they are facing. What is needed is a responsible, empowered, free-thinking workforce where all the players are responsible and committed to collaborating, achieving objectives and seeking growth and new possibilities. The old style of 'control and command' has clearly outlived its usefulness.

Stress in organisations

The last three decades have produced unprecedented rates of change that demand increasing flexibility from the workforce. For example, the inability to achieve a reasonable life/work balance plagues many of us.

When the coach works with life/work balance issues, the concepts of competency and commitment may prove useful. For instance, peak performance at work occurs when there is a balance between commitment and competency. Obviously, if the worker's commitment exceeds the level of competency then he or she feels overwhelmed, overly challenged and unsure. The coach could work with the individual to either lower his or her level of commitment or increase the degree of competency. On the other hand, if the coachee's level of competency exceeds his or her commitment, then the person will be bored and frustrated. Such a situation can occur if the person has decided to allocate more time and energy towards homelife than work.

The coach can also look at the following issues in relation to life/work balance:

➤ examine time wasters

➤ explore instances where the executive experiences lack of fulfilment or feels underemployed

➤ determine the executive's values and prioritise these

➤ establish what is most important to the executive at this particular stage of life

➤ discuss possible trade-offs the executive might have to make in achieving more life balance.

Research shows that male executives who enter therapy most commonly present with depression, anxiety, substance abuse or dependence disorders. Executives also experience work-related stress including:

➤ workaholism

➤ success addiction

- role overload

- role underload

- role conflict

- role ambiguity

- career development challenges

- co-worker stress and management stress

- stress related to structures within the organisation such as incomplete or ambiguous communication systems

- customer demands.

Stress can also result when our innate tendency to bring about stability, harmony and routine in our lives is blocked. We all seek control over our lives. Yet the impact of change undermines this sense of stability and control. For example, changes in technology and production have resulted in automation, the need for retraining and the loss of many jobs. Rumours about the stability of our organisation, organisational demands that render our education obsolete and the prospect of numerous job changes can be destabilising and cause us to feel powerless.

Certainly, change is all around us. It has even been suggested that most dominant cultures have declared change to be an important, independent goal or principle that overrides the essence of what a culture really is and provides. According to this viewpoint, espoused by Schabracq and colleagues, a culture is a collectively shared strategy to prevent stress. The essence of a culture is to provide standard solutions to standard problems to set us free for activities that matter to us. Yet the current pursuit of change, sometimes for its own sake, has resulted in increasing stress for most of us.

There is a considerable amount of literature on the flattening out of management. Of course, increased efficiency and cost reduction are the prime objectives and benefits of this structural change. However, there are also disadvantages, and fallout. The loss of corporate intelligence is extensive. Furthermore, individuals who survive downsizing are left with 'survivor guilt', and anxiety about the security of their own position. As a result of downsizing, there is often an overload of work on those remaining in the organisation. Stress and burnout are becoming increasingly common.

Restructuring and mergers can impact negatively on those in the organisation. We are all aware of the 'new broom' syndrome when incoming managers introduce changes, sometimes trivial and senseless, just to leave their mark. Business literature also suggests that many mergers fail because of a lack of vision, goals and strategy. Sometimes mergers are based on personal ambition rather than on commercial reality. However, it is employees who often have to deal with suspicious, sometimes resentful colleagues from different corporate cultures and backgrounds.

As more and more organisations seek to become part of a multinational network, individuals face new challenges which place heavy demands on their adaptability skills. Working with colleagues from different cultures, the physical effects of travel, and time zone differences can be added sources of stress on top of increasingly demanding, complex and challenging jobs. Personal relationships may suffer, individuals have little time for themselves and work becomes the entire focus of their lives. Fatigue can result in confusion, impulsive decisions and looking for short-term wins at the expense of long-term strategies.

Temporary employees who may perform relatively simple tasks are not immune from change-induced stress. Their future is also unstable, making financial planning impossible. Their security needs are not met, working conditions offer little chance for development, their skills are frequently under-utilised and they generally receive little support from management. Research shows that low autonomy, a low variety of skills and under-utilisation of skills are detrimental to health and wellbeing and may even contribute to premature death.

The coach's role in dealing with organisational stress

The following table demonstrates the coaching needs of individuals in three categories. These categories can serve as a blueprint for specific target areas in a coaching program. They can also serve as a guide to what issues to explore when working with individuals from the different categories.

Table 2.6   Coaching needs across the organisational structure

Temporary employees

➤ Supervisors and managers require leadership and coaching skills

➤ Stress-prevention skills

➤ Time-management skills

➤ Career training and development—explore the labour market and job flexibility

Full time professionals and temporary consulting professionals

➤ Life/work balance

➤ Interpersonal skills

➤ Team skills

➤ Assertion skills

> Conflict-management skills

> Stress-prevention skills

> Coaching skills to work with temporary employees

> Decision-making skills

> Self-marketing skills

Core nucleus of executives

> Coaching skills

> Leadership skills

> Team-management skills

> Delegation skills

> Stress-prevention skills

> Personal and technical mastery skills

> Life/work balance

> Change-management skills

Change can be costly. However, while the cost of coaching can be high, so is the cost of not attending to these needs. Research suggests the following repercussions of introducing change without coaching and supporting those involved:

> low morale

> poor quality services and products

> poor internal communication

> increased conflict in the workplace

> increased lack of life/work balance with negative impacts on health and work performance

> difficulties in staff retention.

Learning organisations

It is a widely held though erroneous belief that change from the outside in the form of new organisational structures and processes will result in enhanced performance and increased business competitiveness. Coaching however emphasises personal fulfilment and learning as the way to organisational growth. It seeks to develop and enhance the congruence between the self and one's professional role in an organisation. These aims can only truly reach fruition within an organisation that values and supports personal mastery, learning and development.

What is a learning organisation?

The concept of a learning organisation is becoming as clichéd as the notion of change management. Perhaps it is important for us to look beyond the rhetoric.

A learning organisation is a group of people who are on a continuous, never-ending search for new and better ways to adapt to change, and enhance performance. Learning and improvement can only thrive in an atmosphere where learning is truly valued and where it is accepted, even expected, that questioning and exploring creative solutions and new possibilities are the norm. Creative learning organisations are accepting of change, open to new approaches, able to make mistakes and learn from them, able to accommodate diversity and committed to solutions. Creativity is related to risk-taking and risk-taking involves the possibility of failure. Failure has to be expected.

Argyris, for instance, differentiates organisations in terms of how they learn and compete over time. His Model 1 organisation is characterised by institutionalised self-censorship; it is defensive and limits truthful, honest communication. The only views encouraged and expressed are those sanctioned, indeed imposed by the organisational culture. As a result, the organisation is working out of a system of 'invalid knowledge': for example, people will not deliver bad news at a meeting for fear of the consequences. Management practices in such organisations tend to induce worker apathy and decreased effort. People are encouraged to be passive and dependent, power remains at the top and job specialisation leads to boredom and stagnation. According to Argyris, organisations succeed when they refine their processes but also refine their assumptions about the way the world works. There is frequently a gap between the theories espoused and the theories in use in many organisations. These theories can vary, and if this gap persists nothing changes and nothing is overturned.

In Model 2 organisations there are better conversations. These organisations promote and diffuse knowledge and are therefore better equipped to assess reality. As a result, they obtain superior business results. The organisation's value system dictates the nature of human relationships within the organisation. Relationships can be shallow and mistrustful with little encouragement of true expression. Or they can be more humanistic. For example, in a democratic value system human relationships are related to the organisation's internal system, adaptation to the environment and achievement of objectives. Human relationships are also effectively influenced through authentic relationships and internal commitment.

In learning organisations individuals develop and enhance their interpersonal competencies within a psychologically safe environment. Research, such as that done by Edmondson, shows that team members engage in learning behaviours in a climate of perceived psychological safety. If individuals do not engage in learning behaviours there will be a decrease in the organisation's ability to solve problems.

Self-mastery in a learning organisation

According to Senge, a learning organisation is one in which people continually expand their capacity to create the results they truly desire. He sees personal mastery as one of the five disciplines of a learning organisation. Others suggest that it is the cornerstone. Self-mastery is not simply an accumulation of technical and operational information. It involves the wise and beneficial use of this information. Self-mastery demands that we observe ourselves, face reality and choose a vision and a future. It involves changing ourselves and ridding ourselves of conditioned, automatic responses to which, some claim, we are biologically hardwired.

Self-mastery requires courage and practice. It demands self-awareness regarding our thinking, our self-limiting beliefs and our conditioned emotional responses. We have to challenge and reframe these beliefs and behaviours. The views of others have to be welcomed, accepted and integrated. Such personal mastery occurs on a personal and organisational level. If management values and practises this it will spread. In turn, the learning organisation will produce empowered adults who develop trusting and committed relationships in an open, creative environment.

It is widely accepted that successful individuals are constantly learning. They seek information and experiences that they then apply to new situations. Active learners pursue self-knowledge, and are reflective and intuitive. They analyse and leverage their strengths and seek to overcome challenges and limitations. Active learners question and are not afraid to admit that they do not know. Leaders today need these personal qualities if they are to embrace and master the forces of change that impact on them and their organisations. They also have to encourage and support a culture where these qualities flourish.

As well as establishing a culture that is learning based, organisations and the external or in-house coach have to be aware of how individuals learn best. Individuals have to be in charge of their own learning. For instance, at Dell University, Cone introduced 'on-demand learning' where learning was reduced to the smallest, most useful increments and the learner was in charge. He distinguishes between three kinds of learning. The first type, 'learning to know', involves the acquisition of general knowledge about the company and its processes and systems. 'Learning to do' entails the quick acquisition and immediate application of specific skills to specific jobs. Finally, 'learning to know and do' includes the acquisition of both the big picture perspective and the pragmatic techniques needed to accomplish something.

According to this approach, learning today has shifted from the traditional importance of knowing something to knowing how to find out information. Learning should be synchronous with work, it should not be presented as 'overload', and people should know just enough to complete the task.

Finally, according to this model, the best learning happens quickly. As coaches within organisations, we require an understanding of what has to be learned and how it can be learned most effectively.

In order to establish or develop a learning organisation, the coach works with the team or individual members to enhance creativity in an open and trusting environment. Coaching is guided by the notion of creative tension. By definition, change is destabilising. If the coach or the organisation seeks harmony, the coaching initiative may end in compliance and collusion, and any real problems may be swept under the table. The coach has to be willing to grapple with ideas and solutions and create an atmosphere of creative tension and critical thinking.

Models of organisational change

Change is always occurring somewhere in an organisation and on some level, regardless of which particular change model is employed. Change is not a one-off phenomenon nor is its effectiveness contingent on the degree to which it is planned. Furthermore, the trajectory of change is more often spiralling, or open-ended, than linear. All of the following insights are more likely to be relevant and useful if organisations and coaches focus on 'changing' rather than 'change'.

Indeed, there has been a shift in the management and coaching vocabulary from 'change' to 'changing'. This alteration suggests a greater recognition and appreciation that change is a continuous process. It underpins our existence—both on a personal and organisational level. It is no longer appropriate or helpful to suggest a change program that is finite. Coaching change programs are instituted to create conditions where change is welcomed, created and managed on a continuous basis.

Establishing a pilot coaching project

Research shows that between 50 and 70 per cent of organisational change efforts fail. Many organisations are capable of designing change programs but not implementing them. Perhaps this is because short-term goals intervene and are too overwhelming to allow for focus on the long-term objectives.

There is a widely held belief among organisations and coaches that cultural changes have to begin at the top and filter down. Yet this traditional top-down approach to change has not had great success. Peter Senge claims he has never seen a successful organisational learning program rolled out from the top. Every successful change initiative starts on a small scale.

According to this approach, deep change only occurs through real personal growth—through learning and unlearning. Relying on the CEO or the 'guru' with all the answers means compliance rather than commitment. In this paradigm, there is no one person in charge. Real, sustainable, significant change only occurs when there are talented, committed local line leaders and 'seed carriers' or internal networkers who build informal communities of practice, such as coaching, within the organisation. As well, executives cannot play the hero because they have to coach and mentor those in the organisation. If change initiatives are to succeed, there has to be interplay between these three types of communities of practice.

While it is necessary to get sponsorship from the top, the 'seed' of coaching can be planted in a particular unit or department. It can begin as a pilot project and once it has succeeded it can move horizontally or vertically throughout the organisation. Then, the organisation's culture changes completely, although this change is never stagnant. It is continual, and individuals in the system are open to changes, possibilities and opportunities for growth.

Challenges to the pilot group

We find Senge's research on establishing pilot change groups to be especially applicable to coaching change initiatives. Senge and his colleagues (1999) identify specific challenges facing a pilot change group. For example, during the initiating phase people in the pilot group need time off from their usual responsibilities to devote to the coaching project. They also require coaching, support and mentoring to learn and do the required work. Furthermore, the proposed new skills have to be connected closely to the real work of the organisation and the pilot group has to act out the espoused values and behaviours. Once the pilot coaching project has taken off, the challenge is to maintain momentum. Members of the pilot group may become anxious and concerned about their vulnerability and inadequacy. They may question the change effort. Furthermore, the change efforts can run into measurement problems. Finally, the pilot group may become arrogant, and the company divide into 'believers' and 'non-believers' in the coaching initiative. In terms of redesigning and rethinking systems, the pilot group may want more autonomy and conflict can result. Instead of building on previous successes, each new group or unit may have to start again. Finally, the pilot group can lose focus of the overall strategy when faced with the day-to-day demands of the project.

Continuous versus episodic change

Continuous change

It is nearly impossible to offer any succinct account of all the models of the change process. There are numerous theories of change that posit different sequences and different growth mechanisms. For instance, models of change can employ life cycle metaphors, evolutionary sequences or they can approach change from a conflict and resistance perspective. One model of change however that has particular relevance to the coach's specific role is change as a continuous or episodic process.

The phrase 'continuous change' is used to group together organisational changes that tend to be ongoing, evolving and cumulative. A common presumption is that change is emergent and is situated and grounded in continual updates of work processes and social practices. The role of the change agent is to manage language, dialogue and identity. Change agents have to make sense of change dynamics that are already under way, recognise adaptive emergent changes, make them more salient and reframe them. They explain current upheavals, where they are heading, what they will have produced by way of a re-design, and how further intentional changes can be made at the margins.

The coach enables groups to create a shared set of meanings and common thought processes. As discussed throughout this book, this occurs mostly through conversations. Research (e.g. Werke 1999) suggests that the most powerful change interventions occur at the level of everyday conversation. Good and powerful conversation is vocal, reciprocating, issues-oriented, rational, imaginative and honest. Change agents produce change through various combinations of these six kinds of speech. These speech acts occur in different combinations to create four different conversations: conversations of change, understanding, performance and closure.

Episodic change

Episodic change on the other hand refers to organisational changes that tend to be infrequent, discontinuous and intentional. Episodic change occurs during periods of transition when organisations are moving away from their balanced state. There is a recognised misalignment between the organisation's structure and perceived environmental demands. Episodic change tends to occur in response to events such as technology changes or internal events such as changes in key personnel. The role of the change agent in episodic change is that of the prime mover who creates change. The coach as change agent focuses on larger gatherings, there are more issues on the table for immediate action and the change initiative is concentrated into shorter periods of time.

Research suggests that large-scale change in very large groups is counterproductive because size and participation tend to be negatively related. Large group settings tend to induce stereotyping, decreased ownership of ideas, increased abstraction and less willingness to express unique thoughts. The challenge for the coach as the prime mover is to neutralise these tendencies.

There is a growing understanding of the specific ways in which change agents can be effective prime movers. Language interventions, as discussed above, are becoming a crucial means for agents to create change.

Theory E and Theory O

We find the approaches to organisational change discussed by Beer and Nohria (2000) to be helpful. They are called Theory E and Theory O. Theory E (economic value-driven change) is driven from the top with extensive help from consultants, and financial incentives. Change is planned and programmable. The purpose behind the Theory O (organisational capability-driven change) model is the development of the organisation's capacity to implement strategy and to learn from actions taken. Its focus is on the development of a high-commitment culture. Here change is emergent and less planned. Both approaches clearly have validity although neither achieves all the objectives of management. Beer and Nohria suggest it is possible for companies to integrate the two models sequentially or simultaneously.

The role of the coach—guidelines for introducing a coaching change program

In order to help coaches establish whether an organisation is ready to engage in a coaching change intervention we have adapted the following guidelines from Beryl Levinger. These include the following:

1   What is the history of change in the organisation? How have people responded? It is important to reflect on this in order to recognise strengths, weaknesses and past obstacles. Similar barriers could arise in the context of the current change initiative.

2   Is there a willingness on the part of the coach, the coachees and the organisation to openly and trustingly explore the following questions:
    ➤ What is our mission?
    ➤ Where are we going?
    ➤ What is our blueprint for action?
    ➤ What resources (budget) do we have available?
    ➤ How do we evaluate our successes? How do we know we are on track?

3   Is there a likelihood that consensus can be reached on the following issues:
    ➤ Where are we in terms of our strategic plan, vision and mission?
    ➤ What gaps do we need to fill—socially, politically and culturally?
    ➤ How do we respond to those needs?
    ➤ Who are our key stakeholders? How do we respond to their needs?
    ➤ What are our core values?
    ➤ What is our model of change?

4   Is there an impending crisis or threat to the organisation?

5   Is there a deeply held belief about, and commitment to, coaching from management?

6   Do the stakeholders share a common understanding about what coaching involves?

7 Are there competent, trained and committed 'sponsors' on the coaching pilot or project management team?

8 Is there a consensus on the mandate of the coaching team?

9 Is there a consensus on how the program might be carried out?

10 Is there an agreed-upon coaching model to be used?

11 Is there an agreed-upon time frame for the coaching program?

12 Are there resources for the coaching project team to:
   ➤ clarify the organisation's mission and values?
   ➤ identify the clients and stakeholders?
   ➤ assess the internal and external environment?
   ➤ identify the strategic issues facing the organisation?
   ➤ formulate strategies to deal with these?
   ➤ convert vision into goals, strategies and action plans?
   ➤ review project feedback to stakeholders?
   ➤ reassess and realign expectations and goals on a continuous basis?
   ➤ make adjustments to the overall plan?

13 Will the coaching project team have access to data (internal and external) that will affect and aid the coaching project?

Resistance to change in organisations

As noted earlier in this chapter, many organisations either abandon their change efforts completely or only partially succeed with their change objectives. Resistance to change is clearly a major factor in these outcomes. Argyris (1991) defines resistance as the thoughts or actions individuals, groups and organisations employ to defend their usual way of dealing with reality.

The organisation may be contributing to this fear by inducing change but still punishing risk-taking behaviours. Changes may have been introduced before but if the culture does not accept and embrace change, these change initiatives may have failed. People may have become cynical and developed a sense of futility. If the organisation fears conflict then change solutions are not proposed because they are seen as causing disagreements.

The coach has to identify the specific fears within the organisational culture. If they remain amorphous in nature they cannot be challenged. Generalised fears manifest as anxiety that can be paralysing and result in inertia and resistance to change. The coach has to help the individual or organisation to recognise and nominate the specific fears about change. It is then possible to take action which, in itself, begins to dissolve the barrier caused by anxiety.

Change can be resisted in indirect ways. For example, an organisation may want to hold on to the old system and just modernise it when really a total overhaul is necessary. Some churches face this same shift in thinking—from local community to fragmented, multiple communities, from one faith to multiple faiths and a multicultural, pluralistic model. Yet the tendency is to try to retain the current paradigm.

In the chapter on overcoming resistance (see Chapter 11) we focus mainly on resistance from the individual coachee. Here we wish to review the nature of resistance within an organisation. That is, we discuss resistance as it may impact on:

➤ The in-house or external coach who is introducing a coaching program to an organisation that is working to establish a culture of coaching.

➤ The coach who is working with executives to develop and enhance their leadership skills.

➤ The coach who is working with leaders or managers to adopt a coaching style.

➤ The coach who is working with an executive or leader on enhancing personal or operational mastery skills within an organisation.

Psychological and emotional resistance to change

We are all familiar with new leaders meeting resistance and, ultimately, failure when they try to introduce change. One reason for this failure is that change agents do not consider the emotional impact of a change in leadership. Our experience supports Carr's (1999) contention that, depending on how closely aligned individuals are with the outgoing leader, they will respond to the changed circumstances with anger, frustration, despair, happiness or ambivalence. For example, members of an organisation who have identified closely with the outgoing leader and his or her ideals and vision may experience a type of narcissistic injury. Consequently, they will be slow to accept change and form new attachments. Conversely, those individuals who were less closely aligned with, or had less emotional investment in, the leader may be happy with the change, or possibly ambivalent.

Any coaching change initiative has to acknowledge and contend with these emotional responses. The coach has to appreciate that certain individuals may experience a dislodgment of identity and, indeed, may undergo a process of grieving. These individuals require time and assistance to help them through this process.

Change programs, including coaching, can create other perceived losses by those in the organisation. For example, there may be a loss of social status for some individuals who perceive their position in the previous hierarchy to be undermined or even replaced. There can be a loss of well-established social networks. Furthermore, some of the changes may be regarded as unnecessary, and the ensuing loss of corporate knowledge and intelligence can cause added stress and cynicism among staff. There can be blaming, and decreased creativity and productivity.

Organisational regression

Recent research suggests that to understand organisational change one must first understand organisational inertia—its content, its tenacity and its interdependencies. Personal or organisational regression is a form of resistance to or protection against change. According to Kilburg (2000), under certain external environmental pressures or due to the internal psychological and physical forces present in leaders and their followers, the behaviour of individuals and the organisation as a whole can become dysfunctional. The forces of regression triumph. By regression, we mean a partial or symbolic return to more infantile patterns of reacting or thinking.

Some of the potential consequences of organisational regression include problems such as psychological and emotional imbalance, substance abuse, physical health problems, stress and burnout. There can be increased absenteeism, performance problems, career derailment, group conflicts, market losses and competitive failures. When working with change, it is imperative that the coach is aware of the regressive forces within the organisation. Unless these are acknowledged and dealt with they will persist and undermine any change initiative.

Personal style and resistance to change

As a general rule, there is more resistance to change in an organisation that is hierarchical and rigid than in one that is flexible and informal. As yet there does not seem to be any definitive research on the types of individuals who are most likely to resist change. Attitudes to change depend to a great extent on how the proposed changes impact personally on each member of the organisation.

Resistance can arise from feelings of insecurity or from a threat to the individual's feeling of competence. Some individuals feel comfortable with old systems and fear learning new ones. Such reluctance can manifest as complaining, camouflaging errors, withdrawal, apathy, overt frustration and anger. It is important though that the change agent recognises that these behaviours are signs that individuals are going through the change process. Some simply require more direction and support than others.

There are some indicators the coach may find useful in recognising those members of the organisation who are more vulnerable to resistive behaviour. These include:

➤ Some individuals, including CEOs and senior managers, may recognise the need for change but are unwilling to personally alter their own behaviour. That is, they accept the need for structural changes but resist personal change.

➤ Individuals with a low tolerance for ambiguity (i.e. the ability to cope with ambiguous situations, unclear information and unpredictable or rapid changes in the environment) are more likely to resist change.

➤ Some individuals have an extremely strong need to exert their power. They may wish to control the coaching agenda and are constantly involved in power struggles with the change agent.

➤ Individuals with an external locus of control (i.e. they feel they are not in control of their own destiny) may feel helpless and overwhelmed by change.

➤ Sperry (1996) has established that individuals with paranoid, narcissistic, obsessive-compulsive and passive-aggressive tendencies are more likely to show resistance to change.

➤ Certain individuals may be mistrusting of outsiders such as an external coach. They may see the coach as an intruder who does not possess adequate knowledge of the organisation and is therefore unaware of the repercussions of the proposed changes.

Matching to minimise resistance

It may be that resistance to change is a result of the coach failing to match the style of the organisation or the individual. The coach may be perceived as being too young, too old, too conservative or too modern for the particular organisation's culture. Such perceptions may simply constitute a rationale for those individuals in the organisation who are reluctant to participate in the proposed change intervention.

In order to prevent these potential derailments, the external coach has to be cognisant of these stated or implied objections. A thorough coaching needs analysis of the organisation would establish the organisation's culture as well as the expectations the organisation has of an external provider. Matching these needs is a question of experience, openness to learning and political savvy on the part of the coach. After all, it is the key stakeholders whom the coach must satisfy. Clearly identifying and meeting their needs (as discussed in Chapter 3) serves to offset many of the potential difficulties inherent in matching the style of the organisation.

Resistance as conservation

In the above section on psychological and emotional resistance to change, we briefly discussed the sense of loss experienced by many individuals in the face of change. Yet, as noted by Senge and his colleagues, change can entail loss at another level. Change agents tend to criticise individuals and organisations for resisting change. Yet, people within the system may be trying to conserve certain elements such as financial cash flow, innovation or technological expertise that they see as being at risk in the change process. Of course the system may also be trying to conserve undesirable elements such as an autocratic hierarchy or high levels of pressure and stress.

The coach requires a thorough knowledge of the forces of conservation at play in a particular organisation. Coaching programs that fail to recognise what the organisational system wants to maintain are doomed to failure. Regardless of what progress is made, there will be forces that push back against these changes. Part of the coach's role in initiating and maintaining a change program is to first establish any potential obstacles to the stated goals of the coaching program. There also has to be a built-in review process that allows for ongoing recognition of the 'push back' mechanisms or 'compensatory feedback', reflection and a shifting of emphasis on goals and strategies. Introducing and maintaining change is a dynamic process. If the change program is rigid and not open to feedback from the system, stagnation will occur.

The coach has to 'educate' the coachee about the principles and patterns of homeostasis and conservation within the organisation. In this way, the executive also learns not to take these forces personally but to work with these by anticipating resistance and appreciating what might be being conserved. The executive has to be aware of flaws in the system that might be holding people back, such as not giving them the required information to change or the required coaching and support to deal with the changes.

The coach's role in reducing resistance to change

Below are some general guidelines for the coach to employ when trying to minimise resistance to change in any organisation:

1   Announce changes promptly. Ensure that plans are in place to disseminate information instantly and in an orderly fashion, so that everyone is informed at the same time. The coach should ensure that the groundwork for the changes is laid or the change initiative can be undone by rumours.

2   Make sure you can clearly articulate:
    ➤ why change is necessary
    ➤ the specific benefits to all key stakeholders including those who have to facilitate, implement and adjust to the changes
    ➤ the financial benefits of the coaching program. These must be related to the business unit's costs. A coaching program will only succeed if individuals can see the financial rewards. The other payoffs are usually seen as a bonus, at least at first.

3   Brainstorm with those involved prior to implementing the program.

4   Avoid trivial changes.

5   Nominate the forces 'for' and the forces 'against' change—for example, conduct a detailed force-field analysis that nominates the major 'pushing for' and 'pushing against' forces. Clearly articulate what you see as the forces of conservation—both positive and negative. Show how your change program will deal with these.

6   Be aware of potential resistors who want to 'conserve' the status quo. Do not presume people will adjust. Resistance has to be tackled otherwise people will undermine the changes on a subterranean level. A general rule when dealing with resistant individuals, depending on their power, is to align them by offering explanations and support. If this fails it may be necessary to get rid of the resistance, or at least minimise its effects. This could involve the coach discussing the issue with the sponsor/driver of the coaching program and having both parties reach a solution such as excluding the individual(s) from the program. One could be dealing with what has been called 'an emotional plague' that can spread throughout the organisation and undo the change efforts.

7   Ideally, balance an unpopular change with a popular one.

8   Enlist an outside service to evaluate the changes and success of the program. An outside evaluation guarantees objectivity and can assist the coach in reviewing objectives and strategies for the next stage of the initiative. Because of the perceived need for independent, objective evaluations, we have found ourselves conducting more and more assessments and evaluations of coaching programs. For instance, we evaluate the coaching needs of an organisation and assess the coach's suitability for a particular coaching program and whether the coach requires further resources such as a network of specialist coaches to refer to when necessary. We evaluate the progress of both the coachees and the organisation.

Summary Coaching is a structured process focused on outcomes, whereby a coach works with an individual or team to clarify issues, challenge self-limiting beliefs, modify outdated responses, generate solutions and take action to enhance performance. The leader or individual then applies these skills to his or her own staff, thereby developing and fostering a genuine learning organisation. It is increasingly recognised that coaching cultures are necessary for organisations to manage change, grow and develop. A genuine culture of coaching is epitomised by individual action and responsibility that occurs within a climate of authentic, empowering and committed relationships.

The coaching process —guidelines and protocols

The purpose of this chapter is to provide guidelines on the various stages of the coaching process. By process, we mean the steps involved in the establishment, progression and development of the coaching partnership. Although certain sections of this chapter, for example the coaching needs analysis, are more pertinent to coaches working in organisations, the general stages of the coaching process are relevant to coaching across all specialty areas.

The specific process model that we employ involves four phases: (1) establishing the coaching partnership; (2) action planning; (3) the coaching cycle; and (4) evaluation and follow-up. The time frames suggested here are only guides. The period of time taken to move through each phase depends on the coachee and the complexity of the coaching issue. The coach's discretion, intuition and experience should determine the pace and timing of the coaching intervention. At times the coach may have to adopt a more directive role, particularly if the required changes and improvements are urgent. At other times, the coach may deem it wise to match the coachee's pace and move through the phases at a slower rate.

The four phases of coaching

Phase one Establishing the coaching partnership

- ➤ Meeting with management—coaching needs analysis, the coach–client protocol
- ➤ Proposal of services
- ➤ Coaching contract
- ➤ First contact with the coachee
- ➤ First coaching session—the coaching agreement
- ➤ Second coaching session—assessment
- ➤ Report to management

Phase two Action planning

- ➤ Establishing values, vision and specific goals
- ➤ Developing action strategies

Phase three The coaching cycle

- ➤ Review
- ➤ Reassess
- ➤ Feedback

Phase four Evaluation and follow-up

- ➤ Evaluation
- ➤ Final sessions—closure
- ➤ Preventing slippage
- ➤ Follow-up plans

Phase one Establishing the coaching partnership

Meeting with management

As with any client relationship, the first meeting with a prospective client is critical to the success of the coaching intervention. Coaches may be contacted by an organisation interested in either external coaching for one or more of their key staff, or setting up an in-house coaching program. Conversely, the coach may contact the organisation and arrange a meeting to discuss the

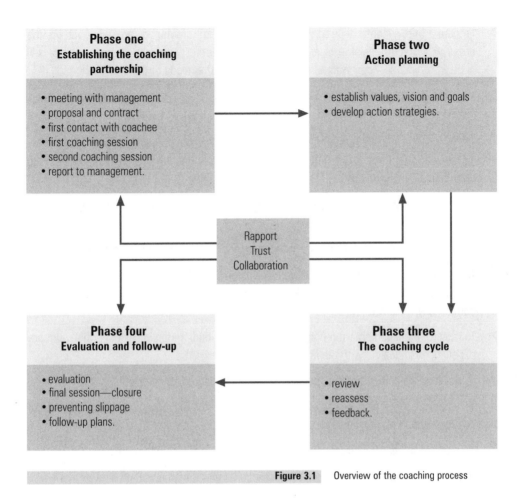

Phase one **Establishing the coaching** **partnership** • meeting with management • proposal and contract • first contact with coachee • first coaching session • second coaching session • report to management.	**Phase two** **Action planning** • establish values, vision and goals • develop action strategies.
Phase four **Evaluation and follow-up** • evaluation • final session—closure • preventing slippage • follow-up plans.	**Phase three** **The coaching cycle** • review • reassess • feedback.

Rapport
Trust
Collaboration

Figure 3.1   Overview of the coaching process

services he or she provides. Regardless of the nature of the initial contact, the coach can benefit from having a structure for the first meeting. Some guidelines include:

1 Prior to the first meeting with management

➤ Ask yourself:
- What is the purpose of the meeting?
- What do I want to achieve?
- What do I want to come away with?

➤ Do a background search on the organisation, including any current changes or challenges the company may be facing.

- Prepare a brief synopsis (one to two minutes maximum) of who you are, what you do, the areas which you specialise in and why you are meeting with management. Do not sell yourself or your services. Rather, establish and meet the needs of the organisation.

2 Goals of the first meeting with management

- To learn about the needs of the organisation.

- To demonstrate, through questioning and reflecting, that you have listened and understood what management has said.

- To show that you understand and appreciate the specific and unique challenges facing the organisation.

- To demonstrate that you are aware of the company's strengths and achievements.

- To establish, through your presence, your words and your interpersonal style, that you are a responsible, reliable, knowledgeable coach who individuals in the organisation could comfortably work with.

- To assure management, through your questioning and general dialogue, that you are experienced in dealing with the issues/needs that arise.

- To reach an agreement on the coaching practices to address these needs.

- To agree on the logistics of the coaching program, for example, the venue, number of sessions, reporting procedures, evaluation methods, etc.

- To agree upon financial arrangements.

- To show how coaching can benefit the individual(s) and the organisation (see below).

3 Relaying the benefits of coaching

Obviously, the coach has to relate the benefits of the coaching service to the particular individual or organisation. However, there are several generic benefits of coaching that the coach can build upon and tailor to the specific organisation. For example, some functions and benefits of an external coach include:

- opening up new opportunities and options for learning and development solutions

- providing an objective and fresh point of view

- providing specialist coaching knowledge, skills and abilities

- maintaining a neutral, non-political stance

➤ acting as a catalyst for change by impacting on the way people learn

➤ maintaining confidentiality without compromise

➤ training key personnel in the organisation to adopt a coaching role

➤ training key individuals in the organisation to establish a coaching culture.

4 Conducting a coaching needs analysis

There are several steps involved in analysing the coaching needs of an organisation. Prior to this, however, it is essential to address the following two issues. First, in our experience and that of our colleagues, some clients expect an external solution and not one that involves any real alteration of their personal behaviour patterns. Essentially, as mentioned previously, some organisations are searching for 'a quick fix' and the coach has to hastily dispel these expectations. One method of doing so is to briefly explain how people learn and the time frame involved. The coach can use the following table:

Table 3.1 Stages of knowledge acquisition

Knowledge

Depending on the complexity of the skill, knowledge acquisition can take an hour, several hours or longer.

Understanding and practice

A coachee may learn how to perform a new skill but understanding the psychological processes involved and practising it until the desired level of competence is reached can take weeks, even months.

Transfer of knowledge

Even when the coachee is highly skilled in a particular area, it can take several months before he or she can creatively transfer these skills to other areas of his or her work or personal life.

The second issue which demands the coach's attention is the manner in which the coaching needs analysis is conducted. Some managers may feel angry or humiliated that they have to call in an external agency. Feelings of anxiety can be triggered and managers may adopt a defensive and unhelpful attitude. It is important that the coach is sensitive to the manager's anxieties, and takes care to appreciate and acknowledge the organisation's successes and its willingness to embrace change. Furthermore, the coach should not present himself or herself as a 'guru' with all the answers. After all, it is in the very first meeting that the seeds of an interactive, collaborative and trusting relationship are sown.

Step one **Establish who the stakeholders are**

As we discuss in the chapter on evaluation (see Chapter 17), it is critical that the coach establishes who the key stakeholders are in the planned coaching intervention. In our experience, the likelihood of a coaching intervention being successful is considerably higher if the needs of all stakeholders are assessed and met.

Coaching interventions are essentially programs of change. And as we all know, change involves costs. These costs include financial investment, time and personnel. Importantly, as we discussed in Chapter 2, there are also considerable psychological costs associated with change. The coach has to recognise the costs to the key stakeholders of the planned change.

We define the key stakeholders as all those individuals who control the resources necessary for the success of the coaching intervention. Three main groups of stakeholders have been identified. These are:

➤ *Opinion leaders* Those individuals who can influence others in relation to getting the project up and running. These may include the CEO, general managers, managing directors or directors of learning and development.

➤ *Process owners* Those individuals who are responsible for the work processes in the coachees' field of operation. These may include senior managers and team leaders.

➤ *Resistors* Those individuals within the organisation who have the power to disrupt the coaching program at any stage. It is crucial that the coach either aligns such individuals or is somehow able to exclude them from the equation. Ideally, the coach should include these individuals in meetings, in conducting the coaching needs analysis and in determining evaluation measures. Recognising and working with individuals who have the power and propensity to destabilise the coaching process requires a considerable amount of 'political savvy' on the part of the coach.

Step two **Gather information on the organisation**

When conducting a coaching needs analysis, the coach can gather information about the organisation on three levels: the organisational level, position level, and personal level. While we provide a series of questions to guide coaches, both in-house and external, in collecting this data these are not necessarily intended as a formal guide. That is, depending on the scope of the planned intervention, the coach can use the questions at any stage throughout discussions with management. If the organisation is intending to introduce a significant coaching program, then the coach may wish to include the following questions in a formal survey to the key stakeholders.

Organisational level

✓ What does the decision maker(s)/organisation know about coaching?

✓ What do the individuals (prospective coachees) know about coaching?

✓ How receptive are they to coaching?

✓ How does the organisation view coaching with regard to fitting in with the current learning and development programs?

✓ Has the organisation employed any coaching or mentoring programs in the past?

✓ How successful were they?

✓ What factors contributed to their success? or failure?

✓ How is the current learning and development program meeting the needs of the organisation?

✓ How is it not meeting these needs?

✓ What are the standards used to measure and evaluate the current learning and development program?

✓ Is the organisation satisfied with these standards?

✓ What involvement would Human Resources personnel and trainers have in the coaching program?

✓ What is the current organisational climate (e.g. morale, absenteeism, staff turnover) like?

✓ Have any system changes affected performance levels recently?

✓ Does the organisation have a policy regarding people management and career development?

✓ Why does the organisation feel it requires external assistance now?

Position level

✓ What are the job descriptions of the prospective coachees?

✓ What major competencies or skills (e.g. personal skills, operational skills, relationship-building skills) are required?

✓ Has the organisation isolated any specific gaps in performance in these three areas?

✓ Of these, which is the most critical—that is, what should be the initial focus of the coaching intervention?

Personal level

✓ Is there a performance appraisal system in place?

✓ Does the coach have access to the results?

✓ Does it identify gaps in performance?

✓ Is there a system in place to work with individuals on the identified gaps?

✓ What training and development programs are already in place to enhance performance?

5 The coach–client protocol

The coach's own version of the coach–client protocol below should be given to management at the first meeting. It contains a summary of the coach's qualifications, services offered and a review of what the coachee can expect from the coaching partnership.

Ideally the coach, whether in-house or external, should talk briefly with the nominated coachee prior to the commencement of the coaching sessions. It is a means of establishing initial rapport and of giving both parties the opportunity to determine if they can work together. It also allows the coach to determine whether or not he or she has the requisite knowledge, skills and abilities to work with the individual.

If, for any reason, it is not possible to conduct this preliminary meeting, it is extremely important that the prospective coachee receives a copy of the coach–client protocol prior to session one. It gives the coachee time to review the document and prepare any questions about it for the first session. Importantly, it is a means by which the coach can attempt to minimise the coachee's anxiety about what is involved in the coaching alliance.

The coach–client protocol—a template

Who is ...?

(Provide a brief description of yourself, your qualifications and the services you provide.)

_____

_____

_____

_____

_____

Some benefits

(List some of the major benefits of coaching in general and the specific benefits of your particular coaching services—you may wish to adapt these to the individual client.)

_____

_____

What is involved in a coaching session:

➤ What the coachee can expect during the coaching process (e.g. support, challenge, a safe environment, etc.).

➤ What the initial interview session involves (e.g. a discussion of the coaching agreement, establishing roles and expectations, an explanation of how the coaching sessions work).

➤ What subsequent coaching sessions involve (e.g. assessments/structured interviews and profiling designed to highlight those features of the individual's personal and operational mastery skills as they impact on work performance)

and

(Working with specific personal or operational skills as highlighted during the assessment phase. Emphasise that proven coaching techniques and interventions are adapted and applied to help enhance the individual's job/task performance level to help them reach their goals.)

How long will each session be? _____

How many sessions will I need? _____

Will I be given any homework? For example, self-monitoring, various tasks, and exercises are recommended so that feedback can be given in the following coaching sessions.

_____

Will our sessions be confidential? _____

Nominate the rules of confidentiality you adhere to. _____

Will there be any written reports about me? For example, any reports submitted by me to management will be viewed by the coachee prior to submission, etc.

_____

_____

Proposal of services

Having established the coaching needs of the individual or the organisation, the next step for the external coach is to present a proposal of services to management. The proposal should be submitted as soon as possible after the initial meeting and a covering note should be attached to the proposal indicating the time the coach will call to follow-up. The proposal should be brief and contain the following information:

A proposal of services

1 **Background** Briefly describe the circumstances that led to the proposal, for example, who made the initial contact, when it was made, who was present at the first meeting with management.

2 **Identified needs** If the proposal is for a coaching program that will involve large sections of the organisation, briefly outline the coaching needs of the entire organisation as established through the coaching needs analysis and discussion with management. Identify the groups or individuals nominated for coaching by management and specify their particular coaching needs. If the proposal is for a few individuals, simply focus on their identified needs.

3 **The coaching program** Outline the program, that is, the number of sessions involved and the generic content of the sessions, such as assessment, exploring values, goal setting, action planning, etc. Establish evaluation and review processes such as reports to management.

4 **Establish the costs of the coaching program**

5 **Nominate the terms of payment**

6 **Establish the commencement date and period of services**

Once the proposal has been accepted, a contract of services should be sent to the accounts department or the nominated liaison person.

The coaching contract

There are various formats for coaching contracts and many coaches have their own preferred method of contracting. The following contract is simply a blueprint that outlines the essential elements that should be included.

Contract of services

Client _____

Address _____

Contact name(s) _____

Coach _____

Address _____

Other contact name(s) _____

Coaching services _____

Commencement date _____ Expected completion date _____

Number of participants _____

Fee _____

Payable to _____

Fee schedule Payable in full before _____ or by 2 payments _____

First payment _____ payable before _____

Second payment _____ payable before _____

Terms of engagement and confidentiality agreement

   1 Brief and fee structure

   2 Fee payment/schedule

   3 Additional charges

   4 Suspension of work

   5 Termination of work

   6 Confidentiality and non-disclosure statement

   7 Liability

   8 The terms of engagement will apply unless modified in a subsequent letter and signed by the consultant and client. The signing of this form by the client constitutes an acceptance by the client that the consultant has been appointed/contracted to perform the agreed upon services as arranged by the coach and the client.

9   The coachee is responsible for his or her own achievements and success, and the coach cannot and does not promise that the coachee will take any specific action or attain specific goals.

10   The coach does not provide counselling or therapy.

Signed for and on behalf of client _____

Date _____

Signed for and on behalf of coach _____

Date _____

First contact with the coachee

As mentioned above, the coach ideally should meet with the coachee prior to the first coaching session. If this is not possible, the coachee should be given a copy of the coach–client protocol to bring to the first coaching session.

The first contact with the coachee can be anxiety provoking for both parties. It can be helpful if the coach prepares a brief interview or a series of questions to ask, or information to give to the coachee. The following guidelines might be useful:

1   Introduce yourself and give a brief summary of what you do.

2   Ask what the prospective coachee knows about coaching.

3   Clarify your role as a coach.

4   Ask the prospective coachee in what ways coaching might help him or her.

5   Ask which specific issues or problems the coachee wishes to address in the coaching sessions.

6   Ask the coachee how he or she feels about being coached.

7   Briefly explain the logistics of the coaching program.

The first coaching session

The coach has to be armed with a solid knowledge of the philosophical basis of coaching and the structure of the coaching process, and be trained in the competent use of various coaching tools and techniques. Such knowledge and competence will allow the coach to approach the first session with confidence and the intention of listening and truly understanding the coachee's current situation. The coach's listening and questioning should be guided by two overriding concerns:

1   In what ways does the coachee want my help?

2   Do I have the necessary knowledge, skills and abilities to work with this person?

The general aims of the first session(s) are:

➤   to form a collaborative and interactive partnership

➤   to establish a safe, trusting environment that will facilitate change

➤   to begin to establish oneself as a supportive, trustworthy, non-judgmental person who is nonetheless willing to challenge and confront when needed

➤   to explore the catalyst for the coachee's decision to seek coaching

➤   to establish a broad overview of what challenges the coachee is facing and what he or she expects from you.

It is usually helpful to begin the session by discussing the coach–client protocol and any concerns or questions the coachee may have about it. In our experience, it is the issue of confidentiality that concerns most coachees. The coach may need to take the time to discuss the limits of confidentiality in more detail until the coachee feels more secure about self-disclosure.

The coaching agreement

The most effective way to establish the expectations of the coaching alliance—remembering that this may be causing the coachee considerable anxiety—is to discuss the coaching agreement. The agreement, as shown below, is between the coach and coachee, not the coach and management. Both in-house and external coaches should employ this agreement which details both the coach and the coachee's responsibilities as collaborative partners. It also serves to set the limits or boundaries of the relationship.

The coaching agreement

Between _____
(Coachee)

and _____
(Coach)

In undertaking to meet with you I am committing myself to meeting at the time(s) we have agreed upon and providing a safe setting within which we can explore issues and difficulties and move towards change. I will endeavour to facilitate you in this process.

In undertaking to see me for coaching you are committing yourself to seeing me regularly at the agreed time and optimising the use of the time we have together. Being honest and objective, as best as you can, is essential. Your intent to grow in excellence and make increasingly worthwhile contributions by providing value-added work is a key to a successful coaching experience.

To be coachable, you must ensure that:

➤ your intent to change and desire for change are serious

➤ you are ready to work and receive feedback

➤ you are willing to try new ways of learning, be truthful, keep to your commitments and inform your coach immediately when things are not working for you

➤ you are willing to explore, challenge, and change thoughts, feelings and actions that you recognise are self-defeating

➤ you understand that your coach will be focused on you and your best interests, not just your goals

➤ you understand that your coach will educate, support and encourage you while you do the work and reap the benefits of your efforts

➤ you are willing to give the coach the benefit of the doubt and try new concepts or different ways of doing things

➤ you recognise the value and worth the organisation is placing on you by investing in your personal development.

Confidentiality

The coaching service is confidential except in the following instances:

1 The progress of these sessions may be discussed with senior management.

2 If you give me information for the purpose of discussion with others.

Cancellations

If you wish to change the time of a session please let me know well in advance. If you do not arrive on time and have not cancelled by the beginning of the session, I will assume you are coming. If you miss the session without notification, you or your organisation will still be charged for the session.

Duration and termination

Once I have agreed to see you my commitment is open-ended. I will see you for as long as we agree coaching is useful. You may, of course, finish seeing me at any time. I ask that you give me a minimum of one month's notice of your decision to stop. It is better to plan the ending in advance and allow for a degree of 'closure'.

Records

Any written notes are securely kept and are confidential.

Policy documents

These cover areas of client information and our professional code of ethics. They will be made available on request.

I have read and understood this agreement.

Name:_____   Signature:_____
                    (Coachee)

                                             Date: _____

Name:_____   Signature:_____
                     (Coach)

                                             Date: _____

The angry coachee

Individual coachees respond in different ways in the first meeting with the coach. For instance, a coachee who has been referred for coaching may react angrily to the situation. He or she may spend a considerable part of the first session expressing anger, frustration and a sense of injustice about being referred for coaching. Depending on the extent of the coachee's grievances, the coach may be wise to postpone discussing and signing the coaching agreement until the next session.

An angry coachee may sign the agreement out of compliance rather than true commitment. Allowing the coachee to 'let off steam' might be necessary for the coach to establish himself or herself as a neutral, non-judgmental person who is able to contain the coachee's feelings. The coach could give the coaching agreement to the coachee and request that he or she brings it to the following session.

Scaling and profiles

In most cases, the first session involves discussing and signing the coaching agreement, and broadly discussing the coachee's concerns. It is at this early stage that the coach can introduce the concept of scaling. It involves asking coachees to express themselves using a number scale. For example, 'On a scale from 1 to 10, how satisfied are you with your work performance?'. Scaling is not only an efficient means for the coachee to express himself or herself but is a useful technique to establish priorities for action, for example, 'On a scale from 1 to 10, how important is this to you?'. Scaling is also a simple method of measuring progress throughout the sessions.

It is during the first session that the coachee's goals will begin to emerge. However, at this stage, the coach is still 'diagnosing' the situation and it would be premature to begin to formally establish goals. Essentially, the coach is building up a picture of the coachee in relation to his or her current work and life situation, values, how committed he or she is to the coaching program and the coachee's personality style.

During this exploratory stage, we find it helpful to administer the following brief assessments or profiles (see Chapter 4):

1 A biographical profile

2 A life balance profile

3 A values profile

4 The coaching commitment profile (see Chapter 6)

These profiles provide fertile ground for dialoguing and serve to clarify the coachee's issues. Towards the end of the first session then, the coach and coachee usually have a general idea of the topics or areas that will dominate the coaching alliance.

It is recommended that the coach suggest that the coachee complete an out-of-session assignment for the following meeting. The purpose of this is to maintain continuity between the sessions and to establish the central role of 'homework' or assignments in any successful coaching enterprise. The task may ask the coachee to monitor the occurrence of a particular behaviour or thought pattern that is impacting on his or her work performance.

Second coaching session

The goal of session two is to assess the coachee on various aspects of his or her life and work performance. Many of the issues surrounding assessment and the assessment protocols are discussed in Chapter 4. For now we shall simply note some of the assessment instruments the coach can employ during this session. Again, the use of the various assessments at any stage of the coaching cycle depends on the coach and the coachee. We are only offering guidelines.

The following profiles are appropriate for all coachees:

➤ A learning profile

➤ A personality profile

For the business coach working with business owners or managers, the following instruments are recommended:

➤ A vision/mission statement

➤ A business owner's profile

➤ A coaching needs analysis for business owners

When working with managers and executives to enhance their work performance, the following profiles are useful:

➤ A work performance profile

➤ A self-assessment competency profile

➤ A job analysis profile

➤ A personal development plan

➤ A competency feedback profile—to be given to the coachee's nominated colleagues.

If the coachee's needs revolve around leadership skills, the coach can administer the following:

➤ A leadership competencies wheel

➤ Areas of leadership profile

➤ Qualities of leadership profile

It is generally recommended that coachees complete these assessments in the session rather than later when they may respond in a more studied, less spontaneous fashion. The results of the assessment can be discussed with the coachee after the completion of each profile or all together in the next session.

A report to management

Depending on the arrangement made with management, the coach may be required to write a report outlining the results of the coachee's assessment and the agreed upon goals and coaching strategies. In our coach training workshops, students frequently raise the issue of the possible conflict between confidentiality and report writing. We have found that the easiest way to avoid any betrayal of confidentiality is to have the coachee read and sign-off on the report before it is submitted to management. Of course, management has to be informed of the coach's report writing process at the very first meeting.

Individual coaches frequently have their preferred way of writing reports. The following headings are only guidelines to the content of a management report. These include:

1 *Management feedback*   What management has discussed with the coach and the areas they nominated for improvement, for example interpersonal style with colleagues, time management, general managerial skills or team building.

2 *Feedback from the coachee*   Based on the assessment profiles and discussions with the coachee, outline the coachee's view of the current work situation, his or her stated attitude to coaching, and the areas the coachee has targeted for coaching.

3 *Value to the organisation*   List the technical or operational skills that the coachee brings to the organisation, such as advanced strategic planning skills and superior decision-making abilities.

4 *Major strengths*   List the coachee's personal strengths, for example loyalty and persistence.

5 *Some behavioural indicators*   List personality characteristics, beliefs and habitual patterns of behaviour that impact on the coachee's work performance. An example of this could be that the coachee avoids giving feedback, both positive and negative—such behaviour is related to issues of assertiveness and expressing feelings.

6 *Action plan*   Outline the goals and strategies that the coach and coachee have agreed upon.

The coach may give a brief outline within the report of what has been covered so far. This will be determined by the stage the coaching intervention is at. The outline should include what topic or issue was addressed, what strategies were employed (e.g. assertive techniques, role-playing, challenging self-limiting beliefs) and how these have played out in the workplace so far. If management has requested specific information, for example what would be the ideal working environment for the coachee or what are the keys to managing the coachee, then these should be included in the report. Finally, the coach should nominate when the next—usually final—report will be submitted.

Phase two   Action planning

Establish values, vision and goals

At this stage of the coaching process, the coach and coachee should have discussed and explored the coachee's assessment results. The coachee's values will have been established, if not fully explored, and both partners should have a reasonable idea of the coachee's vision and general goals.

Together, the coach and coachee can review the coachee's job performance in detail. The coach can question and encourage the coachee to explore any habitual thoughts, feelings or behavioural responses that may be contributing to the difficulties at work. The coach and coachee discuss the coachee's strengths and challenges, the coachee's vision of the future and the overall objectives of the coaching relationship.

The coach and coachee may also talk about the process of change and explore any resistance on the part of the coachee. The coach, too, should be aware of any resistance on his or her part towards working with the coachee or the particular issues that are being addressed.

The coach and coachee now move from the general to the specific and work on establishing specific personal or organisational goals. As we have already discussed the steps involved in goal setting in our previous book we shall not discuss the process in any detail here. However, we reiterate that goals should be clear and specific, appropriately difficult and challenging, time limited, and measurable.

As part of establishing strategies and action plans to achieve the stated goals, the coach and coachee can conduct a costs–benefits analysis or a force-field analysis (see Chapter 14) of the advantages and disadvantages of the planned changes. Together, they can address issues such as who will be affected by the planned changes, how they might respond and how these individuals can be aligned to the proposed changes. Because we have discussed action planning in our previous book the topic will not be explored in any great detail here however the following questions could be incorporated into an action plan.

An action plan outline:

1   What is my learning plan and action plan?

2   How important is it to me on a scale of 1 to 10?

3   What will I do?

4   When will I do it?

5   Where will I do it?

6   What strategies do I need to accomplish the plan?

7   How will I demonstrate that I have attained my goal?

8   How will my colleagues recognise my new knowledge and skills?

Phase three   The coaching cycle

Once the coach and coachee have established the goals and strategies of the alliance, most of the remaining sessions are devoted to reviewing the coachee's progress and addressing any obstacles or difficulties that may arise. The coach gives feedback to the coachee, and goals may be reviewed and reassessed in an ongoing cycle. The coach supports, challenges, congratulates and stretches the coachee in order to enhance performance, ensure the transfer of skills from the sessions to the workplace and encourage increasing self-awareness and self-responsibility in the coachee.

The following diagram illustrates the flow of each session within the continuing coaching cycle.

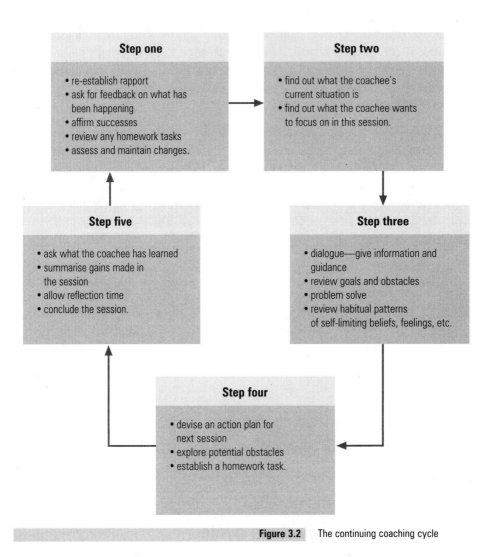

Figure 3.2   The continuing coaching cycle

Session indicators

It is perhaps timely to briefly discuss some indicators which can show whether the coaching session is working well or not. Of course, certain indicators may suggest different interpretations for different coachees. However, we believe that the following list of indicators has general applicability to most coaching sessions.

Indicators of a successful session

➤ The coachee reports successes and gains since the previous session.

➤ The coachee feels free to report failures as well as successes.

➤ The coachee suggests what he or she would like to work on.

➤ The coachee seeks information and asks questions.

➤ The coachee challenges the coach and contributes his or her own ideas.

➤ The coachee accepts responsibility for his or her choices.

Indicators of an unsuccessful session

➤ The coachee reports only failures since the previous meeting.

➤ The coachee is critical of the coach and his or her techniques.

➤ The coachee is disengaged, withholding and 'absent'.

➤ The coachee appears unconcerned or unenthusiastic about the meeting.

As we discuss in the chapter on overcoming resistance (see Chapter 11), the coach can employ various techniques to deal with these barriers. The coach may employ listening and questioning techniques to determine the coachee's current concerns. Or the coach may choose to support or confront the individual regarding his or her obvious reluctance. In many respects, the way the coach responds to these negative indicators depends on his or her relationship with the coachee and the coach's skills in dealing with such situations. The general guiding principle is that the coach recognises these 'symptoms' and brings them into the open immediately.

Phase four   Evaluation and follow-up

Evaluation

As we mention in Chapter 17, evaluation is an ongoing process. Each session usually begins with an evaluation of the progress the coachee has made in the interim. The coach and coachee are also encouraged to assess themselves on an ongoing basis through the use of self-assessment profiles as described in Chapter 4. Evaluation also provides an opportunity for the coach to offer a summary of the results of the coaching intervention, his or her evaluation, and recommendations for follow-up coaching.

Final sessions

Preventing slippage

The coach and coachee must develop strategies to ensure the coachee maintains his or her gains and skills and that slippage does not occur. A useful method to prevent relapse is for the coach and coachee to work on the following questions just prior to the termination of the coaching contract:

➤ How confident are you about following the action plan?

➤ What might prevent you from following it?

➤ What will be the hardest part for you?

➤ How will you know when difficulties arise? What will the signs be?

➤ What resources do you have to assist you during these times?

➤ How will you remind yourself of what you have learned? For example will you:
  – keep a log or journal to recall what you have learned?
  – involve significant others in giving you feedback?
  – receive reminders from the coach, such as e-mails or faxes?
  – share the action plan with others in your workplace?
  – take advantage of follow-up coaching sessions over a particular period of time?

The emotional aspects of ending a coaching relationship

Coaching is a personal relationship—a genuine connection which develops between two parties over time. Endings are not easy. They are an emotional event accompanied by implications of rejection and abandonment as well as regeneration and new beginnings. The coach has to face certain questions regarding the ending of a coaching assignment. Some of these include:

➤ What is my capacity to recognise that a coaching assignment has reached its limits?

➤ What criteria do I use to establish whether it is time to end the relationship?

➤ What are my feelings about ending the relationship? and about endings in general?

➤ Am I tempted to end the relationship when faced with no progress, or resistance? What skills do I have to overcome this tendency? What support networks do I have in place?

➤ How do I deal with a coaching relationship that is terminated prematurely by the coachee or the organisation?

There are some general indicators that the coaching intervention has reached a natural conclusion. The rate of change may have slowed down and the coachee may appear to be consolidating and transferring the skills he or she has acquired. The coachee may appear less interested in the sessions. He or she may not produce any new material or issues to deal with and it may seem that the coach is going over old ground. Finally, the coachee may be satisfied with what has transpired so far in the sessions, and more insightful and resourceful than before.

The coach has to recognise these signs and discuss his or her observations with the coachee. It is important that the coach summarises and celebrates the coachee's successes and encourages the coachee to reflect on the coaching relationship. Even if both parties agree that further coaching sessions are not required at this stage, the coach can build in follow-up sessions or arrange telephone or e-mail contact.

Follow-up sessions

In addition to ensuring that the coachee continues to progress, and apply the learned skills, follow-up sessions also bring a sense of gradual closure to the relationship. They can serve to extend the coaching partnership for a considerable period of time, depending on the needs of the coachee or the organisation.

A guide to follow-up questioning:

➤ What is working with the action plan?

➤ What is not working with the action plan?

➤ What successes and disappointments have you experienced?

➤ Have you 'slipped' in any way?

➤ Have any circumstances changed that mean we need to review the action plan?

➤ What do we need to do to get back on track?

➤ What do we need to do to maintain your gains?

Summary As we have mentioned regularly throughout this chapter and indeed throughout the book there is no one process that can encompass the richness and complexity of the coaching alliance. Coaching is, by definition, a dynamic interaction that entails flexibility, spontaneity and creativity. We have outlined and discussed some of the components of the coaching process that we have found to be critical to a successful coaching enterprise.

PART TWO
Coaching tools and techniques

In coaching literature the terms 'tools' and 'techniques' tend to be used interchangeably. For our purposes we have found it useful to distinguish between the two. When referring to tools we mean instruments, like a stethoscope. There are numerous tools the coach can add to his or her toolkit. These include assessment instruments, evaluation tools, 'challenging' exercises and relaxation exercises. We need to learn how to skilfully use these tools.

The term 'techniques' refers to the way in which we use the tools. The word technique derives from the Greek *techne* meaning art and the word performance derives from the Latin *performare* meaning to give form to. A technique therefore, is the art of using a tool, or the way in which the tool is used.

The purpose of these tools and techniques

The tools and techniques presented in this section of the book serve several purposes. These include the following:

➤ assessing the needs of the coachee and/or the organisation

➤ gaining insight into, and knowledge about, the coachee

➤ increasing the coachee's self-awareness

➤ increasing the coachee's range of choices

➤ developing and enhancing the coachee's personal and technical skills

➤ challenging the coachee's self-limiting beliefs and attitudes

➤ promoting self-responsibility and self-direction in the coachee

➤ evaluating the outcomes of coaching interventions.

The tools and techniques we provide ultimately aim to transform or change the coachee. The accompanying instructions offer guidelines for the coach to enable them to produce something different within the coachee or the organisation.

As responsible professionals it is imperative that coaches understand and are competent in the use of the behavioural change tools and techniques we discuss in this section. They are not intended as cut-out recipes to be added to a coaching cookbook. Although we supply guidelines for using the various techniques, our experience as coach educators has continually shown that coaches require supervised training by a trained clinician/psychologist in learning how to use the various tools and techniques that are available. Indeed, our specialist workshops on specific coaching tools and techniques developed out of this perceived need. Coaching is about change, and change is fundamentally a psychological process. It involves emotions, thoughts, motivation and actions. For example, working with emotions, challenging beliefs and overcoming resistance are particular areas where coaches require supervision and mentoring by a trained psychologist to ensure that they are using the techniques appropriately and correctly.

In Chapter 1 we distinguished between coaching which develops operational mastery skills (hard skills) and coaching which aims to develop and enhance personal mastery skills (soft skills). Yet the psychological foundations of the two types of coaching differ only by degrees. Certainly, coaching to enhance soft skills focuses on exploring and working with values, beliefs, emotions and resistance. However, even when the coaching focus is on hard skills such as strategic planning or developing appraisal systems, the same psychological processes are at play albeit to a lesser degree. Therefore coaches, regardless of their specialty niche, have to be skilled in recognising and working with the psychological processes of the individual and the organisation.

Ongoing training, learning, and development are of course not restricted to coaches. Professionals in other areas such as law, medicine and psychology are required to undergo a period of internship and supervision. Furthermore, given that the motto of coaching is 'lifelong learning', coaches themselves are expected to pursue continuous learning. Ongoing training and mentoring should be a coach's number one priority.

None of the tools or techniques discussed in this section of the book are deemed mandatory or even suitable for use with every coachee. A coach should be provided with ethical guidelines in the use of psychology-based tools. These should be provided by the coaching school when the coach undertakes their training. The coach should also ensure that the coach trainer is a licensed psychologist.

Each tool is appropriate for a particular context—namely the coachee's specific needs and agenda, and the stage the coaching process is currently at. Each tool has to have relevance to the task at hand. The particular technique the coach employs depends on the coach's skill and the coachee's readiness to experiment with the technique. We agree with Mahoney (1991) that techniques are ritualised methods of human relatedness and communication. The tools and techniques discussed here only assume meaning when they are embedded in the coaching relationship. They are only useful when they are carefully chosen and applied to a specific coaching situation with a specific individual coachee in mind.

Tools and techniques—some general guidelines

1   The type of technique the coach chooses to use depends on how he or she assesses and 'diagnoses' the client's situation. However, time constraints also have to be considered. These can dictate whether, for example, the coach chooses a direct, action-oriented technique such as role-playing or a more intensive and time-consuming technique such as working with emotions or self-awareness.

2   A coachee's issues can be worked with on a continuum of intensity and depth. For example, at times a simple relaxation technique (see Chapter 13) may be sufficient to calm and centre a coachee. On other occasions, a coachee may be extremely distressed about a workplace incident. In this case, the coach would explore the issue in greater depth. He or she would discuss the coachee's response, feelings, self-talk and beliefs about the incident. The choice of intensity and depth depends on the emotional availability and openness of the coachee as well as the coach's skills.

3   Timing in the use of a technique is also critical. For instance, if a coachee broaches a difficult topic towards the end of a session, the coach can relegate it to the following session and conclude the current meeting with a review of achievements attained so far.

4   Coaches need a variety of tools and techniques to call on. Refining our theories, models and techniques is done outside of session times. When we are face-to-face with the coachee our attention should be totally focused on the individual. We listen, observe and then decide which technique would be the most appropriate.

5   We have to be knowledgeable about the techniques we employ and use them systematically. Understanding the psychological foundations of techniques, and knowing how, when and why the technique works allows us to give a clear rationale for its use to the coachee.

6   The coach can be directive in terms of which technique to use. If, for example, the coach believes that a coachee is struggling with self-awareness, then he or she can direct the coaching sessions toward this area.

7   The questions we ask, the assessment instruments we use and the techniques we choose all serve to influence the coachee. Our position is never neutral. Our techniques guide the coachee in certain directions, along certain paths and towards certain outcomes. Our influence is clear. Yet we must use this influence to support what coachees want, and to expand their choices so that they lead more fulfilling, self-directed lives.

8   There are a number of self-coaching techniques the coach can teach the coachee to enhance the coachee's control over his or her own life.

The coach's notebook

While each coachee and coaching partnership is unique, there are specific tools and techniques that are applicable to specific coaching issues across the board. Many of our students have found it useful to keep a coaching notebook to assist them in selecting and recording the most appropriate techniques for particular coaching issues.

As well as guiding coaches in the selection of techniques, the notebook can serve as a useful and efficient tool for establishing a database for the individual coach. Over time, it allows the coach to track outcomes and any difficulties associated with a particular technique.

The coach's notebook

1   **The issue:** What is the coaching issue or problem?

2   **The goal(s):** What do we want to achieve in the coaching partnership?

3   **Time frame:** What time frame do we have to accomplish these goals?

4   **Tools:** What tools do I have at my disposal? What tools can we use?

5   **Techniques:** How will we use the tools? Which technique(s) will be most useful?

6   **History of use:** Which technique(s) have I successfully used in the past for this issue?

7   **Results:** How will the results be recorded in the notebook?

8   **Outcome:** How effective was the technique(s)? What difficulties were encountered with this technique(s)? How can I circumvent these difficulties in the future? What alternative tools and techniques can I use in the future for a similar issue?

Assessment issues and profiles

In our previous book we raised several issues pertinent to coaching and assessment. We discussed some of the reasons why executives might object to a battery of formal tests. These included anxiety about comparisons with others as well as a reluctance towards being typecast. We also suggested guidelines for coaches to offset such responses. Nonetheless, assessment remains a major concern for coaches. The purpose of this chapter is to discuss some of these challenges and to provide a series of profiles to assist the coach in the assessment process. The profiles are intended to serve as assessment guidelines or templates for the coach. They can be viewed as a starting point, and with time and experience the coach can add to the various profiles.

As with any form of assessment, the coach should employ these profiles judiciously and with sensitivity. Before administering a profile, the coach should explain the purpose and benefits of the assessment to the coachee. It is crucial that the coachee recognises that assessment is not only a useful means of exploring and 'diagnosing' his or her unique situation, but also a building block in structuring a personalised development plan or desired outcome list. It is important that the profiles not be seen as 'just another series of tests'.

Coaches working within organisations have to be particularly alert to the coachee's history of assessment and diagnosis. Are these results on record and does the coachee have possession of them? How might the results be incorporated into the current assessment? Is further assessment even necessary? Having administered some or all of the profiles, the coach should provide a summary sheet of the 'results' to the coachee. Any report to management (discussed in Chapter 3) should include a summary of the key assessment findings.

Why is assessment necessary?

Coaches derive information about coachees from various sources. This includes information from:

➤ formal assessment or a series of structured discussions

➤ journals or diaries the coachee may keep

➤ the narrative 'story' the coachee tells

➤ observation during the coaching sessions

➤ feedback from colleagues, peers, friends and family.

As mentioned above, assessing the coachee presents coaches with several challenges. The coach has to make a well-informed choice as to the extent he or she will employ assessment in the coaching process. Second, coaches have to choose the particular instruments they will employ. Not all assessment instruments are available to all coaches. As most coaches are well aware, certain tests can only be administered by a registered psychologist (e.g. intelligence tests such as the WAIS-111) or by a licensed provider (e.g. the MBTI). Any standardisation in terms of a battery of tests for all coaching assessments is therefore not feasible.

One way the coach can overcome some of these difficulties is to employ a series of structured interviews or structured discussions such as those provided below. These instruments or profiles are designed to tap into areas similar to those covered in formal testing. However, such interviews are qualitative rather than quantitative in nature and do not make any claims regarding reliability and validity. They do however serve a crucial function—they provide the coach with information that is directly pertinent to the coaching intervention.

Finally, the coach can use assessments to promote his or her practice. The various profiles can be used with existing clients. For example, the executive and manager who is being coached to adopt a coaching style would find the values profile, the work performance profile and the learning profile particularly useful when coaching their staff. Importantly, the profiles can also be presented to prospective clients. After all, the various types of assessments represent the breadth and the depth of the coach's expertise. They also present a clear and valuable blueprint of what coaching is all about.

Benefits of assessment

Clearly, there are numerous benefits to be derived from assessing a coachee. For example assessment:

➤ identifies purpose and personal values

➤ identifies the coachee's strengths and weaknesses

➤ identifies the competencies necessary for success

➤ induces self-awareness by having coachees focus on aspects of their behaviour they may not have considered previously, such as personality style, communication style and how others perceive them

➤ offers the coach a broader perspective on the coachee's world through third-party feedback (e.g. 360-degree performance appraisals)

➤ helps the coach recognise the uniqueness of the individual

➤ assists the coachee to recognise recurrent patterns of behaviour and how these may be adaptive or unhelpful.

Factors that may interfere with assessment

Before outlining and discussing the profiles mentioned below it is useful for the coach to be aware of certain dynamics that can play out during the assessment phase and, indeed, throughout the coaching sessions. The coachee may employ manipulation and avoidance tactics to evade self-discovery and self-understanding. These behaviours can be a means of gaining and maintaining control and may be motivated by vulnerability and fear.

These mechanisms of control, which most of us employ to varying degrees, are not uncommon in successful individuals. It is, in a sense, the negative side of their ambition, drive and leadership qualities. The need for control can manifest as stubbornness and an exaggerated sense of independence. In the workplace, this can translate into ineffective delegation, an autocratic style of management and high levels of stress, both to the individual and to his or her co-workers.

In the coaching relationship, these strategies for gaining control often present as a refusal or inability to accept help. For instance, powerful leaders may attempt to maintain their leadership role in the coaching transaction. They wear the battle armour of the leader and insist on maintaining the leader's persona or mask of invincibility. They may be operating within a habitual framework of automatic behaviour and solutions. Unless the coach is able to penetrate this shield any real change or growth remains unlikely.

How does the coach deal with this issue? First, the coach has to be cognisant of the control mechanisms the coachee is employing and challenge him or her with this insight. It is crucial that the coachee acknowledges that the role he or she plays in the workplace is fundamentally different from that expected of him or her in the coaching relationship. Any exaggerated sense of independence, entitlement, or mistrust and combativeness are inappropriate in the coaching context. It may be that the coachee is unaware of his or her controlling behaviours. The coach has to present the leader with solid evidence to show how his or her typical role is being played out in the coaching sessions. Through reflection the coachee can become more aware of his or her behaviour and that in itself can be self-correcting.

Finally, as discussed in Chapter 10, the coach has to develop an atmosphere of trust and relaxation where the leader's battle antennae can switch off. It is only when the coachee is relaxed, and psychologically and emotionally removed from the demands of the leader role, that he or she can begin to be open to any guidance, direction or support from the coach. To facilitate the transition from the role of leader to that of coachee, coaching sessions ideally should be conducted on neutral territory, in a relaxed, safe environment away from any cues from the 'battlefield'.

Types of profiles

We have developed a series of profiles that can either be administered to the coachee in a pen and pencil format, or provide guidelines for dialogue between the coach and coachee. These include:

1   Individual profiles
    ➤ A biological profile
    ➤ A life balance profile
    ➤ A values profile

2   Small business profiles
    ➤ A vision/mission statement
    ➤ A life/work balance profile for business owners
    ➤ A coaching needs analysis for business owners

3   Organisational work performance profiles
    ➤ A work performance profile
    ➤ A self-assessment competency profile
    ➤ A job analysis profile
    ➤ A personal development plan
    ➤ A competency feedback profile

4   Leadership profiles
    ➤ A leadership competencies wheel
    ➤ Areas of leadership profile
    ➤ Qualities of leadership profile

5 Personal style profiles
- ➤ A learning profile
- ➤ A personality profile
- ➤ A profile for team members

6 Self-assessment profiles
- ➤ A post-session review for the coachee
- ➤ An ongoing review for the coachee
- ➤ A self-assessment profile for the coach

Individual profiles

The three life issues profiles are suitable for use by coaches conducting life skills coaching, executive coaching or business coaching.

1 A biographical profile

The biographical profile is designed to be used by the coach as a guide for structuring questions about the coachee's current life situation. It can also be used to obtain a broad picture of the coachee's needs and ambitions.

 Exercise **A biographical profile**

1 Tell me a little bit about yourself:

- ➤ your age
- ➤ your work history
- ➤ your family
- ➤ your important personal relationships
- ➤ your interests and hobbies.

2 What brought you to the coaching session? What was the impetus or catalyst?

3 What do you think will be your role in our collaboration?

4 Are you living the kind of life you want?

5 What's missing from your life right now?

Exercise

6   Have you thought about what you need to do to fill this gap?

7   Have you worked with anyone or tried any particular techniques to achieve your goals or make your life more fulfilling?

8   How do you learn best?

9   What do you think is holding you back from achieving what you want?

10 How do you think the changes you make as a result of our working together will affect others around you?

11 Are there any significant 'missed opportunities' in your life?

12 How much control do you think you have over your life?

13 If someone who knew you intimately were to describe you, what three words might they use?

14 How can you build on your strengths?

15 If you had your 'ideal life', what would it look like?

2 A life balance profile

Wheels of various descriptions are commonly employed in coaching assessments. They have visual appeal and can be used again at the end of a coaching intervention to determine the coachee's progress. Coachees can be encouraged to complete the wheel several months and a year or two after the coaching sessions have ended. They are a good measure of progress and serve to keep the coachee on track.

Exercise

If the centre of the wheel represents 0 (no satisfaction) and the outer rim of the wheel represents 10 (complete satisfaction) shade in the area that best represents how satisfied you are with each aspect of your life.

3 A values profile

We have found that some coachees are not aware of, or have not thought about, their purpose or values. When this occurs it is usually more time efficient for coachees to complete the values profile in their own time and bring it back to the next coaching session for discussion.

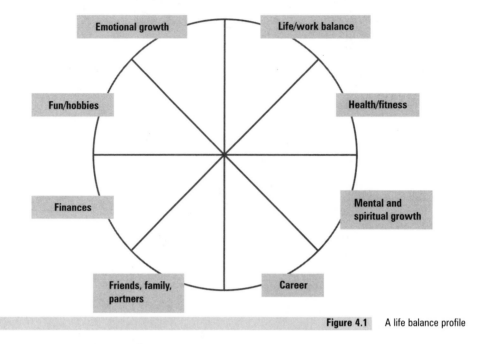

Figure 4.1   A life balance profile

 ## A values profile

1   What do you think is your purpose in life?

2   What do you love doing?

3   In what specific ways do you express your purpose in your life?

4   How much importance do you place on the role of values in your life?

5   Tell me five values that are important to you.

6   Of these five values, which three are the most important to you?

7   Which of these is the single most important value for you?

8   How does your life reflect your three most important values? Give examples.

9   Do you ever think or feel that you may not 'live up to' your values?

10   Would you like to reassess or change any of your core values?

11   Do you experience any conflict of values?

12   If you do have a conflict of values, how do you solve it?

13   Are there any particular individuals you admire? Who are they? What is it about them that you admire?

Small business profiles

1 A vision/mission statement

In coaching literature the terms 'purpose', 'vision' and 'mission' are frequently used interchangeably. Each of these terms is a summary of what is possible and desirable about the future. An individual may make a personal vision statement that defines his or her purpose and direction in life and may also design a vision statement for the business or company. Establishing a vision/mission statement helps the individual to clarify and establish business values and goals. Successful action planning is more likely to follow on from goals that are in accord with the individual's true values and purpose in life.

Developing a mission statement usually takes time. The coachee can be encouraged to observe the mission statements of others, brainstorm ideas with the coach and write a tentative statement that can be clarified, refined and redrafted over the coaching sessions. The following questions are guidelines for the coach when working on a vision/mission statement with small business owners, owner/managers and entrepreneurs.

 Exercise

Some personal questions:

1   What are your beliefs about 'good' and 'not good', 'realistic' and 'unrealistic' in relation to your life purpose or mission?

2   Is there a metaphor that encompasses and sums up your life purpose?

3   What legacy do you wish to leave behind?

4   What peak experience(s) in your life profoundly affected you in relation to your purpose?

5   How important is a mission statement to you?

Some operational questions:

1   What are your basic beliefs about the service(s) you provide?

2   What are your company's beliefs about these services?

3   What is your company's competitive edge?

4   How devoted are you to customer service?

5   Would your customers recognise this? How?

6   What do you want your public image to be?

7   What is unique about you and the services you provide?

8   List 12 words that define this uniqueness.

9   Can you put these words in a sentence to define your purpose/mission?

10   How will you communicate this vision/mission statement?

2 A life/work balance profile for business owners

Before establishing the needs of the business, it is essential that the coach has a good understanding of the individual business owner's balance in other areas of his or her life. The coaching sessions may revolve around growing the business and strategic planning but they may also focus on other aspects of the owner's life and how these impact, either positively or negatively, on the business. As mentioned previously, the current demands of work and the inability for many of us to achieve a satisfactory balance between work and other areas of our life is one of the most important challenges we all face.

Exercise

A life/work balance profile for business owners

1   What is the nature of your business?

2   How long has the business been in operation?

3   How long have you been in the business?

4   How many hours a week do you spend on the business?

5   Do you feel you are having enough time off?

6   When was your last holiday?

7   Do you have enough time:

➤ for yourself   Y/N

➤ for your family   Y/N

➤ for your friends   Y/N

➤ for hobbies/relaxation   Y/N

8   How much more time (in hours per week) would you like:

➤ for yourself

➤ for your family

➤ for your friends

➤ for hobbies/relaxation

9   Have you tried to get more balance in your life?

➤ What methods did you use?

➤ How successful were they?

10   If you could wave a magic wand, what would your life look like?

3 A coaching needs analysis for business owners

The coaching needs analysis for small business owners, entrepreneurs or individuals wishing to establish a business focuses on two aspects—the individual's personal skills needs and the logistics of operating a successful business.

A coaching needs analysis for business owners

Some personal mastery questions:

1   What do you enjoy most about your business?

2   What do you enjoy least about your business?

3   What are the major challenges facing your business right now?

4   Of these challenges, which is the most critical?

5   How have you attempted to deal with this challenge?

6   How successful were you?

7   In retrospect, what could you have done differently?

8   Are you being as productive as you wish to be?

9   Do you often think and say, 'I haven't got enough time!'?

10   Are you doing too much by yourself?

11   What are your major 'time wasters'?

12   Is time management something you could benefit from?

13   How can you become more effective?

Some operational mastery questions:

1 Does your business have a mission statement?

2 What are your core business values?

3 Do you have a business plan?

4 Do you have a marketing plan?

5 Do you have a strategic plan?

6 What are your business's strengths?

7 What are its weaknesses?

8 What opportunities does the business have?

9 Have you missed any opportunities recently?

10 What are the current threats to your business?

11 Have you considered creating a larger or new stream of income?

12 What do you need to learn in order to achieve this?

13 What is holding you back from achieving this?

14 What 'excuses' do you use for not moving ahead?

15 How can I as a coach help you?

16 How do you want me to coach you?

17 What do you want to gain most from our coaching relationship?

Organisational work performance profiles

The following profiles are useful for coaches working with individuals in an organisation. They focus on the coachee's professional values, required job competencies, strengths and weaknesses, and overall work performance.

1 A work performance profile

The work performance profile serves to elicit information about the coachee's specific work situation, including the requisite competencies for the position, the individual's personal and professional strengths and weaknesses and the possible benefits of coaching to the individual and the organisation. The coach may use the profile as a guide to a structured discussion in the coaching sessions or may ask the coachee to complete the questionnaire in their own time.

Exercise

A work performance profile

1 List three values that influence your professional life?

2 What is your current position?

3 How long have you been in this position?

4 What are your major job functions?

5 What are the job specifications for your position?

6 What are the stated competencies for your position?

7 Which aspects of your work do you enjoy most? Why?

8 Which aspects of your work do you enjoy least? Why?

9 How supported do you feel in your position?

10 On a scale of 1 to 7 where 1 is poor and 7 is excellent how would you rate your relationships with your:

➤ colleagues

➤ peers

➤ staff

11 What are your particular strengths in your position?

12 How can you build on these strengths or use them in new ways?

13 Which aspect(s) of your work would you like to enhance?

14 What are your weaknesses in your position?

15 What might be contributing to your weakness?

16 What are the benefits of enhancing this skill(s):

➤ personal benefits?

➤ organisational benefits?

➤ team benefits?

17 How will enhancing your skills contribute to the company's growth?

18 Have you received feedback on your work performance? Can you tell me about this?

19 Have you undertaken any development courses or special training to enhance your work performance? Were these beneficial?

20 What resources do you need to help you develop/enhance your skills?

21 Have you done any 'personality style' assessments? Can you tell me about these?

22 What do you see yourself doing in five years? ten years?

23 How does this vision relate to your current life and work circumstances?

24 Are you fulfilled in your work?

25 Are you doing what you really want to do?

26 What do you want to change most about your current work situation?

2 A self-assessment competency profile

Self-assessment by the coachee of his or her personal and technical skills can provide valuable information to guide the coaching intervention. The following profile can be given to the coachee to complete before or during the first or second coaching session.

Personal and technical skills profile

Personal skills	Organisational skills	Leadership skills
emotional connection	administration	troubleshooting
decisiveness	analysing data	strategising
self-belief	planning	motivating
self-esteem	presentation skills	promoting
empathy	resourcefulness	persuading
emotional control	decision making	influencing
resilience	problem solving	developing trust
communications skills	negotiation	directing
people skills	delegation	visioning
assertiveness	flexibility	leading
lightheartedness	time management	clarifying values
endurance	systems management	coaching others

Exercise

1 Can you list three areas from each group that you are competent in?

Personal skills:

_____

_____

_____

Organisational skills:

_____

_____

_____

Leadership skills:

_____

_____

_____

2 Can you list three areas from each group that you would like to develop further?

Personal skills:

_____

_____

_____

Organisational skills:

_____

_____

_____

Leadership skills:

_____

_____

_____

Exercise

3   Overall, which three skills are you most efficient at?

_____

_____

_____

4   Which three skills are you least efficient at?

_____

_____

_____

3 A job analysis profile

The job analysis profile examines aspects of the individual's job in terms of the behavioural demands it places on the coachee. It also raises issues regarding the coachee's learning and development needs, and future plans. The profile, which is relatively brief, may be useful when time constraints or the nature of the coaching intervention do not allow or warrant more detailed assessment.

Exercise

A job analysis profile

1   What are your specific job tasks?

2   What specific skills are required for your job?

> ➤   interpersonal skills?

> ➤   behavioural skills?

> ➤   technical skills?

3   What results are expected from you?

4   How difficult is your current job? Do you need further training or coaching? In what areas?

5   How much authority do you have?

6   How do you react under stress?

7   How do you work as a team worker?

8   Describe your leadership qualities.

9   How does your personality fit with your job?

10 What are your current development plans

> ➤ for training?

> ➤ for coaching?

> ➤ for future positions?

4   A personal development plan

The personal development plan is a useful tool for the coach and coachee to employ when bridging the gap between the assessment or diagnostic stage of the coaching program and the action phase.

A personal development plan

1   Identify ways in which you can apply your strengths (e.g. as identified in the self-assessment competence profile) to other areas of your work such as building more effective teams?

2   How can you close the skills gap you have identified?

3   What are the benefits of developing these skills?

> ➤ for you personally?

> ➤ for the organisation?

4   Which skill(s) is it most important to develop?

> ➤ for you personally?

> ➤ for the organisation?

5   What resources do you need to close the skills gap?

6   What action plans do you need to set in place to close the gap?

7   What is the measure of success for each of these skills?

5 A competency feedback profile

As well as gathering data from the coachee about his or her work performance, it is extremely helpful if the coach can obtain data from the coachee's colleagues. Usually the coach engages in initial informal discussions with senior management or the referrer. However additional data from the coachee's colleagues on how the individual is performing in the specific areas nominated for coaching can guide the coaching process, especially in the assessment and evaluation phases.

The following guidelines can assist the coach in conducting what is essentially a 'mini' 360-degree performance appraisal.

Step one   Ask the coachee's permission to approach four or five of his or her colleagues with the intention of having them rate the coachee on those aspects of performance that are the subject of the coaching brief. It is important to refer to the colleagues as 'supporters'. They are not critics and the sole purpose of gathering information from them is to facilitate the coachee's growth and the development of essential competencies.

Step two   Inform the coachee that you will contact the four or five colleagues and that their feedback will remain anonymous.

Step three   Devise a brief appraisal form relevant to the skills being addressed in the coaching intervention.

For example:

Exercise

I am an executive coach working with _____ on her leadership qualities. She has nominated you as one of the colleagues I could approach to establish her current performance in relation to specific aspects of her leadership role.

The information you give me is confidential. The feedback given to _____ will be anonymous.

Please rate _____ on the following aspects of her leadership role:

1	2	3	4	5	6	7
Not at all		Sometimes		Often		Always

1 She is comfortable taking responsibility for important decisions and justifying them, when necessary.   ....

2 She delegates work when necessary.   ....

3 She gives honest and constructive feedback to people who are performing badly.   ....

Exercise

4   She is willing to step forward and address difficult issues.   ....

5   She establishes and maintains good, supportive relationships
    with her team members.   ....

6   What do you think is _____ greatest strength as a
    leader? Please give some examples.   ....

7   Which aspect of _____ leadership skills could be
    enhanced? Please give some anecdotes to support your choice.   ....

Step four   Contact each colleague by telephone and arrange to e-mail the appraisal sheet, requesting that it be returned by a certain date.

Step five   Discuss the feedback with the coachee. Names are to be kept confidential and the coach has to be judicious in feeding back comments that may be unhelpful or destructive.

Step six   Midway through the coaching sessions, e-mail the 'supporters' the same set of questions.

Step seven   Compare the scores and comments with the previous appraisals, and give feedback to the coachee.

Step eight   Towards the end of the coaching partnership, e-mail the supporters the same set of questions. Repeat Step seven.

Leadership profiles

There are numerous leadership models that emphasise different skills and competencies. While it is beyond the scope of our book to review these models in detail, we provide several profiles that we have found useful when coaching for leadership skills. None of these profiles is definitive or suitable for all occasions. Leadership involves a very complex set of interpersonal, technical and thinking skills. The coach may not have the mandate or time to develop all the nominated competencies. Leadership training may be necessary to allow the leader a broad overview of the requirements for success.

The following profiles are an attempt to break down the multifaceted aspects of leadership into readily accessible self-rating units. The profiles can serve as a starting point for discussion and as a guide for the coach and coachee to isolate particular aspects of leadership to enhance and improve in the coaching conversation.

1 A leadership competencies wheel

As well as asking the coachee to complete this wheel, the coach can also (with the coachee's permission) request that several of the coachee's peers and colleagues rate the coachee on the competencies wheel. The ratings by the coachee and the feedback from colleagues can then be used to determine and guide the issues addressed in the coaching sessions.

Exercise If the centre of the circle represents 0 (no satisfaction) and the outer rim represents 10 (complete satisfaction), shade in the area that best represents your level of satisfaction within each area of your work life.

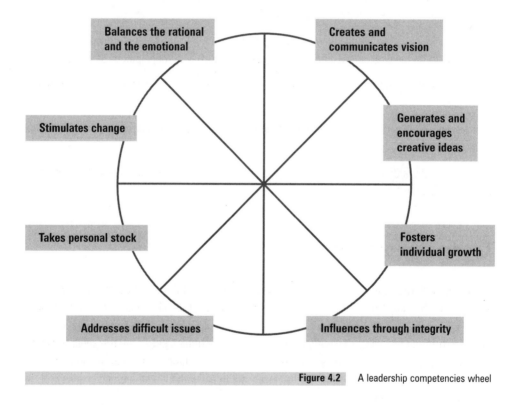

Figure 4.2 A leadership competencies wheel

2 Areas of leadership profile

The following list of leadership responsibilities can guide the coach and the executive or manager to isolate specific aspects of leadership to develop. In addition, it can provide a checklist for the coach to recognise his or her competencies or limitations as a coach in the various areas.

Checklist

Areas of leadership profile

Place a tick next to three areas you would like to work on:

- ☐ Communication—interpersonal and organisational
- ☐ Delegation and empowering others
- ☐ Managing change
- ☐ Strategic planning
- ☐ Building and managing teams
- ☐ Working with virtual teams
- ☐ Decisiveness
- ☐ Persuading and influencing others
- ☐ Developing and communicating vision
- ☐ Promoting learning and development in the organisation
- ☐ Presentation skills
- ☐ Managing conflict
- ☐ Negotiation
- ☐ Goal setting and action planning
- ☐ Giving feedback
- ☐ Conducting performance appraisals
- ☐ Problem solving
- ☐ Dealing effectively with stress and pressure
- ☐ Life/work balance
- ☐ Managing time and prioritising

Other _____

Prioritise the three areas you have ticked above.

1 _____

2 _____

3 _____

3 Qualities of leadership profile

This profile highlights the three main qualities of leadership: self-awareness, interpersonal skills and thinking skills.

Exercise **Self-awareness profile**

1   How often do you deliberately seek out feedback on your behaviour and leadership qualities?

2   How often do you reflect on your behaviour?

3   In the course of a typical work day, how much attention do you pay to your feelings?

4   How quickly do you recognise what others are thinking and feeling?

5   Are you able to easily modify your communication style to suit the situation?

6   How successful are you at harnessing conflict in a productive and creative way?

7   Do you find it easy to describe yourself?

8   What do you consider the essential or critical qualities of a leader?

9   How would you rate yourself on these qualities?

10 How do you think your colleagues would rate you on these qualities?

11 Which of the following leadership styles do you most identify with?

➤ *Visionary:* architect of change, questions tradition

➤ *Traditional:* decisive, follows through on commitment

➤ *Negotiating:* gets job done, challenges, is adaptable

➤ *Charismatic:* strong interpersonal skills, persuasive, influencing, excellent communicator

12 Give a few examples of how you enact this role or style.

13 Can you list three of your personal strengths?

14 Can you list three of your personal weaknesses?

15 What attempts do you make to modify these weaknesses?

16 Which personal skills(s) related to your leadership role would you most like to enhance?

Exercise

Interpersonal skills profile

Rate yourself on the following items:

1	2	3	4	5	6	7
Not at all		Sometimes		Mostly		Always

1 I trust my emotions and learn from them. ....

2 I am honest with people close to me. ....

3 I am capable of long-term commitment in a relationship. ....

4 I try to listen to others without making snap judgments. ....

5 I question others to obtain clarity and understand them. ....

6 I am always looking for ways to enhance my communication skills. ....

7 I clearly communicate my expectations. ....

8 I ensure people have the competencies and resources to perform the required tasks. ....

9 I foster autonomy and self-empowerment. ....

10 I am familiar with different styles of conflict resolution and can match the technique to the situation. ....

11 I feel confident about using rational and logical arguments to persuade others. ....

12 I am able to inspire others by appealing to their values and aspirations. ....

13 Others consider me to be charismatic. ....

14 I am acutely aware of the pressures facing me in my position. ....

15 I have strategies in place to lower my stress levels. ....

16 I am familiar with the stresses and pressures facing my colleagues and staff. ....

17 I can usually balance the demands of the organisation with a genuine concern for my staff. ....

18 I deliver on what I promise. ....

A thinking skills profile

Rate yourself on the following items:

1	2	3	4	5	6	7
Not at all		Sometimes		Mostly		Always

1   I analyse data quickly and efficiently.   ....

2   I am aware of the impact of my decisions on both the short- and long-term plans of my company.   ....

3   I think laterally and 'out of the square'.   ....

4   I confront ambiguity and complexity with genuine interest.   ....

5   I encourage new ways of looking at old problems.   ....

6   I am solution-focused rather than problem-focused.   ....

7   I regularly update my professional knowledge.   ....

8   I have various problem-solving techniques that I apply as the situation demands.   ....

9   I am comfortable testing hypotheses rather than always having to provide a definitive answer.   ....

10   I try to expand the various methods by which I learn.   ....

11   I have the knowledge and skills to lead the organisation through various stages of change.   ....

12   I rapidly process information.   ....

13   I am receptive to new ideas and new paradigms.   ....

14   I communicate my ideas clearly and succinctly at all levels.   ....

Personal style profiles

1 Assessment of learning styles

Research indicates that successful people are aggressive learners. Yet some studies suggest that only 10 per cent of individuals are naturally active learners. One of the underlying premises of coaching is that coaching is all about change which, as we have stated previously, is all about learning. The coach can work with individuals to develop and enhance their ability to learn. As a first stage in this critical process, it is important to be aware of the coachee's typical approach to and style of learning.

One of the most frequently employed assessments of learning styles is the learning styles questionnaire (LSQ) (Honey & Mumford 1987). As noted in our previous book, Honey and Mumford believed we have different preferences for learning. They isolated four styles:

1   *Activists* enjoy new experiences and excitement and learn best when thrown in at the deep end.

2   *Reflectors* like to listen, review and analyse before making a decision.

3   *Pragmatists* learn best by putting ideas into practice.

4   *Theorists* prefer exploring and synthesising ideas and information.

The LSQ can be particularly useful for a coach in the following situations:

➤   when working with a team or group

➤   when working with leaders and managers who are responsible for the learning and development of others

➤   when coaching an individual in transition who may be experiencing difficulties acquiring and absorbing new information.

The following learning profile can be valuable to the coach who does not have access to the LSQ. It provides guidelines for a structured discussion between the coach and coachee regarding the coachee's learning style and learning needs.

Exercise A learning profile

1   When was the last time you sought out a new learning experience?

2   What obstacles might prevent you from learning?

3   When faced with a completely new area of learning, do you usually view it as an exciting challenge or just something else to contend with?

4   Do you learn best from material presented in a visual form or in a written format?

5   Are you more likely to remember what you see or what you hear?

6   Do others describe you as logical and analytical?

7   Do you have any existing models of hypothesis testing and problem solving?

8   Do you prefer a lot of detailed information and preparation time before you begin working on a project?

9   Do your feelings play a significant role in your actions?

10   Would you consider yourself to be pragmatic?

11   When presented with new ideas are you quick to adopt them?

12   Do you think a great deal about an issue before you act?

13   Are you more excited about 'the big picture' than the details?

14   Do you learn better through theory or practice?

15   Would you prefer to 'give something a go' and learn from your own experience or seek advice from others?

16   Do you learn best when you're 'thrown in the deep end'?

17   When you acquire new information, do you try to synthesise it and explore links with your existing knowledge base?

18   If you were acquiring a new skill, would you prefer written instructions, watching a training video or being actively involved in a role-play or simulation of the task?

19   What do you most need to learn right now?

20   What might inhibit you?

2 Personality assessment

Personality assessment in coaching is plagued by more difficulties than other areas of assessment. For example, research suggests that personality profiling is more useful in assessing an individual on job performance, satisfaction or commitment in a particular work situation than it is at predicting an individual's performance, satisfaction or commitment across work situations. Such findings have clear implications for career coaches and the instruments they employ.

Interestingly, research also suggests that background knowledge, hunches and applied judgment may be just as valid in predicting emerging leaders as formal instruments such as the 16PF. It would appear then that there is a place for alternative methods of personality profiling.

Prior to outlining the personality profile we have developed, it is useful to briefly discuss some of the most common instruments used in assessing personality. These are the Myers-Briggs Type Inventory (MBTI), the Fundamental Interpersonal Relations Orientation-Behaviour (FIRO-B) and the Enneagram.

The MBTI and *MBTI-Step 11* are perhaps the most well-known and frequently employed personality profiles in the business world. Based on Jung's typology, they place individuals on four dimensions: Extrovert (E) or Introvert (I); Sensing (S) or Intuition (N); Thinking (T) or Feeling (F); and Judging (J) or Perceiving (P). The results of the assessment are given as one of sixteen broad profiles, for example, INTP, ENTJ, ISFP, etc.

The MBTI helps us to understand not only where we as individuals fall on each of these dimensions, it also offers us insights into how others prefer to communicate and how we can best deal with different preference styles. Many coaches are licensed MBTI providers while others coach individuals who have completed the inventory and are familiar with their own style and preferences. It is therefore important that coaches are familiar with the MBTI and have at least a working knowledge of each of the four continuums and how best to listen, understand and communicate with different personality types. The MBTI is used effectively with group or team coaching where differing styles of communication can be a blockage to performance or can, with understanding, enhance interpersonal interactions and team efforts.

The FIRO-B is available to HR personnel as well as psychologists. It measures our behaviour in terms of how it is expressed towards others and what we want from others. Individuals are assessed on the following dimensions: expressed inclusion, wanted inclusion; expressed control, wanted control; expressed openness and wanted openness. Scores on these dimensions form a matrix of 'expressed behaviour towards others' and 'wanted behaviour from others' in relation to inclusion, control and openness. Total inclusion, total control and total openness scores are added to derive a social interaction index. The FIRO-B is not only a useful assessment tool to use on coachees, it can also provide critical insights into the coach's own style of relating to others. After all *inclusion, control and openness* are central to any relationship and knowledge of one's own orientation towards interpersonal relations can provide valuable insights and self-awareness for a coach.

The Enneagram is increasingly employed in coaching. It is informed by a long tradition of philosophy and spirituality dating back to Homer and brought to the west by George Gurdjieff. There are nine basic Enneagram personality types, although these are sometimes labelled differently by various authors. For instance, Riso (1987, 1995) nominates the following nine types: the reformer, the helper, the motivator, the artist, the thinker, the loyalist, the generalist, the peacemaker and the leader. Another typology (Hurley & Dobson 1991) lists the following types: the achiever, the helper, the succeeder, the individualist, the observer, the guardian, the dreamer, the confronter and the preservationist. Others, such as Goldberg (1999) suggest a different classification system.

Such a lack of standardisation may deter many coaches from employing the Enneagram. However, research on the instrument appears to be increasing and at the very least, the questions can be used as a springboard for discussion and for isolating personal and interpersonal skills the coachee may wish to enhance or modify. The various Enneagram inventories provide self-assessment on personality characteristics and offer insights into the individual's strengths and weaknesses, ways of communicating, leading and working with others. As with the MBTI and the FIRO-B, the Enneagram can be a useful tool to assess the coachee and can provide insight and self-knowledge for the coach.

Depending on various factors such as time constraints, the training and mandate of the coach, the coachee's willingness to disclose and the specific coaching intervention, personality assessment can play a variable role. The following general personality profile is a useful guideline for a structured interview or discussion when formal personality testing is not appropriate. It can be used in conjunction with the various profiles provided earlier in this chapter.

Exercise   A personality profile

1   Where would you place yourself on the following dimensions? Please indicate your position with a cross.

Introvert	Extrovert
Confident	Self-conscious
Critical	Accepting
Enthusiastic	Contained
Organised	Disorganised
Leader	Follower
Empathic	Indifferent
Energetic	Lethargic
Highly strung	Relaxed
Easily stressed	Resilient
Competitive	Collaborative
Controlling	Accommodating
Reactive	Proactive
Controlled	Impulsive
Pessimistic	Optimistic

2   On a scale of 1 (lowest) to 10 (highest):

How much does destiny or fate figure in your life?   ....

To what extent do you believe that 'character is destiny'?   ....

How reliant are you on the opinions of others?   ....

To what extent do you live the way you want to?   ....

Exercise

3   How do you typically resolve a difficult situation or conflict?

    ☐ Avoid it

    ☐ Adapt to it

    ☐ Accept it

    ☐ Other _____

4   Name three 'sayings' or 'quotes' that guide your life.

5   Who is your role model(s)? How has that person(s) impacted on your life?

6   When you are reflecting on your life, do you emphasise the past, present or future?

7   Write a brief description of yourself in the third person.

8   What is the one quality you respect most in others?

9   What is the one quality you like most in others?

10 What is one word you would use to sum up the kind of person you are?

3   A profile for team members

Individual profiles of each team member may not be necessary when a team coach is working on strategic planning or developing, and utilising specific team skills. However, if the coach encounters certain difficulties among the team members, for example a conflict of values or a clash of personality styles, it may be useful to administer the following profile to each individual team member. Alternatively, the profile can serve as guide for the coach when conducting exercises to raise team awareness and overcome obstacles to progress.

 Exercise

A profile for team members

On a scale of 1 (a little) to 10 (a great deal), rate yourself on the following:

1   How confident are you that significant changes will result from
    the team sessions?   ....

2   To what extent do you think your colleagues really want to work
    together on team issues?   ....

3   To what extent are you willing to express your true concerns
    and feelings to the team?   ....

Exercise

4   To what extent do you think the other team members are willing to express their true concerns and feelings to the team? ....

5   How much do you know about team processes? ....

6   Do you enjoy working closely with others? ....

7   What is your greatest strength as a team player?

_____

8   What is your greatest weakness as a team player?

_____

9   Name three qualities of a successful team.

_____

_____

_____

10   What might be potential sources of conflict in this team?

_____

_____

11   How do you gain cooperation from team members?

_____

12   How do you best influence others?

_____

Self-assessment profiles

1 For the coachee

The following reviews are useful for the coachee to rate his or her satisfaction with an individual coaching session (Profile 1), and track his or her performance during and after the coaching intervention (Profile 2). The coach can provide these profiles to the coachee to complete on a need-to-know basis rather than as an accompaniment to every session.

Exercise **Profile 1   A post-session review for the coachee**

1   Did I talk about what was most important to me?

2   Did the coach really listen?

3   How do I feel right now?

4   Did I feel supported by the coach?

5   Did I feel encouraged by the coach?

6   Did the coach consider my feelings and thoughts on issues on an equal basis?

7   Did the coach really consider my agenda?

8   How will what we talked about today impact on my life in the following week(s)?

9   Did the coaching session reduce any stress in my life?

10   Do I feel stronger as a result of the session?

11   Do my goals seem closer, more achievable?

12   What assumptions or preconceptions of mine did I challenge?

13   How will that help me now and in the future?

14   Out of 10, where 1 is very low and 10 is very high:

   ➤   What is my level of satisfaction with the session?   ....

   ➤   What is my level of frustration with the session?   ....

15   Did I feel free to voice any dissatisfaction to the coach?

Exercise **Profile 2   An ongoing review of coaching sessions for the coachee**

Review period:

From _____/_____/_____   To _____/_____/_____

1   What were my goals for this period?

_____

_____

_____

_____

2   How did I perform according to these goals? Which goals were met?

_____

_____

_____

_____

3   What did I learn during this period?

_____

4   How can what I learnt from achieving these goals be transferred to other goals I may set in the future?

_____

_____

5   What changes did I make during this period?

_____

_____

6   What was most difficult for me?

_____

7   Was there any single technique or skill that contributed most to my success?

_____

8   Was I at all disappointed or frustrated with any aspect of my performance?

_____

9   How might the coach assist me to avoid such disappointments and frustrations in the future?

_____

10 What are my goals for the next period of coaching?

_____

_____

2 A self-assessment profile for the coach

Many coaches work in isolation and are not in a position to debrief or get immediate feedback on their coaching sessions. The following profile can serve as a guide for coaches to assess their own skills, competencies and progress. It can reinforce the coach's confidence about those areas/skills/techniques at which he or she may excel, and clarify those that require further development. As with all professions, ongoing development is crucial for any practising coach.

It is not intended that the coach review each and every coaching session. The profile is intended as a barometer of where the coach is at in terms of basic coaching competencies. The profile can be particularly useful for the coach working with a large number of coachees in groups or an organisation. It can alert the coach to the extent to which he or she is meeting the individual coachee's needs. These needs are sometimes obscured by the sheer weight of numbers.

Exercise

A self-assessment profile for the coach

1   How well prepared was I for the session?

2   How clear was I on the objectives of the session?

3   How appropriate were the models and techniques I employed?

4   How successful were the techniques I employed?

5   Do I need to develop new techniques?

6   How strongly did I build rapport with the coachee?

7   How effectively did I use my listening skills?

8   How effectively did I use my questioning skills?

9   How truly engaged and interested was I in the session?

10   Did I try anything new in the session?

11   How patient was I in the session?

12   How empathic and non-judgmental was I in the session?

13   What verbal and non-verbal cues did I pick up from the coachee?

14   How effectively did I follow these through?

15   What did I enjoy most about the session?

16   When, if at all, did I feel uncomfortable or bored?

17   What was my level of satisfaction with the session?

18 What was my level of frustration with the session?

19 On a scale of 1 (low) to 10 (high), how effective was I as a coach overall?

20 What do I think the coachee gained from the session?

21 How did I ensure that this learning could be transferred to other situations?

22 What is the single most important thing I learnt from the session?

23 What would I do differently if I could redo the session?

24 Which coaching competencies were highlighted in the session?

25 What action(s) do I need to take to enhance or improve my coaching competencies?

Summary

Assessment is a critical aspect of the coaching relationship. Without it, the coach and coachee can flounder and waste valuable time simply trying to diagnose the coaching issues. Ongoing assessment of the coachee's progress assists the coach and coachee in focusing on and reviewing the achievement of the stated goals and objectives. Furthermore, the coach and coachee's self-assessments of the coaching sessions provide the coach with valuable information to assess his or her own performance.

Personality as a coaching tool

Coaching is about relationships. To this relationship the coach brings his or her knowledge, skills, abilities and self. The coach has to be knowledgeable about, and skilful in, the application of various models, techniques and interventions such as those discussed in this book. However, such knowledge and skills can only be successfully applied in the context of a secure, supportive environment that facilitates growth and development. The creation of this milieu is to a great extent a function of the coach's self or personality.

Personality is a coaching tool and the progress and ultimate success of coaching is significantly dependent on the personality of the coach. In the same way that we expect the coachee to honestly explore his or her personal strengths and weaknesses, it is necessary for us to recognise and work with aspects of our own personality as they impact on the coaching partnership.

Personality characteristics of a successful coach

It is generally accepted that it is not possible to specify the personality characteristics that are necessary and sufficient for coaching success. However, many coaches and writers in the field have nominated various personality features that contribute to desired coaching outcomes. Furthermore, as noted in Chapter 1, coaching borrows from the helping professions such as therapy. In these disciplines certain personality characteristics have been identified that impact positively on the change process. For example, there is an ample body of research that indicates that the most useful and empowering aspects of a helping relationship from the clients' viewpoint are 'feeling understood and supported'. Of course, goal setting, problem solving, action planning and appropriate interventions are equally as crucial in coaching.

From these various sources we have selected the following personality characteristics that can serve as an aid for the coach. These are:

➤ awareness of self and one's values

➤ empathy

➤ authenticity

➤ flexibility

➤ resourcefulness

➤ communication expertise.

Awareness of self and one's values

Freud believed that knowledge leads to transformation; that in the very act of knowing oneself, one transforms oneself. Carl Rogers also emphasised the importance of being aware of and being able to express one's own feelings and attitudes in order to facilitate growth in another.

Many of the coaches we train profess a high degree of self-awareness and self-knowledge. This is frequently true in terms of knowing their style of communication, their preferences, perhaps their 'type' according to the MBTI classification and their limitations in dealing with specific types of individuals. Yet rarely do they question their values. Many coaches nominate integrity, passion and success as their core values. While they accept that others may not share these values, they frequently talk about their own specific values as though they are 'categorical imperatives' or universal truths rather than man-made constructs which therefore have no intrinsic merit or meaning. After all, Nietzsche asked whether untruths could have more valuable effects on life than truths, and whether truth could harm life.

Values affect and determine our goals and actions. Part of the coach's role may be to persuade and influence the coachee. Yet even self-aware coaches sometimes seem oblivious to how their values guide and shape coaching sessions. For example, many coaches value success, competition and drive. Coaches working in the corporate arena frequently do so in a climate that promotes and values globalisation and expansionism. Yet an entire school of scholars, namely the Frankfurt School, claims that such expansionism leads to cultural domination, cultural imposition and cultural fragmentation. While this book is clearly not the arena for a debate about this issue, such a viewpoint highlights some of the questions surrounding the coach's values.

Our values are simply what we consider good, beneficial or life affirming. While it may be impossible, and even undesirable, to operate within a value-free vacuum, we have to accept that our values provide an agenda and underpin the work we do with coachees. Therefore, it is imperative for us to nominate, accept and be able to defend our core values.

Our values are also reflected in our theories about behaviour and why coaching does or does not work. While some authors suggest it is more important for coaches to know how to (rather than why they should) act in a certain way, theories about coaching can guide the coaching process. Many of us have theories about why coaching works but may not have clearly articulated these to either ourselves or others. Being aware of our theories, which are interrelated with our values, and being open to changing them in the face of new experiences and research are crucial aspects of self-awareness in coaching.

As coaches, we need to examine and reflect on our personal and professional experiences. Studying theories from coaching, philosophy, psychology, education, therapy, facilitation and business, and discussions with mentors and colleagues allow a coach to develop a unique theory of coaching that is not simply grounded in intuitive or folksy beliefs about human nature and behaviour.

As coaches we are busy working with others in what we consider to be a process of lifelong learning. Skills and techniques learned in coaching sessions are transferred to the workplace or life situations. The coachee is able to apply the learned problem-solving methods to similar and new challenges. However, the coach also has to engage in a process of self-help and self-coaching. Part of self-coaching involves ensuring that we 'walk the walk, and talk the talk'.

While the phrase 'walk the talk' has been overused to the point of cliché, our actions have to be consistent with our theories and our words. Objectivist philosophy for example claims that honesty and integrity are core virtues. To be honest, one has to be consistent in everything one does. Thought has to be consistent with action. Reality is a synthesised whole, so we have to think in general principles and then be able to apply these principles to broader situations—to our life and, in this case, to our coaching.

Coaches need guiding principles and models in order to be genuine and successful. These principles and models may vary of course, and we are not suggesting that coaches should adhere to those we propose. What is important is that we bring guiding principles, models and empirically validated techniques to the coaching process. Self-coaching ensures that we have first-hand experience of what we, after all, expect of our coachees.

Our work with various coaching organisations suggests that the coaching profession is undergoing transformation. This is also supported by the coaching literature. The first wave of 'feel good' coaching with little theory and substance apart from exhorting others to be happy and fulfil their dreams is becoming extinct. The population is becoming more educated about what coaching can and cannot deliver. Simply enjoying the process of coaching is not enough. Coachees and organisations are demanding more content, more experienced coaches and long-lasting change.

Coaching is about change so one would expect the profession to be continuously reinventing and streamlining itself. If we are to stay informed and remain relevant and viable in the current marketplace, we must clarify and refine our principles, theories and strategies and regard self-coaching as an integral part of ongoing learning, self-awareness and professional development.

Finally, our beliefs about human nature underpin our choice of strategies and interventions in the coaching situation. Most of us have theories about what constitutes a healthy, successful individual, what motivates people and why change does or does not occur. We tend to have beliefs about how much a person's behaviour is a function of genetics and environment and the role of free will and choice in our lives. It is not uncommon for a coach to espouse such beliefs as 'you can do anything if you really want to' or 'we always have a choice about our behaviour'. While such beliefs may or may not be valid, it is important to see how they impact on the coach's expectations of others. For example, stating either implicitly or explicitly that 'it's your choice' can underestimate the difficulty of change for the individual and absolve the coach from dealing with 'resistance' or barriers to change.

Research by Argyris and Schon suggests that under psychologically difficult situations people resort to a set of core values and think in such a way as to control the situation and minimise the expression of negative feelings. They think they know best, that they are better informed and that their motives are purer than others'. What is most interesting about these studies is the suggestion that people are usually unaware of how their thinking and their values contribute to these responses. Self-awareness and re-assessment of our values and beliefs are obviously critical if coaches are to avoid these traps.

Being aware of our values and beliefs assists us to reflect on why we are coaches, why particular strategies are successful or not, and, importantly, if and where our values and beliefs cause blind spots. They may be closing us off to new observations, understanding, new methods and new techniques.

Empathy

The word empathy is derived from the German word *Einfühlung* meaning to feel oneself into another's experience. Through empathy we are able to understand the other's experience and convey this understanding. Stephen Covey's (1998) fifth habit of highly effective people is 'seek first to understand then to be understood'. As Covey notes, empathic listening is not just a technique. It involves listening with the intention of really understanding and really trying to get inside another's frame of reference. It also, importantly, means being open to influence by the other. Other writers such as Hill and O'Brien (1999) also view empathy not so much as a specific skill but more as an attitude or manner of responding with genuine caring and a lack of judgment.

Empathy is not a universal construct. Research indicates that clients can experience empathy on different levels: on the cognitive level, in the affective or feeling domain, or as sharing and nurturing.

Regardless of the way in which it is experienced, it is through empathy, through the coach's attempt to understand what the coachee is thinking and feeling, that coachees feel understood and supported.

Empathy is considered a core ingredient of any helping relationship. The writings of Carl Rogers have provided a framework for the conditions that many practitioners regard as crucial to the change process. An empathic coach, for instance is able to understand the coachee's 'structure of interpretation' or internal frame of reference. Empathy also involves acceptance and a liking and caring for the individual. By acceptance, Rogers meant a warm regard for the other as a person of 'unconditional self-worth', a person of value regardless of his or her feelings or behaviours.

Young (2001) talks about empathy in terms of 'taking a tutorial stance'. By this he means that rather than assuming a hierarchical or authoritarian position with a client, the coach becomes a learner who seeks to understand and learn what it is to be like that person. Empathy is the first step in leaving behind the cultural baggage, world view and prejudices that prevent us from getting inside the world of the coachee.

Research indicates that lack of interest, remoteness and excessive sympathy are major barriers to facilitating growth and change. While coaches who are approaching burnout may present as aloof and uninterested, coaches who are just beginning their career are more likely to err on the side of excessive sympathy. Empathy does not involve merely agreeing with or supporting the coachee. It involves awareness of when we may be too distant or too involved—there must be a balance.

In our training we have encountered several coaches who related incidences of becoming over-involved with coachees especially in the area of life issues. Empathy and concern therefore need to be expressed within the confines of the coach's professional boundaries. As much as we empathise with the thoughts and feelings of the coachee, these thoughts and feelings do not belong to us. Any blurring of these boundaries can result in damage to the coach's wellbeing as well as proving totally ineffectual in helping the coachee.

There are many faces to empathy. For example, in his book *Working with Emotional Intelligence*, Goleman talks about empathy as a social competence. In the workplace it involves: understanding others, developing others, service orientation, leveraging diversity and political awareness. In a coaching context it includes guiding coachees in exploring their values and beliefs and understanding the challenges and choices they face.

Coaches are not, and should not pretend to be, experts in how people should live their lives, solve their problems or carry out their work duties. Guiding and facilitating others to achieve self-understanding and instigate change in order to lead more purposeful, successful lives is what coaching is about. Empathy is critical to these processes. The coach can express empathy through attention, questioning, support, encouragement, affirmation, interest and non-verbal cues. However, as noted previously, empathy cannot be taught. It emerges in the coaching relationship as a function of the coach's personality characteristics.

Finally, empathy is also tied in with self-awareness. Being in tune with our own thoughts and feelings, as well as our physiological responses, provides us with vital information about our current degree of empathy. We can learn to recognise our own bodily signals of anxiety, frustration, boredom or excessive sympathy and what these are telling us about our relationship with the coachee.

Authenticity

Being authentic simply means being true to who we are and what we believe in, and facing reality even though we may not like what we see. Authenticity involves living congruously so that what we know, what we claim to believe and value, and what we do are in harmony with each other. It is also related to self-esteem in that individuals with high self-esteem tend to be more authentic.

In *The Six Pillars of Self-Esteem*, Nathaniel Branden lists six practices which can gradually strengthen self-esteem and, therefore, authenticity. It is worth discussing these in some detail as they are not only relevant to our personal development as authentic coaches, they also provide us with guidelines when working on self-esteem issues with our clients. As noted by the author however, although others can be coached to develop these practices, the task of generating and sustaining them belongs to the individual alone.

1   *Living consciously* This practice involves paying attention to and respecting facts even though we might find them uncomfortable or threatening. We have to be aware of what we are doing while we are doing it and be open to feedback and information relating to our values, goals and work. We must be aware of the external world and also our own inner world so that we do not act out of blindness or self-delusion.

2   *Self-acceptance* A person who engages in this practice is willing to own, experience and take responsibility for his or her own thoughts, feelings and actions. Individuals have to be capable of facing up to the reality of what they think, feel and do without necessarily liking, condoning or judging.

3   *Self-responsibility* This practice serves to remind us that we are the authors of our choices and actions. We are responsible for our life, our happiness and the achievement of our goals.

4   *Self-assertiveness* Individuals who practise self-assertiveness refuse to fake who they are or what they believe in. They are willing to express and defend their thoughts, values and feelings whenever they consider it necessary and appropriate.

5   *Living purposefully* Rather than living at the mercy of outside forces or fate (external locus of control), this practice encourages us to identify our goals and action plans, to monitor these, seek feedback and to reassess on a regular basis.

6   *Integrity* As mentioned above, integrity concerns the integration of our beliefs, values and convictions with our actions.

Flexibility

In *The Complete Guide to Coaching at Work* we discussed some of the particular characteristics and competencies associated with flexibility. These include recognising when to be supportive or challenging, adjusting to the agenda of the coachee and varying one's coaching style in order to suit the individual coachee.

Flexibility can also be viewed from another perspective. Not only should the coach match the coachee's interactive style but he or she should be flexible enough to adapt models and strategies to suit the individual. For example, when dealing with cultural differences, the coach should not view reluctance to disclose as a form of resistance that has to be dealt with in the coaching sessions. Such an approach involves the imposition of cultural values on the coachee. A truly flexible coach will be able to focus more intensely on strategies and actions to change the situation rather than delving into the individual's belief systems and feelings surrounding the issue. Flexibility means we are not tied to static models and strategies.

Another aspect of coaching that demands flexibility is the choice of method for the delivery of the coaching sessions. Some coaches believe that face-to-face sessions or at least telephone contact are necessary to develop the rapport and relationships that underpin successful coaching. E-mail coaching is considered by many coaches to be an insufficiently 'rich' medium to support this development. Yet some studies on mentoring and e-mail suggest that as users begin to comprehend the challenges associated with e-mail they also evolve special techniques for establishing mutual understanding. The point of this discussion is not whether e-mail is an effective medium for coaching. Rather, it is intended to highlight the need for coaches to be adaptable and flexible in terms of their theories, strategies and methods of coaching.

Resourcefulness

Coaches are not experts. While this is true, coaches are expected to be resourceful in terms of the methods, strategies and solutions they bring to the coaching partnership. They have to display creativity in terms of problem solving and be imaginative in the techniques they apply. One model or one solution does not fit all. Being adaptable and willing to research and adopt new techniques is crucial if the coach wishes to remain on the cutting edge of coaching technology.

Resourcefulness can involve taking on clients who face issues and challenges that the coach has not dealt with before. While it is clearly unethical to proclaim competence or expertise in areas one is unfamiliar with, the resourceful coach will become competent in these areas. Researching the issue, speaking and consulting with other coaches who may be experts in the particular area, and paying particular attention to milestones in reaching the individual's goals will equip the resourceful coach with the confidence and skills to meet new challenges.

As mentioned several times throughout this book, the profession of coaching is changing. More and more, coachees are demanding that coaches provide solid content and experience in their niche area. However, one cannot be a coach for all reasons and all seasons. A coach has to have access to a group of professionals such as psychologists, financial lawyers, lawyers, trainers and life skills coaches, that she or he can refer the coachee to or from whom the coach can obtain advice and guidance.

Communication expertise

Because of the core role of communication and dialoguing in coaching, we have devoted a chapter to this topic (see Chapter 8). However, it is timely to mention here one of the core ingredients of good communication—clear thinking. A coach has to be able to think in a logical, rational manner and verbalise these thoughts succinctly and clearly to the coachee. After all, as coaches we frequently work with and challenge the self-limiting or self-defeating beliefs of the coachee. A coach who expresses his or her ideas in vague, ambiguous terms instantly loses credibility. Our thoughts have to be clear and objective, based on reality and facts, not on some inarticulate theory or feeling that is influenced by irrelevant factors or others' view of reality.

Coach–coachee mismatches

It is useful to note that sometimes there will be a mismatch between the personality style of the coach and that of the coachee. An introverted coachee might find the extroverted enthusiasm of the coach irritating. Similarly, a very practical, pragmatic coachee might lose patience with a coach who is seen as being too theoretical.

Socioeconomic and cross-cultural factors might also affect the relationship because these two things impact on our personality. Research suggests there is a better match between individuals from similar socioeconomic, racial and cultural backgrounds. In our experience as global educators, and this is supported by research, we have noticed that cultural differences impact on coaching, particularly in relation to the coachee's level of self-disclosure. Many coaches would agree that life issues frequently are intertwined with work matters. However, some cultures value privacy and self-determination to such an extent that it may prevent them from disclosing and seeking help from the coach on personal or 'life' matters. For instance, individuals from Asian cultures are more likely to try to solve problems themselves or talk to family and friends than see a professional coach. Therefore, they are sometimes reluctant to discuss certain issues with the coach. As coaches we have to be sensitive to these cultural differences and not impose our own values or ways of dealing with problems.

Age and gender are also variables that can lead to a coach–coachee mismatch. For example, generation-Xers may prefer a coaching alliance with a coach closer in age to themselves. They are, after all, more impressed by personal rather than positional power. Other coachees may prefer an older, more experienced coach. Coachees may also prefer to work with a same-sex coach.

While these mismatches may present barriers to coaching, there are ways to at least minimise their impact on the coaching relationship. Setting expectations, providing information about the structure of the sessions (see the coach–client protocol and coaching agreement in Chapter 3) and carefully aligning the values and goals of the individual can counterbalance some of the drawbacks associated with a coach–coachee mismatch.

 Summary

The personality of the coach plays a critical role in the success of any coaching alliance. Assessments, tools and techniques will only be useful if the coaching relationship is situated in the context of an empathic, authentic communication between a coachee and a coach who is self-aware, flexible and resourceful.

Taking ownership

The coaching alliance can be an intense and challenging experience for the coachee. The individual has to embrace the coaching process with an open mind and an honest and frank recognition of his or her strengths and weaknesses. As we all know, facing up to certain facts about ourselves can be uncomfortable, even upsetting. The coachee also has to recognise that he or she is adopting a learning role, and appreciate that this is not an inherent criticism of current abilities but rather an opportunity for growth and personal development.

These demands on the coachee constitute his or her acceptance of owning the coaching process. Unless ownership occurs, coaching is likely to be unsuccessful. The core ingredients of taking ownership are commitment, trust and pride. Of course, the development and maintenance of commitment and trust is a two-way process and, as we discuss in this chapter, has to be generated by the coach.

Commitment

Regardless of how adept the coach is at employing various tools and techniques, and no matter how clever the coachee, the coaching alliance is doomed to failure unless there is commitment on both sides. Unless the coach is able to generate commitment coaching will just be an intellectual exercise. Perhaps the coachee will learn how to perform an existing skill with greater finesse or even acquire new skills, but there will be no real transformation. Values, beliefs, expectations and moods will not be explored in any depth and powerful changes will not take place. These can only occur in a context of commitment.

Commitment is an agreement or a pledge to do something in the future. It is the state of being obligated. Coaching, as we mention throughout this book, is about achieving breakthroughs and change. It involves committing to other options and possibilities, to other values, beliefs and emotions. Coaching demands that the coach and coachee commit to these changes before they occur, before there is any evidence that the changes can be accomplished. Commitment then, is a serious agreement between the coach and coachee and it provides the foundation for the coaching relationship.

Gaining commitment

How is the coach to gain commitment from the individual or organisation? One cannot simply ask for it. Nor is there any simple 10-point plan or set of guidelines that will work for every coachee. The coach has to design and employ specific strategies that will engender and develop commitment in each individual coachee. The following diagram illustrates the cycle of commitment we use as a guide in our workshops, and when coaching individuals and organisations.

As the cycle illustrates, the coachee has to commit to the possibilities that change may bring, even when there is no existing evidence to support this. The coachee has to commit to the unknown. While we can present our credentials, our experience, our professionalism and our confidence, there is as yet no real evidence that the possibilities we envision will be realised. However, we believe that the coach can take some steps to lay the foundation for a commitment to coaching.

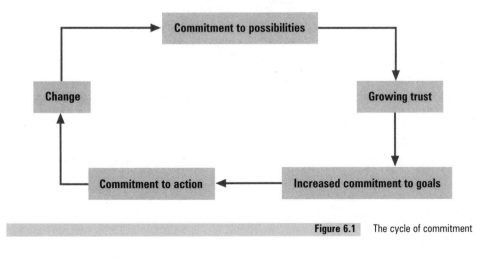

Figure 6.1   The cycle of commitment

1 Establish reliability and predictability

The coachee is more likely to be committed to the coaching process if the coach presents as a reliable professional. For example, the manner in which the coach deals with fees, contracts, and appointment times can signal to the coachee that he or she is reliable. Second, the coach's credentials and apparent experience and expertise in coaching contribute to building commitment. In our experience though, prospective clients do not expect a great deal of information about past clients, success rates or even the tools and techniques we employ. It seems that the critical factor in establishing initial commitment is that coaches present as qualified, certified and experienced professionals who are able to ascertain and meet the organisation's specific coaching needs.

2 Assess the coachee's and organisation's needs

The coach can engender commitment by accurately assessing and reflecting the coachee's and/or the organisation's needs. Although we examined the logistics of how to conduct a coaching needs analysis in organisations in Chapter 3 it is worth noting some of the core skills involved in engaging and aligning coachees. These include:

➤ *Observing, informed listening, reflecting, and articulating the needs of the coachee in order to reveal our understanding of these.* Our experience shows that coachees are more likely to reveal early signs of commitment when the coach asks questions and listens to their needs and concerns rather than 'selling' the benefits of coaching.

➤ *Framing the coaching needs by clarifying, hypothesising, brainstorming and problem solving rather than providing answers.* Anxiety and a need to prove one's value can result in a coach prematurely providing solutions. We have found that the most effective means of establishing a true coaching alliance, from first contact onwards, is to collaborate and cooperate in the search for solutions, rather than advise.

➤ *Focusing on the consulting process itself rather than on one's own agenda.* Again, our experience shows that commitment is more likely to occur when the coachee recognises that it is his or her agenda that is the foundation of the coaching relationship. It is important that the coach is not seen as offering generic problem-solving models or solutions, and that the coaching program is carefully and individually tailored to the coachee's specific needs.

➤ *Clarifying expectations.* The coachee must be aware of what coaching is and what it is not. Importantly, the coachee also has to recognise that change involves time—it is not an overnight miracle fix and can be challenging and, at times, difficult. When armed with this knowledge the coachee can choose to truly commit to the time and effort involved in a successful coaching partnership.

3 Assess the coachee's level of commitment

In order to create a structure on which to build commitment, the coach has firstly to diagnose or examine the individual coachee's beliefs about commitment. We need to know what commitment means to the coachee, how seriously he or she treats obligations, what constitutes reasonable—and unreasonable—obligations, how he or she deals with unreasonable obligations, what fuels commitment and what kills it.

To discover the above elements we have found it useful to establish a history of the coachee's commitments. Usually, we ask the coachee to discuss previous situations that demanded commitment. Some questions to employ in this dialogue include:

➤ What were you committed to?

➤ What motivated you?

➤ What values were at stake?

➤ What maintained your commitment when things were tough and the goal seemed a long way away?

➤ Have you experienced any situations where you did not persevere with your commitment?

➤ What were the reasons for this?

➤ How did you feel about this situation?

➤ What would you change about it if you could?

➤ Tell me how you see yourself at the end of the coaching program (i.e. your vision of yourself).

➤ How committed are you, on a scale of 1 (low) to 10 (high), to the coaching process?

➤ What would it take to move you up the scale?

➤ What could I, as a coach, do to build and develop your commitment?

Establishing the coachee's vision and values is critical to gaining commitment. Unless the goals of the coaching alliance are aligned with the individual's values and vision, commitment is likely to be low.

4 Formalise the commitment process

As we discussed in Chapter 3, commitment can be fostered if the coachee signs off on the coaching agreement form during the first coaching session. The coaching agreement signals that the coaching process is a two-way interaction with obligations on both sides. The coach can then hold the coachee to the agreement and challenge any obvious failure to follow-through on commitments. Without some formal acknowledgment of commitment it is difficult for the coach to confront the coachee later on if they are not fulfilling their obligations. The coach is in a stronger position when he or she is able to say for example, 'In the coaching agreement you committed to …but your actions suggest …'

During the assessment phase the coach can administer a series of questions that will give an indication of the aspects of change that may prove problematic in the coaching intervention. Focusing on these areas can weaken the intensity of any resistance and facilitate change. Below is a coaching commitment profile we have developed:

Checklist

How to use:

✔ pen and pencil format.

When to use:

✔ during the first coaching session with all coachees.

Why use:

✔ to highlight potential barriers and resistance to change.

Exercise

The coaching commitment profile

1   Do you consider your role as a coachee to be totally voluntary?

2   What do you expect from the coaching sessions?

3   How urgent is your need to change? Circle the number on the scale.

1	2	3	4	5	6	7
Low			Medium			High

4   When you are faced with change, how do you usually adapt?

   Slowly ………….   Gradually ………….   Quickly ………….

5   How hopeful are you that you will change? Circle the number on the scale.

1	2	3	4	5	6	7
Slightly			Moderately			Very

6   Who will support your changes?

7   What strengths do you have that will make change easier for you?

8 What obstacles might stand in your way?

9 What 'trade-offs' might you have to make in order to change?

10 On a scale of 1 to 7 where 1 is 'a little' and 7 is 'very much' how prepared are you to:

> challenge your beliefs and attitudes even if they are deeply
held?   ....

> put an end to self-limiting and self-sabotaging behaviours?   ....

> persevere during difficult times?   ....

> examine your values and choices even when it is
difficult for you?   ....

> talk about any fears that may be holding you back?   ....

> try out new behaviours?   ....

> insist on what you want from the coaching sessions?   ....

> accept responsibility for the outcome of the
coaching program?   ....

As we are all aware, a coachee may be responding in such a way as to meet the coach's (or even management's) expectations. However, if a coachee is not carrying out the agreed upon actions and the coach has exhausted all possible avenues for dealing with the resistance or non-compliance it is justifiable to revisit the profile and remind the coachee of his or her commitments.

Of course commitment can change over time as can values, decisions and choices. The coach has to be flexible. It is ludicrous to attempt to hold someone to commitments that are no longer relevant or appropriate due to changing circumstances. In such situations, the coach's role is to work with the coachee to ensure that any change in commitment or values is a logical, rational one and not one based on impulse or an 'easy way out'.

A barrier to commitment

Fear

Everyone experiences fear. In fact, fear drives much of our behaviour. We fear illness, old age, loneliness, rejection, failure and death and many of us have additional personal fears. We may fear for our position at work, that we will be downsized or fall from favour. We fear we do not have the time to complete our work tasks efficiently and that we have lost, or are losing, control over any sense of a life/work balance. Fear can destroy our lives. It is a barrier to performance, effectiveness and the quality of our life and work.

Although the clinical literature distinguishes between fear, which is a response to an identifiable stimulus, and anxiety, which is less intense, longer lasting and not clearly associated with a specific stimulus, both are aversive states which impact negatively on our lives. For instance, fear in the workplace may be a response to a performance appraisal, whereas anxiety may be induced by planned changes in organisational structure. Individuals may feel a vague sense of unease and worry although they are unable to isolate what exactly is causing their concern.

Anxiety and fear can be major obstacles to a commitment to change. However, as noted by Kelly, anxiety is a necessary accompaniment, in fact a precursor to change. Yet anxiety and fear can be overwhelming if not managed effectively.

Specific fears

Individual coachees may be unable to commit to coaching because of an underlying fear. Some of these fears include:

➤ *Fear of success*   Some individuals underachieve because of consciously or unconsciously perceived negative associations with being successful. They may fear that success will undermine or damage their relationships with peers and that it will generate envy and enemies. Success is also accompanied by greater expectations from self and others, and the individual may fear that he or she is unable to continue to perform successfully.

➤ *Fear of failure*   The coachee may feel that he or she will not be able to achieve a desired or set goal and will therefore be a failure in the eyes of self and especially others. The prospect of a promotion can engender such fear and it can manifest in the coachee not committing to gaining or enhancing the skills necessary for the new position. Indeed, some individuals may be committed to failure, to blaming others and to complaining.

Fear of failure is frequently related to fear of reprisal because reprisal is a likely outcome of failure. The tendency to fear failure usually means that individuals are unwilling to take risks and try out new ideas and new behaviours. In turn, this leads to apathy, defensiveness and stagnation within individuals and organisations. If individuals are afraid to fail, then the organisation will not grow and flourish. We learn from our mistakes and from the risks we take. Management must recognise that change and growth involve the risk of failure and be prepared to accept and forgive failure and to learn from it. A coach working within an organisation also has to be prepared to take risks, to fail and to learn.

➤ *Fear of change*   The prospect and implementation of change policies can invoke fear in individuals and organisations alike. The often cited phrases 'we've always done it this way' or 'this has always worked in the past' may be a defensive response to the feared changes.

Restructuring may involve loss of jobs, working with difficult colleagues, market expansion and other changes that can reveal deficiencies in the organisational structure. We may also fear the changes that technology imposes.

Assessing fears

We tend to not talk about our fears although sometimes the coachee will naturally and spontaneously broach the topic in the coaching conversation. Our experience suggests however that the coach cannot rely upon this happening. Therefore, the coach has to either formally or informally assess the coachee's fears. We have found the following three assessment methods to be useful. Depending on the individual coachee and the degree of trust and security he or she experiences in the coaching relationship, the coach can:

1   Ask the coachee to talk about any fears that currently impact on his or her life or might impact on the coaching relationship.

2   Ask the coachee to nominate three fears and rate them on a scale of 1 (very little) to 10 (a great deal) according to how much impact they have on his or her current work and life situation.

3   Ask the coachee to complete the following questionnaire.

Exercise   **A brief fear survey**

How often do you experience the following states? Rate yourself using the scale.

1	2	3	4	5	6	7
Never		Sometimes		Often		Always

Fear of losing control.   ....

Fear of not being able to cope.   ....

Fear of failure.   ....

Fear of success.   ....

Fear of illness and death.   ....

Fear of unemployment.   ....

Fear of rejection.   ....

Fear of ageing.   ....

Exercise

Fear of being downsized. ....

Fear of responsibility. ....

Fear of betrayal. ....

Any other fear(s). ....

Trust

Many of us believe that trust is an absolute belief in the honesty of self or another. Yet leading practitioners such as Solomen and Flores claim that authentic trust does not necessarily exclude distrust. On the contrary, their work in organisations suggests that we have to embrace the possibilities of distrust and betrayal as being an essential part of trust. Trust always involves the possibility of distrust: it entails a risk and is always fragile. Although there is a risk involved in trusting, the outcomes of our coaching partnerships suggest that taking the risk is more than compensated for by the coachees' growing commitment and ultimate progress.

We do not believe that trust is the 'social glue' it is sometimes glibly described as being. Trust is an emotional skill; it is something we choose and a personal investment for which we take responsibility. By trusting, the coach and coachee are responsible for making a commitment, and choosing goals and a course of action.

Developing and growing trust

As Figure 6.1 and the section on commitment illustrate, the coachee has to commit to possibilities and the coach has to work quickly and consistently to foster this initial commitment. However, we have found that in order for this commitment to grow and flourish trust has to develop and be maintained between the coach and coachee.

As part of the coaching agreement, the coachee understands that the coach expects him or her to be honest and open about the work or life situation and any difficulties involved. The coachee will only fulfil these expectations in an atmosphere of trust. There has to be trust that the coaching relationship will be helpful, and that the coach is trustworthy.

Trust is built up over time. It is naïve to expect authentic trust between the coach and coachee at the beginning of the coaching relationship. Initially the coachee may make small disclosures in order to test the coach's reaction. Some hostile individuals may employ criticism of coaching in order to undermine the coach. It is the way the coach responds, that is, the coach's ability to contain these projections and not react in a defensive manner, that can contribute to the gradual building up of trust on the coachee's part. Trust evolves through tests and time. As coaches, we need the skills to facilitate the growth and development of trust. Such skills involve exploring and enhancing self-trust. It is obvious that one must trust oneself in order to generate a trusting relationship with another, yet self-trust is something many of us take for granted or assume we have.

Trusting the self

As coaches we have to trust in our mind and our judgment. In addition, we have to build self-confidence, and trust our emotions and ability to control our moods. We have to reflect on and scrutinise ourselves on an ongoing basis.

Trust is an orientation towards the world. It is the foundation of our 'being in the world'—our sense of security in our own being and our place in the world. According to Erik Erickson (1963), developing 'basic trust' is the first task of the infant. Infants either develop a basic trust or mistrust in themselves and their caretakers. If the infant's needs are met, he or she is more likely to believe that others can be trusted. Research suggests that individuals with a well-developed sense of basic trust display certain characteristics. Using these characteristics as a guide, we suggest that coaches reflect on the following questions:

➤ Are you able to ask others for emotional help when necessary?

➤ Do you tend to focus on the positive aspects of others' behaviour?

➤ Do you have an optimistic but realistic world view?

➤ Do you prefer a balance between giving and receiving?

➤ Are you honest with yourself and others about your emotions?

➤ Are you comfortable with intimacy?

Fear of, or the avoidance of, intimacy has been recognised as one of the major barriers to creating and displaying trust. Intimacy demands an emotional honesty that allows the coach to recognise and acknowledge the limitations of his or her knowledge. We have to feel comfortable saying 'I don't know'. It also involves the coach being able to take risks, and being vulnerable to failure and mistakes.

As we discuss in the chapter on self-awareness (see Chapter 7) and the chapter on emotions (see Chapter 10), the coach does not necessarily have to deal in an in-depth manner with all the disclosures of the coachee. The coach must be prepared however to expand the bounds of acceptable topics. A fear of intimacy on the coach's part will be transmitted to the coachee. As a result the coachee may withhold certain thoughts and experiences for fear the coach is unwilling or unable to deal with certain issues. When this occurs, the depth and potential success of the coaching alliance is jeopardised.

It is obvious then that a coach must possess a well-developed sense of trust in himself or herself. Such trust is as much a function of basic trust and ontological security as it is of trusting in one's coaching skills and techniques. Ongoing development and training in the use of coaching techniques and continuous self-appraisal are critical to this process.

Displaying trust

As well as developing a solid sense of self-trust, coaches can learn how to better display trust to others. Some guidelines for this process include the following:

1 Learn to talk about trust

Coaches cannot ask for or demand trust from the coachee. But they can talk about trust. Indeed, it is essential to discuss the issue of trust. One way of approaching the matter is to discuss confidentiality and ensure that the coachee is agreeable to the terms of confidentiality as outlined in the coaching agreement. Most importantly, the coach has to establish what trust means to the coachee. Otherwise, when a coach adopts a challenging and confronting role, the coachee may feel that trust has been betrayed.

We also suggest that coaches begin the first coaching session with a brief acknowledgment of the apprehension the coachee may be experiencing. It is helpful to also acknowledge that such unease may partly be a function of having to disclose information to a complete stranger. Regularly bringing the issue of trust into the open allows the coachee the freedom and confidence to talk about his or her own expectations, particularly when he or she feels the coach has betrayed trust. Trust, after all, is about relationships. It is a two-way process.

2 Make commitments that command trust

The coach makes a commitment to the coachee. Such a commitment involves staying with the coachee's agenda, exploring significant aspects of the coachee's life (e.g. values, beliefs, emotions), supporting, challenging and encouraging the coachee through the process of change and bringing to bear the most effective tools and techniques to facilitate change.

The coach has to be aware of and accepting of his or her own weaknesses or blind spots. Of course, 'we don't know what we don't know', so it is essential that each coach has a colleague or mentor who can provide honest observations, assessments and feedback regarding his or her performance.

In turn, the coachee commits to being honest about his or her strengths and weaknesses, trying and adopting new methods of thinking and behaving, and transferring learning in the coaching sessions to the workplace or home. Both sets of commitments demand trust from the other party. Coaching will not be successful unless these demands are met.

Distrust in organisations

Free markets, globalisation and converging societies increasingly demand that we trust in ourselves, in others and in technology. However, research suggests that distrust within the corporate world may be at an all-time high. Trust is frequently espoused in organisations. Yet such trust is sometimes a façade and relationships are built on fear and pretence. Many organisations attempt to change from the old 'command and control' style of management but revert to it because they are unable to function in a culture of cooperation and trust.

Lack of trust can impact negatively on organisational creativity. It also prevents individuals from freely expressing their feelings and differences. Instead they resort to defensiveness and sabotage. Poor communication, misperceptions, cynicism, resentment and anger are the results of a failure to build trusting relationships.

Many individuals who work in an environment of distrust are unable to express their fears and uncertainties freely and openly. Such suppression of fear frequently results in the following types of behaviour:

➤ being overly critical of self and others

➤ developing a 'victim' mentality

➤ excessive worrying

➤ adhering to standards of perfection that promote stress and burnout.

While such behaviours are open to modification and change through the coaching process, fear can override any commitment to change.

Some of our students have worked in organisations where distrust was endemic. There was little or no true communication between senior management and middle management, staff were uncertain about what to do, most communication took place on the grapevine, rumours were rife and morale was poor. No one, it seemed, was willing or able to discuss their true feelings and beliefs. In essence, they were governed by fear, denial and hidden agendas.

As coaches, it was extremely trying to work in such an environment. It was virtually impossible to get a true picture of the state of affairs. The coaches were always second-guessing someone's motives and working 'in the dark'. More importantly, the coaching alliance was compromised from the very beginning. The coachees were afraid that being nominated for coaching was indicative of their inability to perform effectively and feared that coaching was a prelude to losing their jobs. The real issues were not addressed because no one was prepared to raise them.

Unfortunately, these experiences are not isolated events. Other students report similar difficulties and obstacles. Therefore, it is important for coaches to accept that coaching interventions are unlikely to succeed in an atmosphere of distrust and fear. Trust should be built on commitment and commitment should be strengthened by trust. Fear sits outside the equation.

Conversely, some coaches have had the pleasure of working in organisations where there was genuine, authentic trust between the CEO and the rest of the staff. There was a consensus on the issues or problems to be addressed in coaching, confidentiality was respected and the CEO sought and shared feedback from the coach and the coachees. The coaching outcomes were, as predicted, highly successful.

Pride

As with trust and commitment, successful coaching partnerships require that the coachee take pride in the coaching relationship. Coachees should be proud of engaging in the coaching process, of their willingness to examine their personal style and shortcomings and to adopt a learning role. If the individual is not proud of his or her involvement in coaching, this may be a signal that he or she is not truly engaged and does not accept ownership of the experience.

It may be that the organisational culture is such that, if the coachee were to discuss his or her involvement with coaching, it may be interpreted as a sign of weakness and incompetence. However, such constraints should not operate on the personal level. It is important that the coach establishes whether the coachee has discussed the coaching alliance with his or her colleagues, family and friends. If coachees are reluctant to discuss their engagement in coaching with family and friends it may signify that they are embarrassed about their perceived weaknesses or shortcomings. If this is so, it may be useful for the coach to explore the coachee's beliefs. The coach may need to reinforce the notion that self-awareness and openness to change require courage, and that the coachee should take pride in committing to this challenge.

Summary We cannot overemphasise the critical role commitment, trust and pride play in any coaching relationship. Coaches cannot take them for granted. They must be vigilant and honest in scrutinising, assessing and developing their own levels of commitment and trust as well as those of the organisation and individual coachees.

Self-awareness

Although the notion of self-awareness is bandied about frequently in self-help literature the term remains poorly defined. For our purposes, we define self-awareness as the state of being aware of our emotions and the thoughts and behaviours accompanying them. According to Goleman, how we attend to and deal with our emotions is a function of our emotional intelligence. Some of us feel overwhelmed by our feelings and thoughts, and feel helpless to change them. Others are accepting of their feelings yet make no effort to deal with them, even though they may be negative and distressing. On the other hand, individuals who are aware of their feelings and recognise and use techniques to overcome any negative states tend to manage their emotions more effectively.

Recent empirical research, as cited by Kilburg (2000), has shown a significant positive relationship between managerial self-awareness and managerial performance. Self-awareness ultimately improves the individual's managerial and leadership skills.

Recognition of the importance of self-awareness and emotional competencies continues to grow within the coaching industry. Some research suggests that it is not the pay and perks that contribute to employee productivity but rather the emotional connection and relatedness employees have to their peers and supervisors. Increasingly, many companies are promoting self-awareness and coaching for emotional development as key elements in assisting employees to develop interpersonal skills.

Developing self-awareness

As individuals we all possess the capacity for and perhaps varying degrees of self-awareness. The extent to which the coach should focus on developing awareness in a coachee depends upon several factors. These include:

➤ the coach's skill in this area

➤ the coachee's capacity for insight and awareness

➤ the extent to which a lack of this quality may be impacting on the coachee's growth and skill development.

However, we believe that some degree of self-awareness is necessary if the coachee is to produce any real, sustainable behavioural change. The ongoing relationship between self-awareness and action learning is demonstrated in the following diagram.

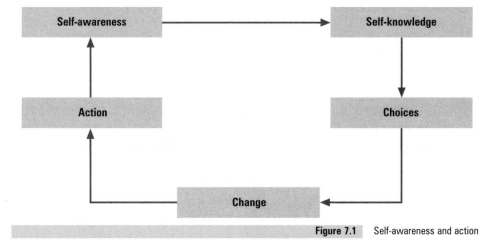

Figure 7.1   Self-awareness and action

Of course, awareness of one's emotions and thoughts does not mean that one has the ability to change these. However, without self-awareness the likelihood of change is minimal. The overall purpose of the self-awareness tools and techniques described below is to encourage and assist the coachee to become more aware of his or her own experiences and, in the process, become more accepting and more responsible for them.

Sometimes when an individual attempts to change there is the possibility that he or she may feel 'divided'. Part of the person wants to change while another part wants to retain the status quo. There can be a constant oscillation between the two parts with the individual feeling torn and frustrated. It can even happen that the more one wants to change the worse the situation becomes. At times it can be useful for us to simply become aware of how we are now. Becoming aware of a feeling, a thought or a situation can often result in some change occurring by itself.

There are various methods already in place to increase an individual's self-awareness. These include 360-degree performance instruments and formal psychological assessment. However the techniques discussed below emphasise the reflective and experiential aspects of self-awareness. It is important to reiterate the point made earlier that these techniques should only be employed in a safe, accepting environment where the coachee feels genuinely free to reflect and openly engage in new experiences.

Self-awareness is a soft skill. Yet so called soft skills frequently impact on the acquisition of hard skills. The coach can promote self-awareness in the coachee in order to familiarise him or her with feelings, thoughts, bodily sensations and perceptions that may otherwise be closed off from conscious experience and be preventing hard learning from taking place.

Techniques for promoting self-awareness

The following tools and techniques, some of which have been adapted from Gestalt therapy and transactional analysis, are designed for the coach working with a coachee to enhance or even induce self-awareness. Many of the techniques emphasise the 'what' and 'how' of an experience rather than the 'why'. Our specialty coaching workshops on self-awareness are a result of the increasing insistence and demand by professional coaches to be trained and supervised by a psychologist in the use of such psychology-based techniques.

1 Being aware in the present

The purpose of this technique is simply to encourage self-awareness in the coachee. The coach does not have to engage in any deep analysis of the coachee's responses. It is the awareness, the experience itself, that facilitates change. The coach's role here is to provide a structure, to teach the coachee the technique, and encourage him or her in the sometimes difficult and protracted process of increasing the awareness of one's experiences.

Checklist

How to use:

  ✔   as an experiential technique to teach the coachee in the coaching session

  ✔   as a homework exercise and an ongoing practice.

When to use:

  ✔   when a coachee appears to be 'stuck' in the past

  ✔   when a coachee seems preoccupied and 'absent'

  ✔   when the coachee appears to be out of touch with his or her experiences, for example, tends to intellectualise, deny or minimise feelings

✔ when a coachee appears overly absorbed in his or her own thoughts and oblivious to the environment or response of others.

Why use:

✔ to increase the coachee's awareness of the external world, the inner world of feelings and the inner world of thoughts and memories

✔ to bring to the foreground any 'unfinished business' that is preventing the coachee from moving forward into the hard learning phase of the coaching program.

Step one   Explain the purpose of the exercise to the coachee.

Step two   Suggest that the coachee spends three minutes of quiet, uninterrupted time to simply be aware. If the coachee requires some structure he or she may say silently, 'I'm aware of…' or 'I notice…' during the three minutes.

Step three   Ask the coachee the following questions:

➤ What did you attend to most during the three minutes?

➤ What was happening inside your head, such as thoughts, fantasies, future plans, past events, etc.?

➤ What was happening inside your body, such as physical sensations, heartbeat, nervousness, emotions?

➤ What was happening in the external world, such as sounds, sights, observing the coach, etc.?

➤ Did you feel bored or uninterested at any stage?

➤ Did you feel anxious at any stage? What made you anxious?

Step four   Depending on which realm the coachee has paid least attention to, design a homework assignment to increase awareness in that area.

Some examples of homework assignments:

➤ *To increase cognitive awareness* (What's happening inside my head?)

Spend three minutes twice a day at a nominated time and just be aware of the thoughts, fantasies and plans inside your head.

➤ *To increase awareness in the bodily realm* (What's going on inside me?)

Exercise

Spend three minutes twice a day at a nominated time being aware of what is happening in your body.

> ➤ *To increase awareness of the external world* (What's happening around me?)

Spend three minutes twice a day at a nominated time and be aware of what is happening in the world around you.

Step five   Awareness of experience is an ongoing process of growth and development. It is a way of life. If the coachee enjoys and benefits from the practice, the technique can be built into the individual's weekly goals. For instance, each week the coach can add one of the following suggestions:

In the three minute awareness periods:

> ➤ *see* and notice details you have never noticed before in a familiar work situation.

> ➤ notice *what* you avoid experiencing in a familiar work situation

> ➤ notice *how* you avoid experiencing things

> ➤ be aware of whether you *avoid* experiencing certain things about *your past*.

Ideally, the coachee will increase the periods of 'awareness' and transfer the skills learned in this exercise to enhance awareness of experiences in all facets of his or her life.

2 Owning our feelings

Some of us skirt around our feelings and experiences and even around our lives. For various reasons we develop the habit of distancing ourselves from our experiences. One of the ways in which we do this is to speak in generalisations or attribute our thoughts and feelings to 'everyone' rather than ourselves. For example, a person who does not accept responsibility for his or her own anger is likely to say, 'Everyone gets angry about . . .', rather than, 'I get angry about . . .' Other expressions which signal a similar failure to own one's experiences include: 'No one likes to be put down in public' (rather than 'I don't like to be put down in public') or 'Most people find…annoying' (rather than 'I find…annoying'). Such dialogue is frequently expressed in organisations where there is a lack of honest and forthright communication and subsequently denial of responsibility for feelings and experiences.

Becoming aware of how people disown their feelings and experiences can be a critical aspect of the coachee's growth, development and change. The following exercises are designed to increase such awareness.

Making 'I statements'

Checklist

How to use:

✔ as an exercise in the coaching sessions

✔ as an ongoing homework assignment.

When to use:

✔ when a coachee has difficulty acknowledging his or her own experiences

✔ when a coachee speaks in generalisations rather than claiming experiences as his or her own.

Why use:

✔ to help the coachee become aware of his or her feelings and thoughts

✔ to increase the coachee's degree of responsibility for his or her thoughts and feelings.

Exercise

Step one   Give the coachee two examples of statements which disown responsibility and the equivalent 'I statements'. (See above for examples.)

Step two   Ask the coachee to add two 'disowning' statements he or she may be in the habit of using.

Step three   Ask the coachee to reframe these two statements into 'I statements'.

Step four   Ask the coachee about any differences he or she notices when making the two kinds of statements. Coachees may report feeling more powerful, more in control and more direct when they use an 'I statement'.

Step five   Set a homework assignment in which the coachee commits to making at least three 'I statements' a day until the next coaching session.

Step six   It may be necessary to review the process. This will depend on the coachee's ability to carry out the action plan, and any difficulties encountered. Otherwise, it is useful to continue to build this task into the coachee's weekly goals until he or she is using 'I statements' regularly and confidently.

Changing our dialogue

The language we use reveals, to both ourselves and others, how we perceive our place in the world. Our language can reflect a sense of control and self-directedness or it can express a victim mentality and a sense that we are at the mercy of others or fate. Changing our language can change our view of the world, our sense of self and our relationship to our actions. It can change our actions.

Checklist

How to use:

✔ as an exercise in the coaching sessions.

When to use:

✔ when a coachee uses language that suggests he or she is evading responsibility for his or her choices, desires and weaknesses.

Why use:

✔ to encourage the coachee to become more aware of his or her own power and freedom and express this through language.

Exercise

Step one   Ask the coachee to complete the following sentences:

I had to _____

_____

I can't _____

_____

I need _____

_____

I'm afraid to _____

_____

I'm unable to _____

_____

Step two   Ask the coachee to substitute the following words for the five beginnings above:

I chose to … (instead of *I had to*)

I won't… (instead of *I can't*)

I want… (instead of *I need*)

I'd like to… (instead of *I'm afraid to*)

I'm unwilling to work hard enough to… (instead of *I'm unable to*)

Step three   Ask the coachee to describe any differences he or she experienced when writing the latter statements.

3 Awareness of choices

Making choices is part of virtually everything we do. From the moment we wake to the time we fall asleep, our day is punctuated by choices, some minor, others critically important. Coaching emphasises the role of choice in any effort to effect change. The coachee has to choose to want to change. While this is true, much of the coaching literature implies that man has unlimited free will and inhabits a world of absolute and unbounded possibilities. Second, it assumes that making choices is a simple process.

Unwillingness to make a choice is sometimes seen as a moral failing where the individual lacks 'the courage to support his convictions'. More often than not however, individuals do not make choices because they do not know how. Rarely are we taught to make choices at school and making a choice is not usually presented as a problem-solving skill that can be learned and improved.

Coaches are frequently confronted with a coachee who is unwilling or unable to choose. The individual may be desperately unhappy in his or her work and yearns for freedom. At the same time, the coachee wants the financial security that the work provides. The individual remains in a state of conflict and ambivalence while the quality of his or her life and work continues to deteriorate.

There are various strategies we can employ to avoid or undermine effective choice making. As noted by Robert Fritz (1989), these include: (1) only choosing what seems reasonable or possible rather than what we really want; (2) choosing the process rather than the result; (3) eliminating all other choices so that only one choice remains; and (4) not choosing to choose or choosing by default.

Self-awareness includes being attuned to the possibilities in one's life and being able to make choices that contribute to a meaningful and fulfilling existence. The techniques suggested below are designed to enable the coach and coachee to work together so that the coachee can recognise options and make more satisfying and rewarding choices.

Recognising choices

Checklist

How to use:
- ✔ as an exercise within the coaching session.

When to use:
- ✔ when the coachee is unable to recognise potential choices or options in his or her path
- ✔ when the coachee is unable to move forward because he or she cannot make a choice.

Why use:
- ✔ to assist the coachee to become more aware of the choices he or she faces and the consequences of making or not making a choice.

Step one   Explain some of the methods (noted above) that individuals employ to make or not make choices.

Step two   Ask the coachee which method he or she usually employs when making a choice.

Step three   Depending on the coachee's response, ask the following questions:

➤ What are the advantages of choosing (or not choosing) in this manner?

➤ What are the disadvantages of choosing (or not choosing) in this manner?

➤ What has choosing (or not choosing) in this way allowed you to do?

➤ What has it prevented you from doing?

Step four   Ask the coachee to nominate a 'choice situation' he or she is currently facing. For example, the coachee may be faced with the choice of remaining in a current job position or applying for a promotion.

Step five   Ask the coachee to complete the following sentences by listing five consequences:

➤ If I choose to remain in my current job…

➤ If I do not make a choice…

These questions may be given to the coachee to complete between coaching sessions, and discussed the following week. Alternatively, they can be worked through in the current session depending on the urgency of the situation.

Taking responsibility for our choices

As well as disowning our experiences, many of us are reluctant to take responsibility for our choices, desires and fears. We have a tendency to blame our situation on others and become weak and passive. Such helplessness is a major barrier to growth and change. Gestalt therapy in particular emphasises that we often have many choices and much power. Reality therapy also underscores the importance of being responsible for our thoughts, feelings and actions.

How to use:

✔ as an exercise to conduct over several coaching sessions.

When to use:

✔ when the coachee cannot choose between two or more alternatives.

Why use:

✔ to enhance the coachee's awareness of the process and consequences of making choices.

Step one   Ask the coachee to describe the choices he or she is currently facing.

Step two   Ask the coachee to write these two (or more) choices on the whiteboard. For example, remaining in a job versus retirement

Step three   Ask the coachee to write the value(s) that are associated with these two choices (for example, security and freedom) next to the two choices.

Step four   Ask the coachee to develop a vision of what his or her ideal life would be like, that is, what does the coachee want? What kind of life does the coachee want to create?

Step five   Ask the coachee to write the vision on the whiteboard.

Step six   Ask the coachee to write the values underneath the vision, for example:

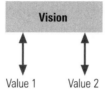

Step seven   Ask the coachee to draw the values as opposing forces, for example:

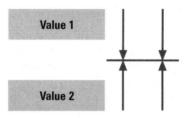

Step eight   Ask the coachee to prioritise, i.e. choose which value is more important in terms of achieving the vision. Write down this choice, for example: I choose…(one value) over …(the other value).

Step nine   Work with the coachee to nominate three goals and an action plan that will contribute towards making the vision a reality.

Step ten   Work with the coachee to nominate three goals and an action plan to help 'manage' the value not chosen (e.g. if it is financial security, then managing this might include working part-time on one's own, budgeting, and cutting down on certain expenses).

Step eleven   Together the coach and coachee should work through the nominated goals and action plans, first paying attention to those goals that will realise the coachee's vision.

4 Ego states, scripts and games

The following techniques are adapted from transactional analysis (TA), first developed by Eric Berne (1910–70). It has subsequently evolved into what is sometimes called the Redecision school of transactional analysis. A detailed account of transactional analysis is clearly beyond the scope of this book. For our purposes we are focusing on techniques that explore *ego states* (the child, the parent, the adult), our *life scripts* (including the injunctions we unknowingly incorporate into our lives) and the *games* we play (the dishonest interactions we engage in). These exercises are designed to foster self-awareness and, subsequently, behavioural change in the coachee.

What ego state am I in?

How to use:

✔ as an exercise within coaching sessions—either with an individual or a group.

When to use:

✔ when the coachee's attitudes and actions appear to be a function of a 'child' rather than an 'adult' state.

Why use:

✔ to increase the coachee's awareness of the various ego states

✔ to achieve a balance between the ego states, with the 'adult' in charge.

Step one   Draw the following table on a whiteboard or give it to the coachee as a handout.

Table 7.1   The three ego states

The child
➤ The 'natural' child—carefree, impulsive, pleasure-loving
➤ The 'adapted' child—compliant, orderly, rebellious
➤ The little professor—clever, observant, manipulative

The parent
➤ The 'nurturing' parent—loving, caring, helping
➤ The 'critical' parent—bossy, directive, punitive

The adult
➤ The objective part of the person—reality-oriented, rational

Step two Ask the coachee to nominate which state he or she mostly functions in.

Step three Ask the coachee to nominate a particular issue he or she is currently dealing with, for example procrastination.

Step four Ask the coachee to respond to the procrastination situation by 'being' in each of the states and speaking about what happens when in each of these states. For example, what does the coachee say, think and feel about procrastinating when in the various child states, the various parent states, and the adult state?

Step five Ask the coachee which state is most active when he or she procrastinates?

Step six Ask the coachee to re-enact his or her experience of the 'adult' state as described in Step four.

Step seven Set the following homework assignment: whenever the coachee is aware that he or she is procrastinating, he or she will ask: 'What state am I in?' and then decide to move into the adult state.

Step eight Continue on with the exercise until the coachee has mastered the problem.

Recognising injunctions

Injunctions are messages from our parents that we have been programmed to accept and that we unknowingly incorporate into our lives. They become part of our life positions and life scripts. Some examples of injunctions are: 'be perfect', 'don't be successful', and 'don't trust other people'.

Checklist

How to use:

✔ in individual or group coaching sessions.

When to use:

✔ when the coachee appears to have deeply entrenched thoughts and feelings that do not seem appropriate to his or her current reality or status, for example, fear of success in a highly competent, apparently ambitious individual.

Why use:

✔ to increase the coachee's awareness of injunctions in self and others

✔ to limit the impact of these injunctions

✔ to develop positive messages to replace these.

Exercise

Step one Explain the concept of 'injunctions' to the coachee using the examples mentioned above.

Step two Ask the coachee to list at least five injunctions that he or she has uncritically accepted.

Step three Ask the coachee to repeat these injunctions using the tone of voice he or she imagines the parent would have used.

Step four Ask the coachee to replace each of these injunctions with another message (an 'allower' message), for example, replace 'don't feel' (injunction) with 'it's okay to have feelings and need people' (allower message).

Step five Set a homework assignment whereby:

1 The coachee first monitors and practises becoming more aware of the injunctions:

> ➤ What are they?

> ➤ When are they most likely to surface?

> ➤ What behaviours or feeling states are they most associated with?

2 The coachee replaces the injunctions with the allower messages he or she has chosen.

Playing games

According to transactional analysis, a game is a put on; a dishonest interaction that ends with at least one player feeling bad. There are three parts to a game:

1 the set-up—a deceptive pretense which hides the true purpose of the game

2 the secret, destructive ulterior motive

3 the pay-off.

There are numerous games that we play. Two games which have particular relevance to coaching are the 'yes-but' game and the 'if it weren't for you' game. However, the following technique can be used with any number of games.

Checklist

How to use:

✔ can be used in an individual or group coaching session.

When to use:

✔ when the coachee continues to complain about and seek help with his or her problem, but is actually resistant to any suggestions made by the coach ('yes-but' game)

Checklist

✔ when the coachee denies responsibility for the circumstances of his or her life, blames others, and either seeks sympathy or is angry and resentful ('if it weren't for you' game).

Why use:

✔ to induce awareness of the games the coachee plays

✔ to encourage the coachee to recognise the pay-off of these games

✔ to develop more honest and adult communication.

Exercise

Step one   Explain the concept of 'games' to the coachee.

Step two   Suggest to the coachee the nature of the game he or she may be playing.

Step three   Describe the three parts of the particular game the coachee may be playing, for example:

The 'yes-but' game:

1   the set-up—asking for help

2   the ulterior motive—to see oneself as a victim, to control the situation or to prove superiority (no one can answer my questions)

3   the pay-off—I'm okay (smart and powerful), you're not okay (you're always wrong).

The 'if it weren't for you' game:

1   the set-up—to explain a person's choices in life, for example, 'I could have been a great artist if I didn't have a child'.

2   the ulterior motive—to deny responsibility, to seek sympathy, to justify anger and resentment

3   the pay-off—to prove I'm not responsible and it's not my fault (I'm okay), you, or my child or God are responsible and you deserve my anger (you're not okay).

Step four   Ask the coachee to think about the game.

➤ Does he or she play the game?

➤ Does he or she play the game often? That is, is it a racket?

➤ In what situations does the coachee play the game?

➤ Does the coachee choose situations and individuals that support the game?

Exercise

Step five   Work with the coachee to recognise which needs are being met by playing the game.

Step six   Together with the coachee work on developing a more adult (I'm okay–you're okay) life position and a new script.

Summary   Working with a coachee to explore and enhance self-awareness requires specific knowledge and skills on the part of the coach. The exercises and instructions described above cannot be successfully employed in a psychological void. As responsible and professional coaches we have to be trained in the use of these psychology-based techniques, and have a clear understanding of why they work and when to employ them. As we frequently note, different techniques are appropriate for different coaches and different coaching interventions. It is only through training that the coach can best leverage his or her experience and background skills in the use of relevant and appropriate coaching tools and techniques.

Dialoguing

Coaching, as we mention throughout this book, is a conversation, a dialogue in which two individuals explore a topic to gain greater understanding. Both Plato and Aristotle believed that conversation was the greatest source of knowledge. Dialoguing is employed in coaching to create new knowledge, to explore possibilities and to generate action. It is a focused conversation between the coach and the coachee and one of the foundations of the coaching partnership. Together the coach and coachee dialogue about the issues to be explored in coaching, ideas, beliefs, feelings, opportunities, obstacles and solutions.

Language is a tool we use to create our reality. It is through language that we give a truthful assessment of how we view a situation. For example, as coaches we make requests to the coachee, including our specifications for a satisfactory outcome. In turn, the coachee makes a promise and a commitment. It is only through language and dialogue that both the coach and coachee are clear about what the coach is asking and what the coachee is responsible for and committed to doing. Coaching involves the coach providing a common language that can open up new ways of seeing, new experiences, new relationships, new meanings and new actions.

Open dialogue

Dialogue between the coach and coachee has to be open and honest, otherwise trust will not develop or be sustained. The coaching climate has to be one in which both the coach and coachee say what they mean and mean what they say. Trust will flourish in an environment where both parties speak with commitment and intention. Honest discussions bring out our best and, as Flores notes, our worst comes out when we behave like robots or 'professionals'. Open, honest dialogue is critical to a successful coaching outcome because the actions we engage in are executed through the coaching conversation. The common language of open dialogue suggests that both the coach and coachee are prepared to examine and overcome their prejudices, assumptions, personal agendas and fuzzy thinking.

Open dialogue also demands that the coach reflects carefully on his or her own use of language. As we know, language has many functions. It is employed to pass information from one person to another, for thinking, for venting our emotions, impressing others, easing social tensions and establishing cohesiveness or solidarity. Knowledge of and practice in employing the language of coaching is imperative for all coaches. Our specialty workshops on dialoguing arose from the perceived need for coaches to be trained and supervised in the art and science of establishing and sustaining a fluid, interactive and dynamic dialogue throughout the coaching intervention. Some questions about language that the coach may reflect on include:

➤ What is my intention here?

➤ What am I trying to accomplish?

➤ How truthfully am I saying what I believe?

➤ How will the coachee respond to what I am saying?

➤ How could the coachee misinterpret what I'm saying?

➤ Am I speaking in order to seek knowledge or to share knowledge?

➤ Am I using language to confront or challenge the coachee?

➤ How does the coachee feel about what I am saying?

➤ Do we have a shared meaning about the words I am using?

One of the most critical features of open dialoguing is that of challenging or confronting. The concept of the samurai warrior can be traced throughout the coaching and management literature. It is chiefly invoked in relation to the coach being courageous enough to face his or her own self-deceptions and challenge and confront those of the coachee. Only through open dialogue can the coach challenge the coachee to move through to action.

For example, the coach can establish the parameters of acceptable language through which the coachee can signify his or her commitment. Statements such as 'I hope it happens' are challenged and converted into 'I will make it happen'. Comments such as 'I wish' are challenged and translated into 'I will do'. Similarly, remarks such as 'It would be good if' are translated into 'I promise I will'. Coaching demands a shared language of action.

Modes of dialogue

Open dialogue is the foundation of two main types of dialogue in coaching. These are transactional dialogue and transformational dialogue.

Transactional dialogue usually takes place when the coach and coachee are expressing ideas, concepts and sharing information. The focus in transactional dialogue is on what is being said rather than how it is being said. Learning occurs through additional information rather than through the process of a change in attitudes, beliefs and feelings. It operates within a rational, logical framework of analysis and problem solving.

Transactional dialogue is most likely to predominate in business coaching where the focus is on the manager's or business owner's technical and operational mastery skills. For example, when a coach works with a manager or owner on strategic planning or performance management processes, the dialogue is likely to be of a transactional kind.

Transformational dialogue is typical of coaching interventions where personal mastery skills are targeted for change. The coach and coachee engage in dialogue that aims to transform the coachee's way of thinking, feeling and acting. Hence, the dialogue engages both partners on an emotional and intuitive level. While the content of the conversation is important, the way in which it is said is critical. For example, the building of trust and commitment is done through transformational dialogue. Changes in habitual emotional responses, insight and 'breakthroughs' are all functions of transformational dialogue.

It is important that the coach is aware of the mode of dialogue that is most appropriate to a particular stage of the coaching process or to a specific coaching issue. Of course, not all dialogue can be neatly divided into either of the two modes we have discussed. However, a skilful coach who is aware of these types of dialogue will be able to recognise when and how to seamlessly move from one mode to another in order to facilitate growth and development in the coachee.

Dialoguing then, whether it be transactional or transformational, underpins the entire coaching intervention. The figure opposite illustrates the five functions of dialoguing during the coaching process.

Barriers to communication

Dialoguing, as with any form of communication, is subject to many forms of interference. Although there is a wealth of literature on communication and communication models, it is useful here to review some of the major impediments to true communication and open dialogue between the coach and coachee.

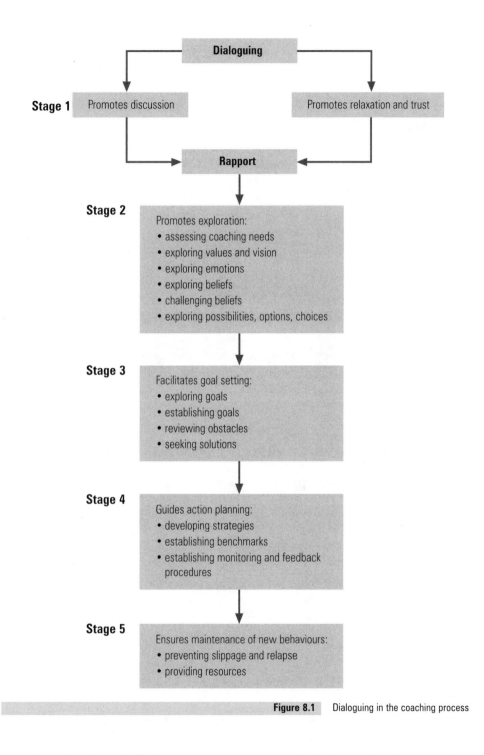

Figure 8.1   Dialoguing in the coaching process

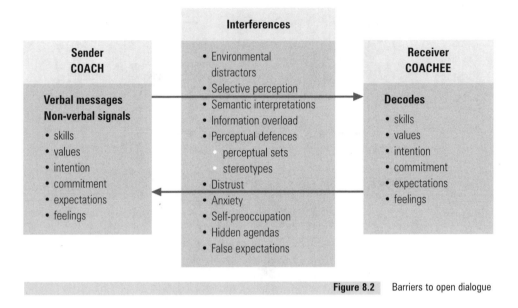

Sender **COACH**	Interferences	Receiver **COACHEE**
Verbal messages **Non-verbal signals** • skills • values • intention • commitment • expectations • feelings	• Environmental distractors • Selective perception • Semantic interpretations • Information overload • Perceptual defences • perceptual sets • stereotypes • Distrust • Anxiety • Self-preoccupation • Hidden agendas • False expectations	**Decodes** • skills • values • intention • commitment • expectations • feelings

Figure 8.2 Barriers to open dialogue

We suggest that through the skilful application of dialoguing, which includes listening, questioning, reframing and offering solutions, the coach can offset many of the potential hazards and interference that prove detrimental to the communication process.

Techniques for overcoming barriers to communication

1 Effective listening skills

Listening is essentially a mental process that involves assigning meaning to sounds. Coaching requires active listening whereby the coach and coachee assume responsibility for hearing the speaker's message correctly. Active listening entails a deliberate effort to understand a message from the speaker's viewpoint. It involves attending to all verbal and non-verbal signals, asking questions to clarify meaning and rephrasing and reflecting to show the speaker that you respect and want to understand him or her.

The listening process, then, is always embedded in a relationship matrix. It involves a true psychological involvement with the speaker. Listening and speaking involve the potential for significant mutual impact. Self psychologists talk of a continuum in the listening process, where one end is a more cognitive form of listening and the other end is an emotional immersion in the speaker's life.

We believe that coaching is about ordinary empathic listening. It is not a distant, intellectual exercise, neither is it total absorption in the other's world. The coach has to be receptive to the coachee's thoughts, emotions and moods so that he or she can sense what the coachee is truly experiencing. However, the boundaries between the coach and coachee have to be clear. The experiences belong to the coachee, not the coach.

As with all aspects of communication, a great deal has been written on listening. For our purposes, we shall first discuss the concept of 'easy listening', and then outline some listening guidelines for coaches as well as some critical barriers to good listening. Finally, and importantly, we discuss what the coach should 'listen for' in order to facilitate growth and development in the coaching alliance.

Easy listening

We suggest that the concept of 'easy listening' (Mermelstein 2000) aptly summarises the ideal coaching conversation. Some of the principles of easy listening are:

➤ Communication occurs in a relaxed manner.

➤ There is a basic, mutual understanding that was easily acquired and expanded upon.

➤ The other's persons feelings are obvious, and the listener is free to follow the content of what is being said.

➤ There is a basic satisfaction and mutual pleasure taken in the listening process.

➤ Both parties tend to speak at the same pace. Each intuitively knows if pauses are meant to be the launching pad for the other or merely a moment for the speaker to catch his or her breath.

➤ Both participants are sacrificing some of their individuality and competitiveness towards the greater good of the conversation and understanding.

➤ Affect (i.e. emotions, moods, feelings) is contagious.

➤ Even serious conversations are more relaxed.

Some listening guidelines for the coach

As we mentioned above, easy listening is the ideal environment for open dialogue. Yet, this is not always achievable. Listening can be hard work. It can be demanding and sometimes frustrating. We have found the following guidelines to be helpful to coaches:

➤ *Always try to find something interesting in what the coachee is saying*.

➤ *Seek understanding.* As stated in Covey's (1998) fourth habit of effective people, it is wise to seek to understand first then seek to be understood. Often as coaches, we listen with our ears but in our mind we are already diagnosing and preparing techniques and strategies that will help 'fix' the person. It is essential that we listen before we go into problem-solving mode. Once in that mode, the coach is closed off to what the coachee is saying and is filtering the coachee's words and actions so that they fit the paradigm the coach has already chosen. Subsequently, hypothesis testing and other problem-solving techniques are given insufficient time and attention because the coach has already formulated the solution.

➤ *Focus on the content as well as the delivery.* Not all coachees are remarkably articulate. If the mode of delivery is uninteresting, the coach has to pay attention to the content and try and understand how the tone of the delivery can contribute to the coach's knowledge about the coachee.

➤ *Withhold judgment until you have the full story.*

➤ *Listen for themes and patterns.*

➤ *Anticipate what the coachee might say.*

➤ *Listen for emotional undertones*—intensity, tone of voice, emphasis, hesitations, rate of speech and other non-verbal signals.

➤ *Paraphrase, reflect, integrate and summarise.*

Potential barriers to listening

1 *Cultural and language differences* These differences can make coaching more demanding and frustrating for both the coach and coachee. It is the coach's responsibility to listen and concentrate intently, and ask for clarification and elaboration whenever necessary. Apart from semantic issues, the coach has to explore what the coachee's words mean to him or her within the particular culture.

2 *Defensiveness* If either the coach or coachee feels threatened by what the other is saying, information will be distorted or blocked-out. Self-awareness and ongoing professional development are essential if the coach is to recognise his or her self-limitations and vulnerabilities. Being in tune with the coachee should allow the coach to recognise when the coachee is being defensive. Gently confronting and questioning the coachee allows the coach to explore the reasons behind the defensiveness. Through honest dialogue we can encourage the coachee to take risks and be vulnerable.

3 *Talking too much* Coaches, almost by definition, are good conversationalists. We are curious, and we like to talk, discuss and exchange ideas and information. While these qualities are admirable, one might say necessary, they can impact negatively on the coaching relationship.

The coach can disrupt the coachee's flow, and sometimes confidence, by interjecting too frequently, asking too many questions and controlling the direction of the conversation.

4   *Fear of silence*   In our experience, we have found that many coaches are somewhat apprehensive about silence. Because coaching is about action and moving forward, the coach may interpret silence as a waste of time, a signal that nothing is happening and no progress is being made. It invokes anxiety. Yet a good listener allows the coachee the time to think and reflect at his or her own pace. As we mentioned in our first book, executives are often so busy providing answers and solutions in the workplace that they have little time to reflect and think. Coaching provides that opportunity.

5   *Self-preoccupation*   If the coach is preoccupied with personal concerns then he or she will not fully attend to the coachee. Ideally, if one's concerns are overwhelming, then the coach should reschedule the appointment. Failing that, the coaching session could be devoted to a more active problem-solving exercise where the coachee is engaged in following his or her own train of thoughts and reporting these back to the coach.

Some general listening skills

1   *Attending skills*   Ideally, the coaching session should be conducted in a private environment with no distractions. Phones, visitors and noise should be eliminated wherever possible. It is only in such a climate that both the coach and coachee are free to listen to and dialogue with each other.

The coach should be positioned at right angles to the coachee, or around, rather than across from each other at a desk or table. Good eye contact, appropriate gestures and a warm tone of voice are all signals that the coach is fully attending to and attuned to what the coachee is saying. Coaches can also demonstrate this through the use of such phrases as 'I see', 'Right', 'I hear you' or 'I understand'.

2   *Encouraging skills*   On occasions, the coach has to encourage the coachee to elaborate on his or her thoughts or feelings. We have found the following statements to be useful:
➤   I'd like to know how you feel about it.
➤   Would you like to talk about it?
➤   Would you like to say something else?
➤   Perhaps you'd like to tell me...
➤   Is there something else I should know?

3   *Clarifying skills*   At times, the coach may be unsure what the coachee is really saying. Some statements to reduce ambiguity and establish clarity include:
➤   What I think you're saying is...
➤   Could you give me an example of...

> I'm not sure I understand you—could you repeat that.

> Could you tell me more about that.

> Can we talk about that some more.

4   *Reflecting skills*   A critical skill in open dialoguing involves the coach restating, in his or her own words, what the coachee is saying—either the content or the feeling that is being expressed. Reflecting, as it is called, reveals understanding and acceptance of the coachee. It also assists the coachee to become more aware of his or her own emotional state. Furthermore, reflecting can help keep the coach and coachee focused and on track. Some typical reflecting statements include:

> Sounds as if you're really…

> You think it's a good idea if…

> You'd really like…

> You think that…

> You believe that if…

> You seem to feel a bit anxious about that.

5   *Summarising skills*   A good listener is capable of succinctly summarising what the speaker has said. The coach can use summarising when the coachee has exhausted what he or she has to say, to tie up loose ends in the session or as an end to the coaching session. Some summarising statements include:

> I'd like to summarise what we covered today.

> In summary…

> We've covered a lot of ground today, particularly…

> Just to sum up…

> It seems to me that the pattern of today's session…

> The themes of today's session seem to be…

A 'listening for' model of dialoguing

Research suggests that the brain processes information at at least four times the speed of the average talker. There is ample opportunity then for the coach to truly listen or for the coach's mind to drift off into a state of receptive vacuity.

Listening with intent can enhance the coach's listening skills and lead to more efficient assessments and effective problem solving. Coaches need to listen for those things that will generate action and accomplish significant and lasting behavioural change. The following table outlines what the coach might 'listen for' at various stages of the coaching process.

Table 8.1 Some 'listening for' questions

Listening for information

➤ What are the coachee's major issues?

➤ What is the unwanted behaviour(s)?

➤ What is maintaining the unwanted behaviour(s)?

➤ What is the coachee's motivation to change?

➤ How does the coachee feel about coaching?

➤ How difficult is this situation for the coachee?

➤ How committed is the coachee?

➤ How easy will it be for the coachee to change?

Listening for emotional states

➤ How is the coachee feeling?

➤ How aware is the coachee of his or her feelings?

➤ How emotionally open is the coachee?

➤ What adjectives would I use to describe the coachee's feelings?

➤ How is the coachee expressing his or her feelings?

➤ Is the coachee taking responsibility for his or her feelings?

➤ How are these feelings impacting on the problem?

➤ How does the coachee feel about being coached by me?

➤ To what extent does the coachee trust me?

Listening for personality characteristics

➤ Is the coachee enthusiastic?

➤ Does the coachee seem to enjoy talking about himself or herself?

➤ What character strengths does the coachee display?

➤ What weaknesses does the coachee have?

➤ What coping mechanisms does the coachee use?

➤ What is the coachee's level of self-esteem?

➤ How resilient is the coachee?

➤ Does he or she blame others?

➤ Does he or she have a sense of humour?

Listening for values and beliefs

Listening for values and beliefs

➤ What are some of the coachee's core values?

➤ How does the coachee express these values?

➤ What are some of the coachee's core beliefs?

➤ Does the coachee express his or her beliefs clearly?

➤ Are there any self-limiting beliefs?

➤ Is the coachee open to having his or her beliefs challenged?

➤ What would be the most effective way of dealing with these beliefs?

2 Questioning

According to Socrates, when we ask a question we already have half the answer. Asking the right questions at the appropriate time is a core dialoguing skill of a successful coach. Our questions guide the coachee in a particular direction—in that sense our questions are never neutral. Questioning is a tool whereby we direct the coaching dialogue.

Questioning serves numerous functions in the coaching context. Through our questioning we gather information, assess and identify issues, highlight critical material and facilitate action and change. Questioning also helps the coachee to edit irrelevant material from his or her life.

There are various forms of questioning, although the individual coach is encouraged to adopt a questioning style that fits with his or her unique coaching method. Mechanical questioning or asking questions from a manual serves only to alienate the coachee and inhibits rapport and trust. Nonetheless, there are generic questions that a coach can employ throughout the coaching sessions.

Some typical coaching questions

Table 8.2 Typical coaching questions

How questions:
How did you think/feel/act?
How often did…?
How did that come about?
How did you react to that?
How have you coped in the past?
How does that fit in?
How would you have liked to have behaved?

What questions:

What happened?

What did you think about that?

What makes you think that?

What did that mean to you?

What might you do differently next time?

What was behind that?

What was important about that?

What did you learn from that?

What made you choose that?

What will you do next?

When questions:

When did it start?

When do you have to...?

When did that first occur?

When did you realise...?

When did you decide...?

When will that happen?

Where questions:

Where does it happen?

Where can we start to make a change?

Where did it all go wrong?

Where do you see yourself in...?

Where will that get you?

Why questions:

Why did you do that?

Why did you act that way?

Why do you think that happened?

Why do you think they responded that way?

Why is this happening?

(Both coaching literature and helping literature caution against the use of 'why' questions. It is generally agreed that 'why' questions can generate defensiveness in an individual and can lead to a never-ending cycle of inference and speculation. Asking 'why' can also deteriorate into an intellectual competition between the coach and coachee. However, we suggest that the sensitivity, warmth and curiosity displayed by the coach can offset many of these potential hazards.)

Clarifying questions:

When you say…what do you mean?

What does…mean to you?

Did I understand you correctly?

Does that sound right?

Am I right in saying that?

Elaborating questions:

Would you like to elaborate on that?

Could you say a little more about that?

Would you like to add to that?

Is there something else you could say about that?

Challenging questions:

What's the evidence for this?

What makes you think this?

Could that be viewed in another way?

Is that logical?

Is that helpful?

Is that an interpretation or a fact?

Confronting questions:

Can you help me here? On the one hand you say…but on the other hand you state…

You claim you…but you…

You claim you're…yet you…

Working with deletions

Occasionally a coachee will omit or delete important bits of information while communicating. The coach can employ questioning skills to challenge the incomplete dialogue. For example:

Coachee: I am angry.

Coach: What are you angry about?

Coachee:	No one listens to me.
Coach:	Who specifically doesn't listen to you?
Coachee:	He made me furious.
Coach:	What specifically did he do?
Coachee:	No one trusts anyone anymore.
Coach:	Who doesn't trust whom, and what are they distrustful about?

Appreciative questioning

The concept of appreciating the coachee's strengths is central to coaching literature and the coaching relationship. Coachees can feel undervalued and 'put down' if the coach fails to recognise and acknowledge their strengths and successes. Indeed, as discussed in Chapter 1, certain coaching methodologies focus on appreciating and leveraging the coachee's strengths rather than concentrating on the problem or issue at hand.

Even if the coach chooses not to construct the entire coaching relationship around the coachee's strengths, it is generally agreed that true behavioural change will not occur without the coach acknowledging and highlighting the coachee's successes. The following questions and requests are designed to tap into and develop the coachee's strengths.

➤ Tell me about some major successes in your life.

➤ What do you attribute these successes to?

➤ Tell me three of your major strengths.

➤ How have they worked for you in the past? Give me some examples.

➤ How can we build on these strengths and apply them in the current situation?

➤ How can we develop these strengths?

Problem-free questioning

The concept of problem-free questioning is somewhat similar in notion to that of appreciative questioning in that attention is taken away from the problem and focused on something else. Essentially, this type of questioning involves engaging the coachee in dialogue about times when he or she did not have the current problem or issue to face. It can be extremely useful when the coachee is stuck and overwhelmed by current circumstances.

The intention of such questioning, as discussed by O'Hanlon and colleagues, is to cause a mental shift to a more positive frame of mind. The coachee may be able to access the previous patterns of thought and behaviour that worked for him or her. Some questions to facilitate this process include:

➤ Tell me about a time when this wasn't an issue for you.

➤ How did you feel then?

➤ What was your life like then?

➤ What strategies did you use to deal with the situation?

➤ What resources did you rely upon?

➤ Why do you think they worked for you?

In our experience, problem-free questioning can serve to remind coachees of previous coping strategies or techniques they may have forgotten.

Specific questioning during the coaching process

The above questions are appropriate at any stage of the coaching intervention. However, we consider it useful to highlight questions that are specific to the particular phases of coaching. The following questions are offered as guidelines for the coach when assessing the coaching topic or issue, when clarifying and isolating the specific coaching issue, when evaluating the progress of the coaching sessions and when terminating the coaching relationship.

Table 8.3 Specific questions to ask during the coaching process

Questions for the assessment stage

➤ Do you think there is a problem or issue that lends itself to coaching?

➤ Why do you think there is a problem?

➤ Do you see any benefits in coaching?

➤ What do you see as your greatest challenge?

➤ What would you like to see happen in the sessions?

➤ What skill(s) would you most like to enhance?

➤ What will be most helpful to you in the sessions?

➤ Where and how do you expect things to be different?

➤ Do you think it is more important to bring about changes in your actions, thoughts or feelings?

➤ Who else do you suggest I speak with about the problem or issue?

Questions for clarifying and isolating the coaching topic

➤ Do we need to do something better?

➤ What aspects can we change?

➤ Do we need to do something different?

➤ What has to change the most?

➤ What is our overall goal?

➤ Where do we start?

➤ What is keeping the old behaviours in place?

➤ How can we interrupt or build upon the old behaviours?

➤ Where do we go from here?

➤ What will be difficult for you?

➤ What might get in the way of you learning new skills?

➤ What resources do we need?

Questions for evaluating progress

➤ Are you finding the coaching sessions helpful?

➤ Is this the area you wanted to explore the most?

➤ Are we working with the issue you wanted to concentrate on?

➤ Are we progressing at a satisfactory rate for you?

➤ What is most helpful to you about the coaching sessions?

➤ What is frustrating you about the coaching sessions?

➤ Do we need to change anything with regard to the coaching relationship?

Questions for the final session

➤ What will help you to maintain the changes you have made?

➤ How will you remind yourself to continue on with your growth and progress?

➤ What aspects may be most difficult for you?

➤ How will you know when you are reverting back to old behaviours?

➤ How can I help you to overcome any potential obstacles?

➤ What resources would be most valuable to you?

Coaching is a relationship that frequently occurs across a number of weeks, months and even years. The coachee can view the end of the coaching partnership as a loss. One way the coach can bridge the transition is to stagger the final few sessions so that there is not an abrupt termination. A follow-up phone call or a face-to-face session in the following two months can also ease the situation.

The coach also has to prepare the coachee for a life after coaching. It is critical that the coachee continues to practise the new behaviours and skills and not relapse into old ways. The questions for the final session will allow the coach to be certain that the coachee has the resources to maintain the newly acquired skills.

3 Reframing

Reframing is a dialoguing skill that involves exploring and challenging a statement and giving it another meaning. Reframing provides an alternative perspective because the conceptual or emotional viewpoint is changed to another 'frame' that fits the facts but changes their meaning entirely. Three types of reframing that we have found helpful include putting a positive spin on things, externalising, and changing tenses. We shall briefly discuss these techniques.

Putting a positive spin on things

When a coachee presents a certain event or behaviour in a negative light, it can be beneficial for the coach to present the same event or behaviour in a positive framework. For example:

Coachee: I've always been weak and indecisive.

Coach: So, you're cautious and careful.

Coachee: He makes me angry.

Coach: What other way could you choose to respond to him?

Coachee: I'm always the last to leave the office.

Coach: You're obviously very dedicated to your work.

Coachee: I've just realised that I've always avoided responsibility for my actions. It's depressing.

Coach: That's a major insight. It can open the door to a new beginning for you.

Coachee: I feel as though I'm selfish and self-centred.

Coach: Maybe you're just taking care of yourself.

Coachee: I'm just self-absorbed.

Coach: Perhaps you're self-reflective and self-referential.

Externalising

Another method of reframing is to externalise a feeling or event. Externalising encourages individuals to objectify and at times personify situations they experience as oppressive. In this way the problem or issue becomes a separate entity that is external to the person. For instance, we have worked with executives who believed they were 'genetically programmed' to get very angry in response to minor provocation. By reframing anger as something which 'comes over' the individual rather than from within, we found that coachees were able to more easily recognise the triggers and symptoms of rising anger. By being aware of the psycho–physiological changes occurring they were better able to work towards self-regulation of their anger.

Changing tense

If the coachee appears to be stuck in a negative mood state the coach can reframe the coachee's experience by referring to it as happening in the past rather than the present. By talking about the coachee's feelings in the past tense the coach sets the stage for the coachee to review the experience, rather than relive it. The technique allows the coachee to bring closure to the experience or feelings, so that he or she can move more easily into another, more desirable state. For example:

Coachee: I'm miserable today.

Coach: You felt miserable. Tell me about how you felt.

Coachee: I felt discouraged.

Coach: So what can we change or do now so that you don't get into that state again?

The use of metaphor in dialogue

The term 'metaphor', from the Greek *metapherein*, means to change or transfer. A metaphor involves understanding or experiencing one thing in terms of another. We regularly use metaphors in our daily life. Some examples include: 'talking to a brick wall', 'swimming against the tide', 'we're at a crossroad' and 'food for thought'. Metaphors capture the essence of our experiences and are replete with information about ourselves, and how we view our place in the world.

Metaphors are used either explicitly or implicitly in most therapeutic settings. It has been suggested that the depths of the mind can be touched by words that speak in images and metaphors, sometimes in a universal, timeless language. Clearly, the coach can exploit the use of metaphor to assess the coachee's situation and to plan appropriate interventions.

The coachee's metaphors are revealing. The coach can use the symbolic language of metaphor to gain an insight into the coachee and add to the individual's understanding of himself or herself. Metaphors help the coach to construct a picture of where the coachee is at, and where he or she wants to be. However, it is critical that the coach explores what the coachee's metaphor means to him or her. Coaches cannot assume a shared metaphoric language. It has to be established through dialogue between the coach and coachee. If this is not done the coach may project his or her own interpretation of the metaphor on to the coachee.

Before discussing two methods of working with metaphors it is relevant to briefly review the coach's own metaphor about his or her role. The language we employ to describe our work has clear implications for us and for coachees. For instance, a coach who defines coaching as 'working with' a coachee is signifying a different role and methodology to the coach who views coaching as 'helping'. Similarly, if a coach employs 'guiding' as a definition of his or her role the implications are vastly different from that of 'partnering with' a coachee. Describing our role as 'teaching' has different implications again. It may well be that there are different metaphors for different types of coaching. While we are not attempting to prescribe a specific metaphor for the individual coach, we do suggest it is useful for the coach to reflect on his or her own metaphor about the coaching role.

1 Working with the coachee's metaphor

Often the coachee will spontaneously describe himself or herself in metaphoric language. Sometimes these metaphors are threaded throughout the coaching conversation and are therefore easily recognised. We have found the following exercise (adapted from Kilburg (2000) and Wahl and Williams (1998)) to be useful when working with stated metaphors.

 Exercise

Step one Be alert to and recognise the consistent use of the metaphor. For example, it is not uncommon for a coachee who is feeling besieged to use language that reflects a battle. Such an individual might talk in terms of 'a battle', 'a struggle', 'territory', 'winning' or 'losing'.

Step two Make the metaphor clear and obvious to the coachee.

Step three Ask the coachee to elaborate on the metaphor.

➤ What are the implications of using the metaphor?

➤ How is the metaphor influencing the coachee's assumptions, beliefs and feelings?

➤ What is the metaphor telling you and the coachee?

➤ What is the metaphor telling us about the coachee's relationship with self and colleagues?

➤ What is true about the coachee and the metaphor?

➤ What new insights can the coach and coachee gain from exploring the metaphor?

➤ How will the metaphor help the coach work with the coachee?

➤ Is the metaphor helpful to the coachee?

➤ Can the metaphor be developed to be more helpful to the coachee?

➤ What beliefs and emotions does the metaphor reflect?

➤ What strengths and weaknesses does the metaphor imply?

➤ How might it be limiting the coachee?

➤ What actions does the metaphor suggest?

Step four   Ask the coachee if he or she would like to change the metaphor.

Step five   Work with the coachee to develop a metaphor that is more life enhancing and more beneficial.

Step six   Request that the coachee experiment with the new metaphor. Review the results in the following coaching session.

2 Developing a metaphor

Frequently, coachees can become 'stuck' in their life or work situation. They may give an unclear or ambiguous account of their experiences. The coach can suggest to the coachee that he or she choose a metaphor that captures his or her essential experience.

Case Study

Working with metaphors

M. S. is a project manager who is feeling unappreciated and frustrated with senior management but is having difficulty communicating his feelings. He believes he is not being given the opportunity to fulfil his potential and really make a difference in the organisation. The coach encouraged M. S. to develop a metaphor that aptly summed up his circumstances. M. S. described himself as the navigator on a yacht. The captain and crew had sailed off without him and he was in a runabout beside them, unnoticed, shouting out directions that no one could hear. The metaphor allowed the coach and M. S. to clarify the work situation and what M. S. was feeling.

Case Study

M. S. was then able to view the work situation in a way that facilitated problem solving rather than just churning over his feelings and frustrations. Subsequently, he was able to approach his colleagues and communicate his feelings clearly about the unsatisfactory work situation and how it could be improved.

The coach may have a metaphor he or she thinks is appropriate to the coachee's experiences. However, as with all the techniques discussed in this book, the coach has to recognise that working with metaphors is not appropriate for all coachees. It is generally agreed that using and developing metaphors is a function of the intuitive mind. Some coachees and coaches may find the abstract, symbolic nature of the language irritating and unhelpful. The intuitive coach would be wise to listen carefully to the coachee's use of language before suggesting that he or she explores or works with metaphors.

Dialoguing and solutions

It is widely agreed that it is not the coach's job to provide solutions for the coachee. Yet many coaches have experienced a coachee who states, 'I don't know what to do. You tell me. You're the coach.' The coachee genuinely may have exhausted all of his or her own ideas. While it is clearly not the coach's role to solve problems unilaterally, he or she can suggest solutions. It is *how* these suggestions are offered and framed that distinguishes coaching from advising.

The coach can frame suggestions or solutions in such a manner that the coachee has the ultimate power to consider or dismiss them. They are offered as possibilities, not answers. Some guidelines for offering solutions include:

➤ Maybe you could…

➤ What about…

➤ Have you thought of…

➤ One way to look at this might be…

➤ You could consider…

➤ Some people find it useful to…

➤ Perhaps you could look at…

Summary

Dialoguing underpins the coaching partnership. It is imperative that coaches are trained, and are experts, in employing various dialoguing techniques. Listening with intent, knowing what to listen for and questioning with intent and purpose establish a context in which a coachee can learn, grow and enhance his or her performance.

Working with self-limiting beliefs

It is generally agreed that our feelings and actions are largely determined by our beliefs about ourselves and others, and current and future situations. The following figure demonstrates the relationship between our thoughts, our emotions, our actions and events.

The notion that it is our beliefs and interpretations that upset us rather than actual situations is not new. In 60 AD, Epictetus noted that men are not worried by things but by their ideas about things. The psychoanalyst Alfred Adler also claimed that it was obvious that we are not influenced by 'facts' but by our interpretation of the facts. More recently, Albert Ellis, who developed rational emotive therapy (RET), asserted that humans largely disturb themselves. It is our irrational and unreasonable beliefs that make us miserable, self-hating and self-pitying about virtually anything.

We base our choices and decisions on a set of truths in which we believe. Yet sometimes these beliefs are not necessarily logical or productive. Indeed, they can be invalid, inhibiting, restrictive, unhelpful and ultimately self-defeating. Many of our fears are the result of a false evaluation of an event. We bring a faulty or illogical interpretation to a situation, do not see what is in front of us and, as a consequence, we can suffer unnecessary misery, anger and anxiety.

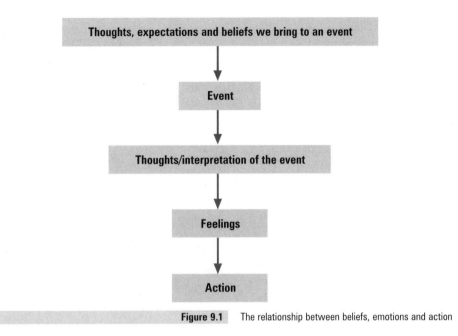

Figure 9.1 The relationship between beliefs, emotions and action

Although our thoughts do influence our emotional state, we have the power to control our own emotional destiny. Each of us has the power of self-awareness and we can observe and challenge our self-limiting beliefs. We can usually change our feelings because we have the capacity to decide to think and feel differently about a situation.

What are self-limiting beliefs?

So, what is the nature of these irrational or self-limiting beliefs that cause us misery and interfere with goal achievement and success? Some philosophers such as Nietzsche, Schopenhauer and Montaigne claim that illusion and self-deception are an integral part of being human. Ellis also believes that humans have an innate tendency to harbour irrational beliefs.

Nathaniel Branden asserts that consciousness is volitional. He claims that we are not automatically rational or reality-focused but have the choice to think or not think. We can choose to learn to operate our mind in such a way that makes us 'appropriate to life'. According to Branden, the 'practice of living consciously' includes having respect for the facts, being present to what we are doing, and seeking information, knowledge or feedback to understand the external world and our inner world so that we do not act out of self-blindness.

It is generally accepted that many of our irrational beliefs are a product of our childhood. They may be internalised messages from parents or other significant figures. Sometimes our negative thoughts are automatic and we are unaware of their origin. Regardless of the origin of these beliefs, cognitive therapists list four major criteria for judging whether a belief is rational or irrational. These are:

1   Is the belief flexible (rational) or inflexible (irrational)?

2   Is the belief consistent with reality (rational) or inconsistent with reality (irrational)?

3   Is the belief logical (rational) or illogical (irrational)?

4   Does the belief lead to largely productive results for the individual and his or her social group (rational) or is it largely unproductive for the individual and his or her social group (irrational)?

Research suggests that we start to question and replace our irrational beliefs when we recognise how these ideas are harming us. Repeatedly seeing the damage our beliefs might be doing to our work relationships, our personal relationships and our health can facilitate change.

Some examples of self-limiting beliefs

According to experts in the field, many of our irrational beliefs are couched in what Karen Horney called 'the tyranny of the shoulds'. Ellis coined the term 'musturbation' to describe behaviour that is absolutist and dogmatic, and revolves around self-repeated 'musts', 'oughts' and 'shoulds'. What are simply our preferences are elevated to the status of demands or facts. Some examples of these irrational beliefs are:

➤   People must live up to my expectations or life is awful.

➤   People must treat me fairly.

➤   I must be approved of or accepted by everyone who is important to me.

➤   I must succeed at everything I do.

➤   If I don't get everything I want, then I can't experience any happiness at all.

➤   The world is a rotten place because it doesn't give me what I must have.

Irrational, distorted or self-limiting beliefs can also take the following forms:

1   *Focusing on the negative*   For example, 'because I can't get the perfect job, I can't see any good happening in my life'.

2   *Minimisation*   For example, 'my success in that assignment was a matter of luck, but my failure in the exam was totally unforgivable and catastrophic'.

3   *Overgeneralisation*   For example, 'my life is clearly out of control because I have been late for work the past two days'.

4   *All-or-nothing thinking*   For example, 'if I fail at any important task, I am a total failure as a person'.

Other common self-limiting beliefs include:

➤   I could never do…

➤   I never finish anything.

➤   I'll be happy when…

➤   If only…

➤   I'm too (old, young, uneducated, etc.) to …

➤   You can't trust anyone.

➤   If you want something done, do it yourself.

Coaching and self-limiting beliefs

The importance of examining self-limiting beliefs in coaching cannot be overemphasised. As mentioned previously, our beliefs largely determine our feelings and actions. Coaching is about change. It is about changing feelings and behaviour. Unless the negative or self-limiting thoughts around an action are explored and replaced, it is unlikely that any real change will occur.

Therefore, it is critical that coaches are competent in assessing and challenging the self-limiting beliefs that may be impacting on the coachee's ability to learn new skills and behaviours. Working with an individual's beliefs is demanding and requires expertise, supervision and practice on the part of the coach. Feedback from participants in our specialty workshops on 'dealing with self-limiting beliefs' has underscored the importance of the coach being trained and supervised by a clinician in the use of these psychology-based techniques.

We recommend that coaches devote at least one entire coaching session to exploring self-limiting beliefs. Regardless of whether such beliefs are apparent or not, skilling a coachee to recognise and confront any irrational beliefs is critical. It is not only useful in the context of any changes that the coaching alliance may demand, it is also an invaluable tool the individual can employ for the rest of his or her life. As noted by many authors, staying rational is a lifelong pursuit.

Clearly, coachees have to decide to examine their self-limiting beliefs and whether or not to change these. Changing our beliefs takes time—it is demanding work. Some coachees may be so entrenched in their beliefs that they are unwilling to change. Others may find the change too time consuming and difficult and may withdraw from the coaching process or display a superficial compliance rather than a true commitment. Fortunately, most coachees engage positively in the challenge and thereby learn and develop.

Research suggests that working with self-limiting or irrational beliefs is more likely to have a successful outcome if the individual coachee meets the following criteria:

➤ He or she recognises that our emotional states and our actions stem from our beliefs.

➤ He or she realises that, essentially, we create our own disturbances.

➤ He or she accepts that we have the ability to change our beliefs and, hence, our emotions.

➤ He or she is prepared to detect and challenge self-limiting or irrational beliefs, internalise changes and continue challenging such beliefs.

The coach's role in challenging self-limiting beliefs

Empathy, affirmation and reinforcement

Changing one's beliefs is difficult. There is frequently a time lag between changes in our thinking and actual changes in our emotional state. That is, we may clearly see that it is not logical or rational to feel anxious in a particular situation yet the unwanted emotions can remain.

Research suggests that it may take several minutes of forceful debate between the rational mind and irrational thoughts each time they surface, over a period of a year or more, in order to change particularly harmful ideas. Of course, if the coachee's ideas are seriously harmful in that they result in depression, severe anxiety or behavioural disturbances such as intense anger outbursts, the coach must refer the individual to a therapist.

It is imperative that the coach prepares the coachee for the difficulty of the task and the need for persistence and practice in challenging beliefs until the desired emotional states occur. The coach has to display empathy and offer affirmation and reinforcement otherwise the coachee may become discouraged and demoralised.

The notion of challenging

Challenging is an accepted role of any coach. It is an invitation or request to a coachee to become more aware of his or her thoughts, feelings and behaviour. Through challenging, the coach highlights and points outs discrepancies, contradictions and irrational ideas that the coachee may be unaware of which may be impeding progress towards goal achievement.

Challenging can be tentative or confronting and it is easier for some coaches to do than others. In our experience, coaches who have a psychology background, particularly in the clinical area, sometimes feel less than comfortable when challenging or confronting coachees. It is as though the idea is somehow at odds with their notions of impartiality and unconditional acceptance of the individual. As a result, they can be too tentative or even avoid challenging the coachee directly.

On the other hand, it is possible that coaches can be inappropriately challenging or confronting. It can be a means of venting their own personal frustrations. It is useful here to bear in mind Nietzsche's comment that any depth or thoroughness is a violation, a desire to hurt the basic will of man's mind which is towards illusion and the surface of things.

One method the coach can use to be clear about his or her intention for challenging the coachee is to ask the following questions:

➤ Am I challenging in order to increase self-awareness (e.g. to facilitate the coachee in recognising that there is more than one interpretation or option in any situation)?

➤ Am I challenging a specific irrational idea or self-limiting belief?

➤ Am I challenging discrepancies in the coachee's account of events?

We have found the following general rules for challenging, adapted from the helping literature, to be useful for coaches when challenging or confronting the coachee:

1 The coachee has to feel supported not attacked.

2 Challenges must not be seen as implied criticism, otherwise the coaching alliance may be damaged.

3 When challenging, the coach has to be empathic and recognise that letting go of cherished beliefs, no matter how self-limiting, can be difficult and distressing for the coachee.

4 Challenging can be culturally inappropriate. For instance, in our training work with coaches from Asia, we are constantly reminded that confronting or challenging a coachee may result in the individual 'losing face'. Challenging may also be seen as insulting to a senior or elder person.

Techniques for dealing with self-limiting beliefs

There are three important reasons why the coach should explore and challenge the self-limiting beliefs of a coachee. These are:

1 It provides the coachee with techniques that can prevent or reduce unwanted negative emotions.

2   It enables the coachee to learn more rational ways to view life, to be more honest regarding self-evaluation and to have more reasonable expectations of self and others.

3   It assists the coachee in realising that we cannot understand ourselves or others without knowing how people perceive or interpret situations.

The choice of which particular technique to employ with self-limiting beliefs depends on several factors. First, the coach has to feel competent in using the technique. Second, the technique has to be appropriate and acceptable to the coachee. Third, if the coach is unable to shift a coachee's self-limiting beliefs and the success of the coaching endeavour is thereby compromised, it is wise to refer the coachee to an expert in cognitive-behavioural therapy.

1   The A to F model

The A to F paradigm is a classic model used for working with irrational or self-limiting beliefs. This model enables coachees to confront their self-limiting beliefs by forcing them to work though the various elements surrounding the belief such as what kind of situations activate the belief, what the self-limiting belief actually is and the consequences of the belief. The coachee can then nominate new and more affective emotions in relation to the particular event or situation.

Checklist

How to use:

✔   as a didactic tool in the coaching session—for all coachees

✔   as a homework assignment for individual coachees.

When to use:

✔   when the coachee is distressed by a particular event or situation at work

✔   when the coachee has voiced self-limiting beliefs

✔   when the coachee has difficulty getting rid of unwanted emotions such as anxiety or anger.

Why use:

✔   to explore self-limiting beliefs and their impact on behaviour

✔   to challenge self-limiting beliefs

✔   to replace these beliefs with more logical and useful ones.

Exercise **Step one** Explain the following A to F model to the coachee—either on a whiteboard or as a handout.

The A to F model for challenging beliefs

A (Activating event or situation)

For example: giving a presentation in front of colleagues.

B (Self-limiting belief(s) about the situation)

For example: I must perform exceptionally well or my colleagues will think I'm stupid.

C (Consequences of these beliefs—emotional or behavioural)

For example: anxiety, poor concentration, defensiveness.

D (Disputing the self-limiting belief(s))

For example: Just because I want to perform exceptionally well, does it logically follow that I must? Am I being realistic? If I don't perform exceptionally well, will my colleagues really think I am stupid? What use is this idea to me? How is it helping me?

E (Effective new beliefs)

For example: Although I prefer to perform exceptionally well, it doesn't mean that I must. There is no evidence that my colleagues think or will think I am stupid if I do not perform exceptionally well. Holding on to this idea will make me more anxious and more likely to perform badly. I can feel concerned but not anxious about the presentation.

F (New feelings)

For example: more confident, able to approach the presentation as a challenge rather than an ordeal.

Step two Review the model with the coachee.

Step three Provide the coachee with a blank version of the model and request that he or she complete the following homework assignment before the next coaching session.

1 Describe the troubling or difficult situation or event. (A)

2 Detect what negative self-talk or self-limiting ideas or behaviour you are bringing to the situation. (B)

3   Specify your unwanted emotions—write down what you felt like doing as well as what you did do or feel. (C)

4   Nominate a new effective emotion(s). (F)

Step four   Review the homework assignment and challenge (D) the self-limiting belief(s) the coachee has identified.

Ask the coachee:

➤   Is this belief logical?

➤   Is there any evidence for it?

➤   How realistic is this belief?

➤   How helpful to you is this belief?

➤   Are you confusing your preferences with demands and facts?

Step five   Work with the coachee to establish effective, new beliefs (E).

Ask:

➤   Is this new belief true?

➤   What is the evidence for this new belief?

➤   How realistic is this new belief?

➤   How helpful is this new belief?

Step six   Ask the coachee to commit to actually challenging the belief by going into the feared or difficult situation (e.g. making a presentation) either as a role-play exercise or as a real life experience. Ask the coachee to complete the following questions immediately after the event:

➤   How did I feel when that (A) happened?

➤   What was I telling myself that brought on the feeling?

➤   How did I dispute the self-limiting belief?

➤   How is my new belief more logical, realistic and helpful?

Step seven   Review the coachee's progress. Make sure the coachee is really recognising (B), changing his or her beliefs (D, E), and not using distraction techniques at (A). Otherwise, if the beliefs are unchanged other events (As) will occur and the coachee will not be equipped to deal with them.

Step eight   At subsequent coaching sessions, ask the coachee:

➤ Are the unwanted feelings about…becoming less frequent than before?

➤ Are they less intense?

➤ Do they last for shorter periods?

Step nine   Depending on the degree of progress the coachee is making, continue to employ the A to F model until the emotional and behavioural changes are stable.

2 Working with fixed beliefs

Another useful technique in dealing with self-limiting beliefs involves asking the coachee to explore the costs and benefits of holding on to a fixed idea. A fixed idea is one that has become divorced from its context and is used as a generalised truth. Fixed ideas can be very powerful because they are intangible and can be applied to any situation.

A fixed idea is usually a conclusion that the individual has reached at some stage of his or her life that has set up an automatic way of reacting to or dealing with life without having to examine specific situations. By definition, a fixed idea is not dynamic or fluid. Some examples of fixed ideas are: 'You have to look after yourself in this life', 'People are stupid', and 'Life is unfair'. The coachee cannot rationalise his or her belief and may be illogical or dogmatic without making any attempt to examine the validity of the belief.

Confronting fixed ideas

How to use:

✔ as an exercise within a coaching session

✔ as a homework assignment.

When to use:

✔ when a coachee presents with a fixed idea.

Why use:

✔ to free up a belief so that the coachee can think more clearly

✔ to enable the coachee to choose to accept or reject the idea.

Exercise

Step one   Recognise the fixed idea when it surfaces in dialogue.

Step two   Rapidly ask the coachee the following questions:

➤ What principles are you operating on here?

➤ What rules are you following?

➤ What do you know about…?

➤ How do you know that?

➤ Why is that?

Step three   Continue questioning the coachee's lack of logic until he or she can recognise that the idea is fixed, and possibly ridiculous. It is not necessary to attempt to replace the fixed idea with an alternative one but rather provide the coachee with the opportunity to recognise how the fixed idea is not an obvious truth.

A costs–benefits analysis of a fixed idea

As we know, our beliefs and behaviours are reinforced or maintained by some kind of 'pay-off' or benefit. We may not always be conscious of this. However, if the benefits are significant and, seemingly, outweigh the costs, the coachee will not be motivated to change. The purpose of this exercise is to encourage the coachee to become more aware of the costs and benefits associated with holding on to a particular belief or behaviour.

The coach must exercise judgment when using any techniques that suggest there are advantages to holding on to certain beliefs or behaviours. A coachee may be unwilling to accept that there are advantages associated with maintaining beliefs or behaviours that are a source of stress and misery.

Checklist ✔

How to use:

✔ as an exercise in the coaching session.

When to use:

✔ when the coach believes that the coachee is unaware of the benefits of holding on to the beliefs and behaviours which the coachee is attempting to change.

Why use:

✔ to help the coachee recognise the pay-offs of certain beliefs and behaviours.

✔ to allow the coachee to develop more effective means of obtaining these benefits while still altering the problematic beliefs or behaviours.

Exercise 🖊

Step one   Ask the coachee to answer the following questions:

➤ What has (the fixed belief or behaviour) helped you to accomplish?

➤ What has (the fixed belief or behaviour) helped you to prevent?

➤ What does (the fixed belief or behaviour) allow you to do?

➤ What is right about it?

➤ Does it leave others at a disadvantage?

➤ In what way has it been a solution?

When working with these questions, it is imperative that the coach encourages the coachee to look at the advantages and disadvantages of the belief or behaviour from all possible viewpoints. For instance, a coachee may have a problem with delegation. He or she believes that 'if you don't do it yourself, it won't get done'. A benefit of this belief might be that it allows the individual to ensure that the work always meets his or her standards. However, it probably also gives the coachee a great deal of power. For example, it might allow him or her to control information and thereby lessen the likelihood or threat of others being able to do the job. He or she is therefore indispensable.

Step two   Ask the coachee about the consequences of his or her belief or behaviour. For example:

➤ What would happen if you did…(e.g. delegate)?

➤ What would happen if you didn't…?

➤ What would not happen if you did…?

➤ What would not happen if you did not…?

➤ When might…(e.g. delegating) be a good idea?

➤ When might…(e.g. delegating) not be a good idea?

3 Countering 'the internal critic'

Many of us have an internal critic or inner voice that criticises us and puts us down. Such a critic is usually created early in life and may be the internalised voice of a critical parent. It could also be an irrational belief we have acquired throughout our life. Despite the pervasiveness of the critical voice, we all have an *observing self* that can give instructions to our *experiencing self*.

'Countering' is a term McMullen uses to describe the production of a self-statement that is incompatible with the critical voice. Counters should not be confused with positive affirmations.

The frequently heralded benefits of positive affirmations have not been corroborated by research. Many individuals expend considerable time and energy using positive affirmations only to give up in frustration. It is difficult to overpower old beliefs and replace them with new beliefs without identifying and challenging the old beliefs first.

Some guidelines for counter statements:

1   They have to be realistic.

2   The coachee has to believe in them.

3   They have to be specific, and not generic positive affirmations.

4   Short counters are usually the most effective.

5   They should be in the same mode as the thoughts or images they are replacing. For example, a negative visual image should be countered with a positive visual image and an angry thought with a calm thought, etc.

Checklist

How to use:

✔   in coaching sessions and as a homework assignment.

When to use:

✔   when the coachee's progress is being blocked by self-criticism

✔   when a coachee lacks self-confidence.

Why use:

✔   to allow the coachee to recognise the source of his or her internal critic

✔   to allow the coachee to develop mastery over his or her own thoughts.

Exercise

Step one   Ask the coachee to nominate the critical voice or the negative self-talk.

Step two   As a homework exercise, ask the coachee to monitor the frequency, intensity and exact wording of each self-criticism.

Step three   Together with the coachee, choose one or two negative patterns to focus on, for example, 'I'll never reach my goals', 'I can't get organised', or 'I'll never be successful'.

Step four   Together with the coachee, identify some counters or statements that will counteract the negative self-talk. Some examples include: 'Nonsense', 'I've been successful in the past' or 'That's not true, there's no evidence for it'.

Exercise

Step five   Ask the coachee to practise the counter statement(s) and monitor the frequency, intensity and exact wording of each self-criticism and its counter.

Step six   Ask the coachee to continue on with the exercise until the critical voice has subsided completely. Regularly review the coachee's progress.

4 Thought stopping

Thought stopping is a short-term response to interrupt and stop the flow of negative and critical messages, and counteract the internal critic.

Exercise

Step one   Ask the coachee to state the critical or negative thought.

Step two   Together with the coachee, choose and create an interruption to this thought such as saying the word 'stop' aloud. Some individuals wear a rubber band around their wrist and snap it and say 'stop'.

Step three   Ask the coachee to substitute a new thought. These replacement thoughts can be spontaneous or planned. For example the coachee might say: 'I'm not going to worry about this presentation' or 'I'll just do my best'.

Step four   Ask the coachee to monitor and practise the thought stopping exercise.

➤ Are the thoughts occurring less frequently?

➤ Are they becoming less intense?

➤ How has replacing the thought been helpful?

Step five   Encourage the coachee to continue practising the thought-stopping technique until the new thought(s) has replaced the critical, negative one.

The coach's self-limiting beliefs

Finally, coaches may also harbour self-limiting beliefs about their role and capabilities. Therefore, it is suggested that coaches examine the following list of self-limiting beliefs and work towards exploring and challenging any ideas that may be impacting negatively on their effectiveness.

➤ I must be liked and have the approval of all coachees.

➤ I must impress management with my expertise.

➤ I must always perform perfectly as a coach.

➤ I should always know what to do and what to say.

➤ I should be able to solve all the problems posed by coachees.

➤ I must be a perfect role model.

➤ I must have the right technique for every possible coaching issue.

Summary Working with a coachee's beliefs plays a critical role in all types of coaching. For example, self-limiting beliefs can impact on an individual's life plan, on an executive's leadership competencies and on a business owner's plans to expand his or her market niche. Coaches require considerable expertise and skill in recognising and challenging any beliefs that are impacting negatively on the coachee's development, and ability to attain goals.

10

Dealing with emotions

The word 'emotions' remains taboo in many workplaces. Emotions are considered too soft, too vague, too abstract and too intangible. With some notable exceptions, many CEOs and managers believe that it is unimportant how employees feel about their jobs. What really matters is that the work gets done. It is as though logic and rational thought rule the workplace and emotions can be obliterated.

Some managers who express these beliefs, often implicitly rather than explicitly, may adhere to McGregor's Theory X of motivation which assumes that workers are lazy and incompetent and can only be motivated through threats and incentives. Emotions, according to this theory, are irrelevant, except perhaps those of fear and anger.

It could be that any talk of emotions is suggestive of dysfunction and, therefore, too close to therapy. Such talk is subsequently threatening and a source of discomfort to many. Although dealing with emotions is generally accepted as a valid aspect of life skills coaching, many organisations remain suspicious and cynical about the relevance and importance of emotions in the corporate world.

Yet organisations are made up of individuals with emotions. People do not switch off their emotions when they enter the workplace. Indeed, it is through emotions that people relate to each other and build up a shared reality. We have feelings about our workplace and jobs. We can be happy, sad, angry, bored or afraid in the workplace and these feelings impact on our performance.

If emotions are ignored or if there are strict instructions regarding how to handle them, the organisation can suffer in two ways. First, the unexpressed negative emotions manifest in backbiting, sabotage and passive–aggressive resistance. Morale is damaged and the resulting tension raises stress levels and impacts on productivity. Second, the organisation fails to capitalise on the energy generated by positive emotions. The company's vision and goals are more likely to be realised by enthusiastic, trusting staff who feel free to express their emotions and communicate honestly and authentically.

Of course, the importance of emotional effectiveness is recognised by some organisations. Most of us are aware of the concept of 'emotional intelligence', developed by Salovey and Mayne in 1990, and popularised in Goleman's book. Emotional intelligence training programs have been adopted by the business world, although a report from Rutgers University suggests that most of these programs are ineffectual.

There is a vast amount of information available on emotions, some of which has been transferred to coaching literature. It is perhaps useful to review here what constitutes emotions and emotional effectiveness. Some training packages discuss 'self-awareness', 'resilience' and 'authenticity' under the umbrella term of emotional skills. Yet clearly these concepts are not emotions. Rather, they are personality characteristics that may or may not have an impact on how the individual deals with his or her emotions. Because, as coaches, we work in the domain of emotions, it is imperative that we have clear boundaries and definitions about emotions, what constitutes negative and positive emotional states and which aspects of emotions the coach can work effectively with.

Our coverage of emotions in this chapter is partially guided by Salovey and Mayne's definition of emotional intelligence as the capacity to reason with emotions in four areas:

1   to perceive emotion

2   to integrate it with thought

3   to understand it

4   to manage it.

Naturally, coaches who do not have a background in psychology are hesitant and sometimes apprehensive about working with a coachee's emotions. As a follow on to this we have developed specialty workshops on 'dealing with emotions' which meet the need for coaches to be trained and supervised in the use and practice of these psychology-based tools and techniques.

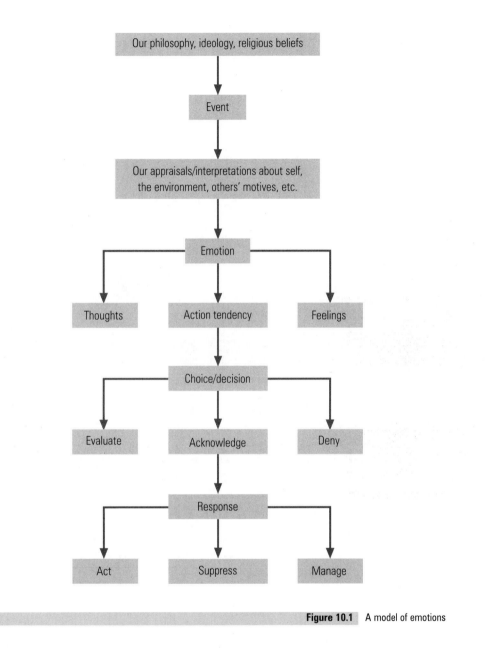

Figure 10.1 A model of emotions

The nature of emotions

Thoughts and feelings

There is no consensus on the definition of an emotion. Frequently, the term is used interchangeably with 'mood' and 'feelings'. However, most researchers in the field agree that emotions are different from moods, which tend to be longer lasting, less compulsive and less intense than emotions.

For our purposes, we view emotions as an affective state with distinctive appraisals and a tendency towards action. As discussed in the chapter on self-limiting beliefs (see Chapter 9), our beliefs and feelings are closely interconnected. Indeed, some authors consider the classic distinction between thoughts and feelings to be a barrier to useful psychological inquiry as it is difficult to separate the two constructs because they are so intertwined.

Our thoughts determine our feelings. They impact on our feelings in two ways. First, our thoughts determine the expectations we bring to an event and how we interpret the event. It is our appraisal of a situation, in terms of our goals, concerns, ego-involvement and unconscious beliefs, that determines our emotional response.

Our religious convictions and our ideology or beliefs about the world precede events and can regulate our response. For instance, beliefs about providence, God or karma can influence our emotional response to an event. Research by Fernandez and Turk (1995) in the area of pain has shown that individuals who held beliefs about 'predetermined' injury and ill-fated circumstances directed their anger towards God. On the other hand, a belief that one is paying back karmic debts from a past life might serve to lessen the impact of unpleasant events.

What we expect from life impacts on how we respond to life events. For instance, many of us expect life to provide us with happiness. Yet Schopenhauer claims that 'the one inborn error of humankind' is the notion that we exist in order to be happy. In fact, he claims it is this expectation that results in our unhappiness and disappointment with life.

The following model of emotions illustrates the manner in which our beliefs influence emotions, and how the choices we make about our emotional states determine our emotional and behavioural response to an event.

Negative emotions

Many of us are not willing to face our own negativity and destructiveness. Self-help books encourage us to focus on the positive and ignore or dismiss anything that reeks of negativity or suffering. We also like our movies to have happy endings. Yet many philosophers and writers suggest that negative emotions are an essential part of human existence. Nietzsche, for example, claims that hatred, envy, covetousness and lust for domination are life-conditioning emotions. He concludes that they must fundamentally and essentially be present in the total economy of life. Authors and poets such as Hesse, Dostoyevsky and Rilke urge us to accept our suffering and not flee from it or resist it. The psychoanalytic tradition also recognises the destructive forces within mankind and asserts that pretending these forces do not exist makes us their victim. Jungian analysts identify an interconnection between 'daimonic' forces and creativity.

Coaching entails change and change may require opening ourselves to life and fully embracing it. We can open ourselves more authentically to the beauty and joys of life if we also acknowledge the shadowy side of human nature.

The stability of emotions

The notion of emotional stability suggests that we can somehow reach a desired emotional state, such as joy, and maintain it. Yet all the laws of emotion work against this idea. For instance, the Law of Habituation as discussed by Frijda (1988) states that continued pleasures wear off, that pleasure is always contingent upon change and that it disappears with repeated satisfaction.

Similarly, Apter's (2001) reversal theory emphasises that every satisfaction, through a process of reversal, turns into a kind of dissatisfaction sooner or later. Apter considers psychological and emotional life to be essentially changeable, inconsistent and even self-contradictory. Buddhist teachings also highlight the impermanence of our existence and view suffering as a function of our attachment to feelings that are always in a state of flux and change.

Classifying emotions

In the academic literature on emotions there is no agreement on how to classify them. However, most emotion typologies include the following negative emotions: anger, fear, sadness, shame, jealousy and contempt while the common positive emotions are joy, happiness and surprise.

Our approach to emotions, both positive and negative, includes the appraisals that accompany them, the accompanying feeling 'state', the intensity of the feeling and the tendency towards action that defines each emotion. It is this information that gives us an insight into the emotional self and also provides guidelines for working with the coachee's emotions. The following assessment instrument has been adapted from the published work by Skiffington and colleagues on negative emotions:

Exercise Assessing emotions in the workplace

How often do you feel this way at work:

1	2	3	4	5	6	7
Almost never		Sometimes		Often		Very often

(Anger)

I feel someone deliberately mistreated me. ....

I feel furious. ....

I want to lash out verbally or physically. ....

(Fear)

Something damaging may happen to me. ....

I feel apprehensive. ....

I worry that something may go wrong. ....

(Sadness)

Something unfortunate happened to me. ....

I feel worried. ....

I dwell on an unfortunate event from the past. ....

(Shame)

Something about me does not deserve admiration/praise. ....

I feel humiliated. ....

I want to conceal something about myself from others. ....

(Jealousy)

Someone I don't care for has met with success/good fortune. ....

I feel envious. ....

I don't want that person's success anyway. ....

These are the negative emotions that tend to be most commonly encountered in coaching situations. The coach can assess these emotional states and then explore, with the coachee, how best to regulate the coachee's emotions.

It may appear that our approach to emotions tends to minimise positive emotions. This is true to a certain extent. We have found that most coachees are willing to discuss and expand upon their positive emotional states such as joy and happiness without any formal assessment. The coach has to consider whether it would be better to explore and regulate negative emotions or focus on and develop positive emotional states.

If a coachee seems to be stuck in a negative frame of mind, perhaps it is more useful to emphasise positive emotional states and develop strategies that enable the coachee to experience more pleasure. Alternatively, if the coachee appears to be denying or repressing his or her negative emotions, examining these could prove beneficial. What is important is that coaches are clear about what constitutes an emotion, how we can measure them and how to employ techniques to enhance or regulate the coachee's emotions.

The function of emotions

Before dealing with emotions and coaching, it is useful to briefly discuss the function of emotions in our life. The Stoics viewed emotions as diseases of the soul that could be cured by proper reasoning. Aristotle differentiated emotions and reasons, and Pascal talked of 'the internal war' between reason and emotion. Darwin, while considering emotions as signals and preparation for action, also noted their atavistic nature because they may have belonged to a time before humankind's cognitive capacities developed.

Psychologists have now accepted that emotions serve a useful purpose. Some of the noted functions of emotions include:

➤ They help organisms deal with major survival issues presented by the environment, including interpersonal encounters.

➤ They can shift behaviours and cast aside beliefs that may not be adaptive.

➤ They signal the relevance of one's concerns to events. For example, fear and anger can signal that our survival is being threatened. Our survival is under threat if our emotional needs are not being met. We require access to all our emotional responses (both positive and negative) so that we have continuous feedback about what we need.

➤ They are involved in and control the management of our goals.

Coaching and emotions

If our emotions are fluctuating and dynamic, how do we deal with them in a coaching relationship? The following general principles are offered as guidelines for the coach when working with emotions:

1   *Responsibility for our emotions*   It is important that we make a clear distinction between what we feel and what we do. Our emotions, moods and impulses give a genuine richness to our experience but it is not helpful to build our life on such a shaky foundation. Emotions

are our signposts and guides but not our master. We do not have to be controlled by our emotions or act upon them.

How we manage our emotions is within our control. It is the coachee's responsibility to be aware of, to acknowledge and to 'own' his or her emotions.

It is through awareness of our feelings that we can open up new alternatives and new choices.

2   *Responsibility for our choices and actions*   Our experiences do not determine what we do but we are responsible for the choices we make based on our emotions. We are responsible for what we do. For example, it is the coachee's choice to yell in anger at a colleague or walk away from the situation.

3   *Emotions have no intrinsic moral value*   Emotions are not good or bad. They are not moral or immoral.

4   *Emotions are neither functional nor harmful in themselves*   An emotion, even a negative one, is not necessarily harmful. Some emotions may be functional when they are of moderate intensity but harmful in certain contexts and when they are more intense.

5   *Emotions can be contradictory*   Gestalt theory proposes that every feeling has two sides. However, the coach should not challenge contradictory emotions the way he or she might challenge or confront contradictory beliefs. Rather, the coach should allow the coachee to explore multiple feelings or multiple aspects of a feeling. Such an approach can allow the coachee to foster increased self-awareness and a greater ability to deal with ambivalence and ambiguity.

6   *Cultural and gender differences in emotional expression*   Some cultures promote the discussion and expression of emotions while others value reticence and privacy. The coach has to be aware of these cultural differences and not impose his or her own cultural values on the coachee. Research also suggests that, even today, males are more reluctant to talk about feelings than females.

The coach's role in working with emotions

1 Self-disclosure

Self-disclosure occurs when a coach relates a personal experience or feeling to the coachee. Research from the helping literature suggests that many clients benefit from the helper's self-disclosure—although usually only if the helper has 'mastered' a problem.

A useful starting point for a coach is to reflect on the following questions about self-disclosure:

➤   Are there any particular feelings I have difficulty discussing because of my own problems or personal discomfort?

➤ What are my beliefs about disclosing my feelings to coachees?

➤ How do I choose to self-disclose?

➤ When would I self-disclose?

➤ When would I not self-disclose?

➤ How would I handle a request for self-disclosure?

➤ When might I be likely to disclose to meet my own needs rather than those of the coachee?

➤ What do I disclose about myself through my clothes, my office, the books on my shelf, etc.?

Some general guidelines are relevant here. These include:

➤ Self-disclosure should be delivered in an objective, narrative format.

➤ Any disclosures should be coachee-focused, that is, related to the coachee's needs rather than those of the coach.

➤ Self-disclosure should not be used as an opportunity for the coach to off-load or simply talk about himself or herself. It should always demonstrate empathy and also offer possibilities for insight.

2 Exploring emotions—some guidelines

As we mentioned previously, dealing with emotions can be challenging and intimidating for coaches, particularly if they do not have a background in psychology. Yet emotions are a critical aspect of behavioural change. As coaches we have to recognise the scope of emotions and understand how they impact on the coaching relationship and on the coachee's life and work. With this in mind, we have developed the following guidelines for coaches when working with a coachee's emotions.

1   *Ensure that the coachee is ready to engage in the session*   Recognising, acknowledging and managing emotions can be challenging and sometimes difficult work for the coachee. It is important that the coachee is ready to do this work. If he or she is distressed or reluctant to talk about feelings, the coach could focus on a behavioural aspect of the situation and deal with the emotional content in the following session. It can be useful to give the coachee a homework assignment, such as self-monitoring of an emotion, in order to move gently into the emotional domain. Being unable or unwilling to discuss feelings at a particular stage in the coaching alliance is not always a sign of resistance.

2   *Provide a safe, contained space for the coachee*   The coach has to provide a psychologically safe, non-threatening environment where the coachee feels free to discuss his or her feelings without fear of judgment. Change invokes anxiety, and the coach has to

be aware of and empathic towards its manifestation in individual coachees. While it would be ideal if coaches could come to each session with 'an empty mind', as the Zen teachers recommend, it is more likely that we bring our own values, feelings, expectations and prejudices with us. Yet, we must aim to maintain a neutral, objective attitude at all times.

3   *Make sure emotions are not the dominant part of a coaching intervention*   Emotions are an integral part of our existence and it is crucial that the coach does not collude with the coachee in minimising or denying emotional responsibility. However, emotions do not constitute the core concern of a coaching partnership. The coach should only deal with the coachee's emotions as they impact on the particular coaching topic.

4   *Recognise your limitations in working with emotions*   While we cannot ignore emotions, it is not necessary to explore them in any depth. If the coach believes the coachee has major difficulties in the emotional realm (e.g. if the coachee is unable to recognise, identify and own his or her feelings or is overwhelmed by the frequency and intensity of certain emotions) then the coachee should be referred to a therapist. It is important that the coach recognises the severity of an emotional problem early on in the coaching partnership. Otherwise, the coach may unwittingly open a Pandora's box.

5   *Clarify your purpose*   Essentially the coach works with emotions in the following four areas:
   ➤ Identifying emotions
   ➤ Clarifying emotions
   ➤ Owning emotions
   ➤ Managing emotions

When working with a coachee's emotions it is useful for the coach to nominate which of these areas he or she wishes to explore.

6   *Don't impose your own emotional language*   It is important that the coach does not impose his or her personal interpretation of an emotion onto the coachee. For instance, many of us feel 'angry' but the realities we experience when we are angry are different. We need to understand the coachee's terminology and have a shared language. It is important that we accept the coachee's description of his or her emotions. We may, of course, question the individual to gain further information and clarification regarding his or her emotional state.

7   *Separate emotions*   Sometimes a coachee reports a blend of emotions. Work with the coachee to separate out the emotions and deal with them one at a time.

8   *Recognise and challenge disguised or 'false' emotions*   A coachee may report what has been termed 'false emotions'. For instance, a senior manager might feel more comfortable

describing his or her feelings towards the CEO as 'angry' rather than 'hurt'. On the other hand, it may be more acceptable for a coachee to describe his or her feelings as 'being upset' rather than 'being angry'. The coach has to feel confident about challenging and exploring false emotions.

9 *Ensure resolution*   It is important that the coach broaches only those subjects that can be resolved within the time constraints of the coaching relationship. We have to ensure that what we start is finished. It is also critical that we do not activate feelings in the coachee that we are unable to deal with in the sessions. A good rule of thumb, especially when dealing with emotions, is to not ask questions unless we know how to deal with the answers.

3 Reflecting the coachee's emotions

One of the primary roles of the coach is to reflect the coachee's feelings. Reflection involves repeating or rephrasing a coachee's statements—including an explicit identification of the coachee's feelings.

The coach should be aware that some coachees adopt the attitude that 'to confess is to be absolved'. That is, they may be happy enough talking about their feelings but do not want, or even think that they need, to change. The coach has to recognise when a coachee is talking as a means of avoiding action, and has to be willing to move from a reflective mode into a more challenging dialogue.

Furthermore, coachees who lack assertiveness skills can too readily comply with the coach's 'expert' reflections. They may assent out of compliance. It is important, therefore, that the coach elicits the coachee's true response to his or her reflections.

Some advantages of reflecting feelings

➤ It can be viewed as less threatening by the coachee. For example, 'you seem upset about that' (reflecting) is less confronting than saying 'how do you feel about that?'(questioning).

➤ It implies that the coachee's feelings are acceptable to you and therefore 'normal'.

➤ It allows the coachee to reflect on what he or she really means. If, for example, the coach reflects 'furious', it allows the coachee to evaluate whether or not this is a true description of how he or she feels. The coachee may then 'correct' his or her own language.

➤ It shows the coachee that the coach is fully engaged and is listening to what he or she is saying.

Reflecting skills

Some guidelines from the helping literature (e.g. Hill & O'Brien 1999) that we have found useful when working with emotions include the following:

1   Understand your intention

Ask yourself what your intention is:
➤ Am I trying to identify the coachee's feelings?
➤ Am I working with the coachee to recognise his or her feelings?
➤ Am I working with the coachee to acknowledge his or her feelings?
➤ Am I working with the coachee to intensify his or her feelings?
➤ Am I working with the coachee to encourage ownership of feelings?
➤ Am I trying to encourage emotional expression?
➤ Am I working with the coachee on techniques to regulate and manage his or her feelings?

2   Choose the most salient emotion

Sometimes a coachee may present with several emotions. It is clearly not possible or even useful to reflect all these feelings. The coach has to determine which feeling is the most powerful or relevant to the topic at hand, and reflect this to the coachee.

3   Observe the person's entire range of communication signals

It is often the tone of voice a person uses that is more expressive and revealing than the words themselves. Non-verbal signals such as smiling can be reflected, for example, 'you seem happy'. Likewise if a coachee is moving around a lot or tapping his or her foot, the coach can state: 'you seem a bit nervous'.

4   Vary the style of reflecting

We are all familiar with jokes and cartoons about therapists or helpers who nod and murmur 'uh huh' regardless of what the client says or who constantly use one phrase over and over such as, 'what I'm hearing is...' It is important that the coach varies his or her style of reflecting so that is does not sound mechanical or false. The coachee can become irritated and withdraw from the conversation otherwise.

Styles of reflecting

1   *Using synonyms*

When a coachee is articulate and willing to describe and discuss his or her feelings, the coach can use synonyms. For example: 'really mad' can be reflected as 'furious' and 'really upset' can be reflected as 'very distressed'. Using synonyms encourages the coachee to think about different dimensions or aspects of his or her emotional experience. If the coachee is a concrete thinker however or not fully trusting, it is better to not use synonyms.

2   *Reflecting verbal content*

A coachee might report a positive event, such as being promoted to group account leader. The coach can reflect this by stating: 'you feel proud of that'. If a coachee describes a negative event, such as not gaining a promotion, the coach can reflect this by stating: 'that was upsetting'.

3   *Projecting your own feelings*

When a coachee reports a particular event, the coach can ask himself or herself how he or she might feel in that situation. The coach's feelings, in conjunction with the coachee's behavioural cues, can then be presented as a hypothesis to the coachee. For example:

➤   I wonder if you feel that…?

➤   Is it possible you feel…?

➤   Maybe you feel…?

➤   It sounds like you feel…

It is important to remember that the coach is hypothesis testing. If the coachee does not agree with these reflections, it should not be seen as a lack of insight or resistance on his or her part.

4   *Avoiding sympathy, over-identification and dogmatic statements*

It is wise to avoid the following styles of reflection:

➤   Sympathy: 'you poor thing' or 'that's terrible'

➤   Over-identification: 'you must feel angry—I certainly would' or 'that happened to me once and I was furious'.

➤   Dogmatic reflections: 'you obviously feel…', or 'you must feel…', or 'clearly, you feel…'

Specific techniques for working with emotions

The following techniques are intended as guidelines for coaches working with emotions. When employing these techniques, as with all the techniques described in this book, the coach has to bear the following in mind:

➤   Make sure you are trained and supervised by a clinician in the use of the techniques. Seek further training or guidance if you lack competency.

➤ Be sure that the coachee is willing to engage in the exercises, particularly those that are experiential.

➤ Only use the techniques when they have a direct bearing on the coaching topic.

We have classified the techniques discussed below into three categories:

1 Recognising emotions

2 Accepting responsibility for our feelings

3 Managing emotions

Recognising emotions

1 Locating the emotion

Before we can manage our emotions, we have to clearly identify them. For various reasons some of us may suppress and deny our feelings to the extent that we are often unaware of what we are actually feeling at any given time. Nathaniel Branden warns us that when we cease to know what we feel, we cease to experience what things mean to us. Existentially, we are at risk.

Suppressing our feelings can also have a deleterious impact on our health. For example, suppressing feelings of anger or fear can result in a state of tension or vague, free-floating anxiety. Similarly, withholding feelings of excitement or enthusiasm can leave the body in a state of unease. Suppressing emotions over a long period of time has been linked with cancer.

When our needs are not met over a protracted period of time, we experience feelings of deprivation and hopelessness. However, because these feelings of deprivation can be painful, we protect ourselves by denying the pain, anger and fear we feel. Sometimes these suppressed feelings manifest as a physical symptom or sensation. The following exercise helps coachees to 'locate' the physical symptom of an emotion they are experiencing.

Checklist

How to use:

✔ as an exercise within a coaching session

✔ as an ongoing homework assignment.

When to use:

✔ when a coachee appears to suppress his or her feelings in a way that prevents him or her from moving forward.

Why use:

✔ to enable the coachee to physically get in touch with the suppressed emotion.

Exercise

Step one   Ask the coachee to describe the physical symptom(s) he or she is experiencing.

Step two   Ask the coachee to tune in to the physical sensation(s). Suggest that the coachee try and relax. Ask:

➤ How do you feel now?

➤ What is concerning you right now?

Step three   Ask the coachee to focus on the specific body part where the feeling is located, for example, the chest, stomach, forehead or shoulders.

Step four   Ask the coachee: 'What can you pick up from your feeling-place?'. Remind the coachee to observe, not analyse.

Step five   When the coachee has a general sense of what he or she is feeling, ask:

➤ Where exactly in your body is this feeling?

➤ What is the shape of the feeling?

➤ What is the size of the feeling?

Step six   Ask the coachee to identify the exact feeling he or she is experiencing.

Step seven   The above steps may have to be repeated until the coachee can confidently nominate his or her feeling. When the coach and coachee feel confident that the feeling has been clearly and correctly named, they should work together on methods of expressing the emotion.

Step eight   Some examples of emotional expression to be explored include:

➤ Talk to someone who cares, who will listen but not offer advice, opinions or suggestions.

➤ Write the feeling down.

➤ Physically express the feeling, for example, pound a pillow (anger), listen to a particular piece of music that induces emotion (sadness) or dance around (excitement).

2 Recognising your coping style

Sometimes we get bogged down in our emotional states. They seem overwhelming and we become 'stuck'. As we know, intense emotional states can impair our cognitive processing skills. We are unable to call upon our resources or recall our past coping mechanisms. The following exercise is designed to help the coachee access previous coping strategies.

How to use:

✔ as an exercise during a coaching session

✔ as a skill the coachee can always call upon.

When to use:

✔ when the coachee is bogged down in his or her feelings.

Why use:

✔ to remind the coachee that he or she has emotional coping skills

✔ to revisit and practise these skills.

Exercise

Step one Ask the coachee to reflect on another time when he or she was overcome by emotion.

Step two Ask the coachee the following questions:

➤ How did you cope then?

➤ What support did you seek?

➤ How did you express your feelings?

➤ Did you try to avoid your feelings?

➤ Did you try to problem solve?

➤ How do you typically and automatically handle your feelings?

➤ What might you do differently this time round?

➤ What might help you cope better in the future?

➤ What will you be like when you change?

Step three Work with the coachee on a relevant technique for managing emotions (see section below).

Step four Give the coachee a handout of the various steps in the exercise for future use.

3 Getting 'unstuck'

Sometimes a coachee may be so entrenched in the past and preoccupied with feelings from the past that he or she is unable to make any progress in the present. The following technique can help situate the coachee in the present.

The coach should only employ this technique when the coachee's 'old' emotions are related to an event that is relevant to the coaching issue. For instance, if the coachee is having difficulty dealing with a senior manager at work and his or her responses are similar to those he or she felt towards a previous boss this technique could be employed. It is not to be used when there is the slightest possibility that it may dredge up traumatic memories or associations.

Checklist

How to use:

✔ in a coaching session within the context of a solid, trusting partnership.

When to use:

✔ when a coachee's emotions appear to be inappropriate and over-reactive in the current context

✔ when the coachee recognises that the feeling(s) may be 'leftovers' from a past situation.

Why use:

✔ to allow the coachee to develop new, appropriate and empowering emotional responses.

Exercise

Step one   Ask the coachee to nominate the feeling that is overly intense, or inappropriate.

Step two   Ask the coachee to nominate a recent incident where he or she experienced a similar feeling:

➤ What does this feeling remind you of?

➤ When did you feel it before?

Step three   Ask the coachee to relax, move into that emotional state and describe the feeling in detail:

➤ Where is it in the body?

➤ Is it tight? burning? heavy?

➤ How does it feel?

Step four   Ask the coachee to close his or her eyes and float back in time to the past incident that involved that feeling.

➤ What do you see?

➤ What is happening?

➤ What are you thinking?

Exercise

Step five   Encourage the coachee to remain in this state. Ask:

➤ What decisions or choices did you make during this incident?

➤ Are there any alternative points of view or interpretations of the situation?

➤ What can you learn from this incident?

Step six   Ask the coachee to rewrite or 'redescribe' the incident as it would be if he or she had the additional resources he or she now has. Ask: How do you feel now?

Step seven   Ask the coachee to open his or her eyes and return to the present.

Step eight   Debrief. Ensure that the incident has not left the coachee with any unresolved, negative or disturbing feelings.

Step nine   Repeat the exercise in the next coaching session and whenever these past feelings intrude upon the coachee's current functioning.

Accepting responsibility for our feelings

Nathaniel Branden claims that nothing does as much for an individual's self-esteem as becoming aware of and accepting disowned parts of the self. Many authors suggest that unless we can accept our self and reality for what it is, we will never be inspired to change.

It is generally agreed that we can learn to accept when we are feeling afraid—we can accept the fear and confront the feared situation. It is, after all, an underlying premise of many therapies. Morita psychotherapy for instance emphasises the importance of accepting reality, accepting oneself and one's symptoms and then setting goals and doing what has to be done anyway.

The following two exercises are adapted from Nathaniel Branden (1994).

1 Owning our feelings

Checklist

How to use:

✔ the coaching session

✔ as an ongoing homework exercise

✔ as a life practice.

When to use:

✔ when a coachee disowns his or her emotions by either projecting them on to others or blaming others.

Why use:

✔ to increase the coachee's self-esteem and responsibility to self.

Step one   Ask the coachee to focus on the feeling you believe he or she is disowning, for example anger.

Step two   Ask the coachee to breathe deeply and gently into the feeling, allowing the body to relax.

Step three   Ask the coachee to 'feel' the emotion—to experience the fear, anger, sadness or disappointment

Step four   Ask the coachee to state: 'I am feeling…'

Step five   Ask the coachee to own the feeling: 'I am now…and I accept it fully'.

Step six   Repeat Steps four and five.

Step seven   Request that the coachee practise this exercise several times daily before the following coaching session.

Step eight   Repeat the exercise in the coaching session until the coachee is truly able to accept his or her feeling(s).

2 Owning our resistance to a feeling

Coachees are not always able to accept that they have certain feelings. When this occurs, the coach can encourage coachees to at least accept that they are resistant to owning the feeling. The Moritists employ a similar tactic and encourage clients to at least recognise their lack of emotional willingness to go on and proceed anyway. Making our resistance conscious and accepting it can tend to dissolve it.

For example, a coachee may have a project to complete but continues to procrastinate. He or she sits around and waits for 'the right moment', or what Sylvia Plath called 'the rare, random descent of the angel'. Meanwhile, the project is not started and the coachee is feeling vaguely guilty and uneasy and is not enjoying the 'not doing'. Through questioning, the coach might determine that the coachee feels anxious about not being able to complete the project satisfactorily. However, the coachee may be unable to accept his or her anxiety. In such circumstances, the following technique can be useful.

How to use:

✔   as an exercise in the coaching session.

When to use:

✔   when a coachee is clearly resistive to owning a specific feeling.

Why use:

✔   to help the coachee recognise resistance as the first stage in accepting a particular feeling.

Exercise

Step one   Discuss your observations and intuitions with the coachee. Ask the coachee to nominate the specific emotion (e.g. anxiety) he or she may be resisting.

Step two   Ask the coachee to recognise his or her resistance to owning the emotion: for example, 'I resist accepting that I am anxious'.

Step three   Ask the coachee to repeat the sentence three times, each time a little louder and with more intensity.

Step four   Ask the coachee to commit to commencing the task in spite of the resistance and anxiety. Nominate and agree upon an initial period of time to be spent on the task. Gradually increase the period of time allocated to the task until it is completed.

Step five   Review and assess what the coachee has learned from the exercise.

Managing our emotions

If the coachee has recognised and accepted his or her feeling(s), the coach can then proceed to work with the individual on strategies to manage this. The following techniques are forms of self-regulation that can assist the coachee in having mastery over his or her feelings.

1 Self-monitoring

Self-monitoring techniques involve individuals observing the occurrence of certain aspects of their feelings and behaviour. Research suggests that such observation has a reactive effect, and in itself brings about a change in behaviour, often in the desired direction. There appears to be some kind of self-regulatory process happening.

Checklist

How to use:

  ✔ as an initial homework assignment.

When to use:

  ✔ as a prelude to introducing behavioural change.

Why use:

  ✔ to increase the coachee's awareness of a feeling

  ✔ to get a baseline measure of a feeling

  ✔ to clarify which aspect of the feeling to work on, for example, accompanying beliefs, emotional intensity, etc.

Step one   Ask the coachee to nominate the troublesome emotion.

Step two   Ask the coachee to monitor the emotion:

➤ How often does the emotion occur?

➤ On a scale of 1 (low) to 10 (high) how intense is the feeling?

➤ What is happening at the time?

➤ What are you thinking?

➤ What do you think about doing?

➤ What do you do?

Step three   Ask the coachee to monitor the feeling over a period of at least three weeks.

Step four   Together with the coachee, determine which aspect of the emotion it would be most helpful to work on, either the frequency and intensity of the feeling, the accompanying thoughts or the behavioural response.

2 Labelling emotions

Labelling (sometimes called 'attention') involves a deliberate and exclusive focus on a feeling. The process of labelling appears to prevent more information from being absorbed and processed. This in turn short-circuits further thinking and feeling. It causes an interruption before thought goes on to make personal attributions, relevance or associations that lead to emotions.

Checklist

How to use:

✔ as a technique that the coachee can learn and apply when needed.

When to use:

✔ when a coachee is feeling overwhelmed by an emotion

✔ when a coachee has difficulty clarifying an emotion.

Why use:

✔ to assist the coachee to clearly differentiate between feelings (e.g. between feeling 'annoyed' and feeling 'furious')

✔ to enable the coachee to modify subsequent actions.

Exercise

Step one   Ask the coachee to nominate the unwanted feeling.

Step two   Together with the coachee list the dimensions of the particular emotion, for example mildly irritated, frustrated, annoyed, angry, furious, uneasy, edgy, nervous, worried, anxious, afraid.

Step three   Ask the coachee to simply label the emotion according to the relevant dimension, for example, 'I am feeling annoyed' or 'I am feeling furious', etc.

Step four   Encourage the coachee to practise the labelling technique whenever he or she experiences 'fuzzy' or intense emotional responses.

Step five   Review the coachee's progress. Ask:

➤ How has labelling your feelings been helpful?

➤ How has it impacted on your emotional states?

➤ How has your behaviour been affected?

3 Reflexive analysis

Sometimes one emotion hides another emotion. For example, anger can mask vulnerability, a fear of loss, or a desire for control in a particular situation. Unless the 'true' emotion is recognised, the coachee will be unable to deal with it, and the life or work situation on which the emotion is impacting will continue to be problematic.

Checklist

How to use:

✔ as a homework monitoring exercise.

When to use:

✔ when one of the coachee's emotions appears to be 'hiding' or 'disguising' another one.

Why use:

✔ to enhance self-awareness

✔ to develop emotion management strategies appropriate to the 'true' emotion.

Exercise

Step one Ask the coachee to specify the (apparent) emotion.

Step two Explain the model of Antecedents, Beliefs and Consequences (the ABC model—see below) to the coachee.

Step three Ask the coachee to consider the following questions when he or she next experiences the emotion:

➤ What makes me vulnerable in this situation?

➤ What am I afraid of?

➤ What do I think I might lose?

➤ What principles or values are at stake here?

➤ What ideas about myself and others are at stake here?

➤ What am I really feeling?

Step four Ask the coachee to monitor these responses.

Step five Review the coachee's self-monitoring responses. Once the 'disguised' emotion has been recognised and renamed, the coach and coachee can work together on an appropriate technique for effectively managing the feeling.

4 Redefining the problem

Sometimes a coach and coachee may work together on a skill which the coachee appears to master. However, the coachee may remain unhappy and not put the skill into practice. The reason for this hesitation may be that what the coachee gains from practising the skill (e.g. increased workplace recognition) is outweighed by the disadvantages (e.g. work responsibilities which the coachee feels inadequate to perform). Redefining the problem can help the coachee to overcome his or her hesitation.

The ABC model

The ABC model is derived from personal construct theory. It is a useful technique to use to explore what might be preventing the coachee from moving towards the stated goal. By questioning the coachee regarding the advantages and disadvantages of a specific behaviour, it is possible to redefine the initial problem.

Checklist

How to use:

✔ within a coaching session with select coachees.

When to use:

✔ when the coachee is not making progress with a seemingly straightforward goal

✔ when the coach intuitively knows that the defined problem may not be adequately addressing the real issues.

Why use:

✔ to explore any advantages associated with holding on to old beliefs and behaviours that may be blocking change.

Exercise

Step one Ask the coachee to nominate:

A: The problem

A1 The actual state: for example—*can't make presentations.*

A2 The desired state: for example—*to make effective presentations.*

Step two Ask the coachee to nominate:

B: Disadvantages and advantages

B1 Disadvantages of A1: for example—*prevents making client contact and ultimately inhibits promotion.*

B2 Advantages of A2: for example—*opens up client contact.*

Step three The next set of questions is designed to elicit what is preventing movement or change on the coachee's part. Ask the coachee to nominate what:

C: Prevents movement

C1 Advantages of A1: for example—*hides feelings of being incompetent and a fraud.*

C2 Disadvantages of A2: for example—*will expose insecurities and fraudulence.*

The problem then becomes redefined as:

A: The problem

A1 The actual state: for example—*feeling incompetent and fraudulent.*

A2 The desired state: for example—*to feel confident and deserving.*

C: Prevents movement

B1 Advantage of A1: for example—*will hide lack of confidence and feeling fraudulent.*

B2 Disadvantage of A2: for example—*will reveal lack of confidence and feeling fraudulent.*

Step four   Redefine the problem once again:

A: The problem

A1 The actual problem: for example—*lacking confidence and feeling fraudulent.*

B2 The desired state: for example—*to feel confident and deserving.*

Step five   Together the coach and coachee work on goals and strategies to address the redefined or underlying issue.

5 Response delay

A particularly effective method of dealing with unwanted responses, such as angry outbursts, involves creating a delay between the impulse and its gratification.

Checklist

How to use:

✔   as an ongoing practice for the coachee.

When to use:

✔   as a practical strategy when it is imperative that the coachee makes immediate changes in behaviour such as anger management.

Why use:

✔   to assist the coachee to implement a behavioural change without having to explore surrounding beliefs and emotions.

Exercise

Step one   Ask the coachee to isolate the troublesome emotion.

Step two   Ask the coachee to nominate the typical action associated with the emotion, for example, yelling abuse at colleagues.

Step three   Work with the coachee to explore the beginnings of or the trigger for the angry response. Sometimes the trigger is not readily apparent to the coachee. Some coachees report just being overcome by rage. Typical 'physical' triggers include: tension around the eyes and forehead, foot tapping and the drumming of fingers.

Step four Ask the coachee to choose an appropriate response delay technique that he or she could use between the trigger and the response. These may include:

➤ Counting to 10 before responding

➤ Taking five deep breaths before responding

➤ Briefly leaving the situation then returning.

Step five Ask the coachee to practise the technique each time he or she recognises the beginnings of an anger response.

Step six Review the coachee's progress and encourage the coachee to continue practising the technique until he or she feels confident about using it regularly and effectively.

6 Developing healthy emotional states

According to the freeze-theory of emotions, when an individual's sources of pleasure are blocked or perceived to be blocked, the natural, 'healthy' move towards pleasure (where the parasympathetic nervous system is engaged) becomes unavailable. If a person believes pleasure will not occur, they 'freeze' the desire rather than discharging it. The pleasure-freeze sets up a physical and emotional state of tension (where the sympathetic nervous system is engaged) that has proven to be detrimental to health.

While the above pleasure-freeze state may appear to be extreme in terms of the average coachee, it is important for the coach to recognise the role of positive emotions in a coachee's life. Dealing competently with negative emotions, as discussed above, is clearly a critical skill for all coaches. However, working with a coachee to develop and enhance positive emotional states is equally important. We have found the following techniques to be useful in engendering positive emotions.

Checklist

How to use:

✔ as techniques or exercises the coachee can learn, practise and incorporate into his or her life.

When to use:

✔ when the coachee's knowledge and skills are being undermined by a lack of confidence or other unwanted feelings.

Why use:

✔ to induce positive emotional states.

Anchoring

Anchoring involves creating an association between thoughts, ideas, feelings or states and a specific stimulus. It can involve any of the five senses. Anchoring is frequently used in neurolinguistic programming (NLP) and hypnotherapy. An example of anchoring would be an association between a particular stimulus (e.g. a piece of music) and a particular emotion (e.g. happiness).

Anchoring can be used in coaching to change undesirable associations and create more positive feelings in the coachee. It can allow the coachee to create a consistent triggering mechanism that will automatically recreate the desired state.

Exercise

Step one   Ask the coachee to choose a feeling he or she would like to access whenever he or she desired, for example confidence.

Step two   Ask the coachee to choose an anchor he or she can use discreetly, for example pressing two fingers together or touching an arm or elbow. The action has to be specific and not one that occurs randomly.

Step three   Ask the coachee to recall a time when he or she felt supremely confident. Ask the coachee to:

➤ notice what they hear

➤ notice what they see

➤ notice what they smell

➤ notice what they feel.

Step four   When the feeling of confidence is intense, instruct the coachee to anchor it by making the chosen gesture (e.g. putting two fingers together). Ask the coachee to hold the gesture for a few seconds and remove it before the feeling subsides.

Step five   Ask the coachee to move around and stretch.

Step six   Ask the coachee to make the gesture again while he or she is thinking of something else and to note the reaction.

Step seven   Repeat Steps three and four at least five times to strengthen the association or connection.

Step eight   Ask the coachee to imagine a time when he or she would like to access the confident state (e.g. giving a presentation to a prospective client). Tell the coachee to make the anchoring gesture. Ask the coachee: 'How do you feel now?'

Step nine   Encourage the coachee to use the technique in a real-life situation and monitor its effects.

Step ten   Review the coachee's progress and strengthen the anchored response as necessary.

Creating positive feelings

It is generally recognised, in both medical and pyschological literature, that positive feeling states impact on an individual's health. Creating positive feelings in the coachee not only has implications for his or her mental and physical wellbeing, it also engenders a sense of control, and an increased likelihood of goal achievement.

Exercise

Step one   Ask the coachee to identify the specific negative feeling he or she may be experiencing (e.g. disappointment).

Step two   Ask the coachee to reflect on the following questions:

➤ Is this a healthy feeling?

➤ How do I want to feel?

➤ What (within my control) would make me feel better?

➤ What am I willing to do to achieve this state?

➤ What am I not willing to do to achieve this state?

➤ What is the first step I can take to feel the way I want?

Step three   Work with the coachee to establish goals and an action plan to achieve the desired emotional state.

The freeze-frame technique

Another useful technique for inducing positive emotional states was developed by Childre. The freeze-frame method allows the individual to interrupt a negative emotional state and gain a clearer perspective of his or her immediate situation. The technique aims to effect an immediate and profound shift in how the person views a situation, thereby breaking the stress cycle by removing its source.

Exercise

Step one   Ask the coachee to nominate his or her symptoms of stress. For example, where in the body does he or she experience the stressful or negative state? It may be tension in the neck and shoulders, an upset stomach or a tension headache. Symptoms might manifest on a behavioural level, such as arguing, feeling 'put upon' or angry outbursts. Ask the coachee to freeze-frame the reaction and step back from the problem.

Step two   Ask the coachee to make a sincere effort to shift the focus away from the negative emotional state or negative thoughts by focusing on the region around the heart. The coachee is to then pretend to breathe through the heart area and focus there for ten seconds or more.

Exercise

Step three   Ask the coachee to recall a positive feeling or a happy time in his or her life. Ask the coachee to experience the feelings associated with that positive state or time. The coachee should try to really experience the feeling rather than simply visualising or recalling it.

Step four   Ask the coachee to use his or her intuition and, staying focused on the heart, ask his or her heart what the most effective and practical way is to deal with the situation. What response would be the most helpful and most life enhancing?

Step five   Ask the coachee to listen to the answer. The answer can provide new perspectives and new ways of dealing with the stressful situation or negative emotional state.

Step six   Together with the coachee, decide on an action plan that involves regular practice of the technique. Impress on the coachee the importance of attempting the technique when he or she is in a minor state of stress. Then, when a seriously stressful situation arises, the technique can be called upon. It is almost impossible to learn and practise this skill once one is in a highly emotional state, be it anger, frustration, sadness or fear.

Summary   Dealing with emotions is not a coach's core concern. However, coaches cannot afford to ignore the emotional aspects of a coachee's behaviour. If they do, significant change is unlikely to occur. Working with the coachee's emotions can be challenging. It is not a skill that can be learned simply from reading a book on the topic. Coaches require a thorough understanding of, and training and practice in, accessing and working with emotional states.

Overcoming resistance

Case studies recounting resistance and coaches' efforts to deal with it are rather scarce in the coaching literature. Yet information regarding a coachee's resistance and the subsequent success or failure of the coaching intervention can offer valuable insights and learning to all coaches. Perhaps one of the reasons for this lack of research is the way in which many coaches view their role and mandate. As coaches we espouse the collaborative, democratic aspects of the coaching alliance. It is the coachee's agenda and goals we work towards and it is the coachee, to a great extent, who determines the nature and pace of change. To work with a resistive coachee may appear to go against the very ethos of coaching. To some coaches it would not be coaching at all.

A surprising number of aspiring coaches state outright that they would not work with a reluctant or resistive coachee. They claim that unless the individual is totally committed to change then the coaching intervention would be in vain. While this viewpoint is understandable, it tends to minimise the complexity and ambivalence that frequently accompanies change. A coach who can rightly claim to be an expert on change should be familiar with all aspects of the change process, including resistance.

Unless the coach recognises and acknowledges resistance, how will he or she deal with it? Some coaches tend to deny or minimise resistance even though the results are superficial change at best or compliance or no change at all at worst. We suggest that some of the reasons why coaches refuse to come to terms with resistance include:

➤ The coach may lack a model or framework for the change process and may fail to recognise that resistance can be inherent in the challenge of change.

➤ The coach is afraid to acknowledge the 'failure' of the coaching intervention as it appears to manifest in the coachee's resistance.

➤ The coach does not recognise or understand resistance.

➤ The coach lacks the models and skills to challenge resistance.

➤ The coach blames himself or herself for the coachee's lack of engagement in the coaching partnership.

➤ The coach blames the coachee for not wanting to change or for lacking commitment to the coaching process. There is no acceptance, for example, that the coachee may be consciously committed to change but unconsciously sabotaging it.

➤ The coach may believe that when the coachee is 'taking one step forward and two steps back' this is a function of difficult goals and may try to alter these accordingly. However, the true reason may lie in ambivalence and resistance on the part of the coachee.

What is resistance?

Resistance refers to a coachee's opposition to change. Most of the research on resistance comes from the helping professions such as counselling and psychology, and from management and organisational literature. Freud first identified resistance as a defence against anxiety. Other therapies attribute resistance to game playing, denial of responsibility, laziness or lack of courage on the part of the client.

Such attitudes can be naïve and at times sadistic and dangerous, particularly in the hands of an unskilled helper. To cheerfully tell a depressed client or coachee that 'you choose to be depressed' is not only untrue but cruel. Coaches have to recognise that there are psychopathological conditions with signs, symptoms and treatments. Yet this is not to deny that some individuals choose to be miserable or engage in other self-sabotaging behaviours. The coach has to be cognisant of when a situation requires expert clinical help and when it can be handled within a coaching framework.

Resistance in coaching tends to be viewed in a less judgmental, less dismissive manner. Along with Mahoney and colleagues, we view the coachee's resistance as a natural response to having his or her core values and beliefs challenged. Coaching can demand that the coachee examine and re-evaluate deeply held beliefs about the self and the world. While this may be necessary for any profound changes to occur, it can nonetheless be a challenging and even frightening process. One must expect some resistance.

Resistance may also be an indication that something is not working in the coaching conversations. Perhaps the agreed upon goals are too easy or too difficult. The coach may not have devoted enough time to examining the coachee's values and subsequently the goals may not truly reflect the coachee's real aspirations. The goals and action plans may even generate a conflict of values within the coachee.

Resistance, either active or passive, can be viewed as a symptom, as something that can be worked with and, ideally, overcome. It is true that coaching is not a panacea, it is not suitable for everyone and some individuals may be 'uncoachable'. However, to dismiss a resistive coachee without attempting to understand and explore the reasons for his or her behaviour is to deny the coachee the potential opportunity for change and transformation.

The coach's resistance

It is not only the coachee who may be resisting change. The coach, too, can respond to the coachee's resistance by 'giving in' and colluding with the coachee's unwillingness or inability to take action. One way to overcome this impasse is to respond to the resistant coachee in the way one would to a more willing participant. That is, by challenging and confronting the coachee (see below for guidelines) the coach does not lose sight of the goals of the coaching partnership. The situation may be unproductive at the moment, but if the coachee has already shown signs of wanting to learn, then the coach can leverage these successes and maintain a solid working partnership despite the current difficulties.

The coach can also resist the coachee's chosen methods and approaches towards achieving particular goals. The coach may feel that such methods are not in the coachee's best interests and may lead to failure or derailment. In such circumstances, the coach is advised to adopt what O'Neill terms 'loyal resistance'. That is, although the coach considers the coachee's methods unproductive, he or she wishes to align with the individual nonetheless to meet his or her goals. Although the coach and coachee agree on the general direction they are taking, there may be disagreement about how to get there. The coach has to provide a solid argument to support his or her objections to the coachee's intentions. Furthermore, it is incumbent upon the coach to suggest alternative solutions. Together, the coach and coachee can brainstorm new options and pathways. However, a coach and coachee can only work together in this way if the coach has already established himself or herself as a loyal, committed and trustworthy partner.

Some manifestations of coachee resistance

Research, as well as our experience and that of our colleagues, suggests the following ways that resistance can manifest itself in coaching:

➤ The coachee constantly 'shifts the goalpost'—that is, he or she identifies a different issue to explore in each session.

➤ The coachee consistently fails to carry out the agreed upon strategies and action plans. Various excuses may be given.

➤ The coachee intellectualises and philosophises about the issue but remains reluctant to translate insights and ideas into action.

➤ The coachee is preoccupied with present grievances, for example being mistreated or unappreciated in the workplace. There is a tendency to blame others and to adopt a 'victim' role rather than instituting any changes.

➤ The coachee feels resentful about being 'coerced' into coaching by management. Although the coachee may claim to welcome and appreciate the opportunity for coaching, the reluctance to actually change belies this.

➤ The coachee remains preoccupied with the past and is unable or unwilling to move forward.

Techniques for dealing with resistance

1 Working with the resistance model

An interesting mathematical model of resistance to change was proposed by Beckhard. His equation is: $D \times V \times F > R$ where:

➤ D equals dissatisfaction with the current situation

➤ V equals the vision of future possibilities

➤ F equals first steps towards the vision, and

➤ R equals resistance to change.

The formula only applies when each of the three elements (D, V, F) are present. It clearly lends itself to coaching for change. The following are guidelines for the coach when working with this model.

1   *Explore dissatisfaction with the current situation* Coaching usually occurs within the context of some dissatisfaction with current reality. Either the coachee or significant others (e.g. the coachee's manager or colleagues) recognise a need for the coachee to develop or enhance a skill. The coach can work with the coachee to explore the costs and benefits of changing the current situation. By increasing the coachee's awareness of the limitations of his or her current behaviour the coach is, in fact, increasing the coachee's level of dissatisfaction.

2   *Explore vision* Assessing and exploring the coachee's values and purpose in life are a core facet of any coaching enterprise. Through clarifying and prioritising values the coachee is frequently able to clearly determine his or her purpose in life. Once the purpose has been defined the coachee is free to develop a vision of what his or her future life should be.

3   *Take action* Having worked with the coachee to establish his or her values, purpose and vision, the next stage in the change process is to set goals that work towards attaining the vision. Setting goals, developing strategies and action planning are, as we know, integral to the coaching process.

2 Dealing with an unproductive relationship

Despite the coach's (and sometimes the coachee's) best efforts it can happen that goals are not being met according to the agreed upon milestones. It may be necessary for the coach to confront the coachee about this lack of progress. We have developed the following two sets of guidelines for the coach when dealing with an unproductive coaching relationship:

A confrontational approach

Checklist

How to use:

✔   as a structured guide for a conversation between the coach and coachee.

When to use:

✔   when the coach feels that the coachee is making insufficient progress and is capable of greater effort.

Why use:

✔   to get the coaching sessions back on track and, if necessary, renegotiate the coaching agreement.

1   The coach should openly describe how he or she feels about the coachee's lack of progress:
    ➤   Use non-emotive language.

➤ Refer to outcomes rather than to the individual's 'personality'.

➤ Accept some responsibility for the lack of progress, for example 'we are not achieving the goals…'.

2 The coach should establish what the coachee thinks is happening and how he or she feels about the degree of progress being made.

3 The coach should record his or her own misgivings. Regardless of whether or not the coachee feels there is progress, the coach should reiterate his or her concerns that the coaching alliance doesn't seem to be working and that little real progress is being made.

4 The coach should summarise the specific goals that have not been met:

➤ Balance empathy with confrontation.

➤ Be supportive but firm.

5 The coach should firmly outline a plan to improve the situation:

➤ Ensure the coachee is aware of the performance gap.

➤ Ensure the coachee understands the required level of performance.

➤ Emphasise that it is the coachee's choice to change his or her performance.

➤ Reinforce that you are there to assist and facilitate the coachee to achieve the desired standard or goals.

➤ Be specific about what has to change—nominate a specific goal.

➤ Suggest how this change can come about—encourage the coachee to examine the costs and benefits of changing.

➤ Establish a strict time frame for the goal to be reached.

6 The coach should clearly establish alternatives if no change occurs in the specified time. For example:

➤ Reassess the values and goals—focus on another coaching issue.

➤ Terminate the coaching relationship.

➤ Set up a meeting with management (if appropriate).

➤ Find a replacement coach.

A compromise approach

Checklist

How to use:

✔ as a structured guide for a conversation between the coach and coachee.

When to use:

✔ when the coach believes that the coachee is incapable of attaining the stated objectives

✔   when the coach believes that a confrontational approach would not induce change and may even damage the coaching alliance.

Why use:

✔   to work with the coachee's limitations

✔   to maintain the coaching relationship

✔   to adjust goals accordingly.

1   The coach should openly describe what he or she thinks about the lack of progress and the status of the coaching relationship.

➤   Use non-emotive language.

➤   Refer to outcomes rather than to the individual's 'personality'.

➤   Accept some responsibility for the lack of progress, for example 'we are not achieving the goals…'.

2   The coach should establish what the coachee thinks is happening and how he or she feels about the degree of progress being made.

3   Reflect back to the coachee what he or she has said.

4   Accept the coachee's explanation and behaviour without judgment or analysis.

5   Collaborate with the coachee and negotiate new goals and strategies.

6   Provide additional support and resources for the coachee.

The above guidelines are simply structures that the coach may choose to follow when dealing with resistance. Each coachee is unique and each coach has a personal style that dictates how he or she deals with issues such as resistance.

It is frequently suggested that a truly committed coach wants more for the coachee than the coachee does. While this attitude is admirable and congruent with the coach's desire to 'champion' and 'stretch' the coachee, it can lead to frustration on the coach's part. If the coachee does not change as quickly or as profoundly as the coach expects, the coach may become disillusioned or angry. This can lead to withdrawal and, ultimately, lack of interest in the coachee.

> **Summary**   Dealing with resistance is one of the major challenges facing all coaches. It is critical that each coach has his or her own model of resistance to bring to the coaching partnership. Such a model involves a theory of resistance, ways to recognise and understand the signs of resistance and ways of working effectively to overcome these signs.

Non-verbal communication

It is generally accepted that our non-verbal messages can be more revealing than our words. Nietzsche stated that 'one can lie with the mouth but with the accompanying grimace one nevertheless tells the truth'. Freud also noted how 'self-betrayal oozes from our pores'. Furthermore, research suggests that where there is a disjunction between verbal and non-verbal messages, observers tend to believe the non-verbal signals. We transmit considerable amounts of information through non-verbal channels. Our posture, gestures, and the pitch, tone and tempo of our voice reveal a lot about our personality, our emotional state, our level of confidence and our trustworthiness. While the coaching literature emphasises how the coach can assess and work with non-verbal cues, it must be remembered that the coach's non-verbal communication also impacts equally on the coachee.

For instance, in the coaching alliance it is often not so much what the coach says but how he or she says it that matters. A critical tone of voice can send the coachee reeling back in time to the voice of a critical parent. The coachee immediately becomes defensive, regardless of how valid the coach's assessment may be. Indeed the coachee may not even hear what the coach is saying because the emotional reaction precludes efficient cognitive processing.

Techniques for working with non-verbal signals

We cannot emphasise enough the importance of recognising that non-verbal signals do not always indicate what we think. While leaning back with one's hands behind one's head may indicate superiority, it could equally mean that the individual is enjoying a stretch. Likewise, folded arms do not always signal defensiveness or being closed-off. It may simply be a comfortable position for the individual. However, if sitting with folded hands is a typical posture for a coach, he or she should explain this to the coachee at the commencement of the sessions.

Similarly, if the coachee uses non-verbal cues that the coach interprets as having a specific meaning the coach should seek confirmation from the coachee. For example, some statements the coach can employ when responding to the coachee's non-verbal messages include:

➤ You're moving around a lot in the chair. Does that mean you're feeling a bit nervous?

➤ When we talk about how your manager might view your behaviour, you fold your arms tightly. Folded arms often signal defensiveness or unwillingness to listen—do you think that applies in your case?

Freud also noted how the unconscious mind of one human being can react upon that of another without passing through the conscious mind. Some of this information is transmitted through body language. Being aware of the coachee's non-verbal cues allows the coach to be more sensitive to what the coachee is experiencing. Furthermore, there are certain NLP techniques the coach can employ to enhance rapport and to effect change in the coachee's behaviour. These include the following:

➤ *Pacing* is a technique to establish and enhance rapport. Essentially it involves 'going along with' what the coachee is doing at the time. For example, if the coachee is speaking softly the coach speaks softly. If the coachee is enthusiastic and gesticulating a great deal, the coach matches these behaviours.

➤ *Mirroring*, which is a type of pacing, means the coach presents a mirror image to the coachee. If, for instance, the coachee raises his or her right hand, the coach raises his or her left hand.

➤ *Leading* is a technique whereby the coach changes his or her behaviour so that the coachee will follow. The intention of leading is to encourage the coachee to change his or her state of mind and access different pieces of information or alternative points of view. For example, a coachee may be slumped in the chair speaking in a low voice. In order to induce a rapid change in mood, the coach might deliberately sit up very straight and speak in a loud voice.

These techniques have to be used carefully and skilfully. If used in the wrong context, or relied upon too much, the coaching relationship will suffer. Furthermore, rapport can be irreparably damaged if the coachee feels that he or she is being mimicked or manipulated. Inducing a rapid change in an emotional state may be less effective than exploring the coachee's feelings and working on strategies to self-regulate emotions.

Non-verbal signals during the coaching cycle

In our experience, certain non-verbal behaviours can be interpreted differently at different stages of the coaching process. The following model of non-verbal communication suggests that there are certain signals the coach can 'read' at various stages of the coaching alliance. Many of the signals listed below may seem obvious or simplistic and coaches may tend to take them for granted or ignore them. Yet coaches, more than any other professionals (except perhaps for those in the helping professions), are responsible for recognising and acknowledging all aspects of behaviour.

It could be that the coach has a long-term contract with an organisation and is therefore reluctant to recognise and challenge any warning signals from the coachee. Yet we must be skilled at reading non-verbal messages and have the courage to interpret these from the very beginning of the coaching partnership. We are, after all, experts in behaviour and behavioural change. That is what we are paid for and therein lies our responsibility to the profession and to the coachee.

Non-verbal signals during the first meeting

➤ *Are the coachee's palms sweaty?* The coachee may be anxious about meeting you, or anxious about the coaching process itself.

➤ *Does the coachee fail to maintain good eye contact?* He or she may feel embarrassed about being 'nominated' for coaching, or may be shy. There could be cultural factors behind this behaviour.

➤ *Does the coachee pull down the blinds in the office or the meeting room?* This can signify embarrassment and may be a reflection of how coaching is viewed within the organisation.

➤ *Does the coachee see you in his or her office and sit in a higher chair than you?* The coachee may need to feel superior and in control. The coach should attempt to rearrange the seating so that both parties are on an equal level.

➤ *Is there a space cleared for you?* If you are expected to work in a cluttered space, this may indicate a lack of preparation for your visit. This can, in turn, signify reluctance or even anger at being coached.

➤ *Does the coachee speak in a monotone?* It is likely he or she may find the coaching situation boring.

Non-verbal signals during the assessment phase

➤ *Does the coachee complete the assessment facing you?* If the coachee turns his or her back on you anger is probably the cause.

➤ *Does the coachee sigh or shuffle while completing the assessment protocols?* Perhaps he or she is concerned about what the assessment will reveal and how this might impact on his or her position in the company.

➤ *Does the coachee hesitate before answering?* Perhaps there is a lack of trust, and uncertainty about revealing weaknesses.

➤ *Does the coachee spend an inordinate amount of time on pen and pencil tests?* Perhaps he or she is pedantic or trying to answer in the most 'acceptable' way.

Non-verbal signals during a 'difficult' session

➤ *Does the coachee frequently change position?* This may indicate anxiety or discomfort with the topic.

➤ *Does the coachee look down frequently?* Perhaps the topic is an emotional one and the coachee is strongly affected by his or her emotions.

➤ *Does the coachee raise his or her voice or speak in abrupt, clipped tones?* The coachee may be angry with you for raising a difficult subject.

➤ *Is the coachee facing away from you?* The coachee may be signalling a lack of interest, disagreement or rejection.

➤ *Is the coachee engaging in prolonged silences?* Depending on the accompanying signals (posture, eye contact), the coachee may be reflecting or may be stubbornly withholding.

Non-verbal signals in the final session

➤ *Is the coachee smiling when you greet him or her?* This would suggest that he or she is pleased with the coaching sessions and feels confident about moving ahead without the coach.

➤ *Is the coachee looking a bit despondent?* Perhaps he or she is not quite ready to sever the connection with you.

➤ *Is the coachee looking sullen or annoyed?* Perhaps the coachee is feeling rejected and is having difficulty ending the relationship.

➤ *Does the coachee seem anxious or restless?* It is possible he or she does not feel confident about maintaining the gains made in the coaching sessions.

Summary Reading a book on non-verbal signals does not make us experts on the subject. Coaches have to not only recognise non-verbal signals but work with them so that the coaching relationship is enriched. Non-verbal communications are open to speculation and inference. They make sense only in the context of the individual and his or her relationship with the coach. It is important that the coach clarifies his or her hypotheses about the meaning of these signals with the coachee.

Relaxation, meditation, visualisation and trance states

The purpose of this chapter is to provide the coach with several relaxation, meditation and visualisation techniques that can facilitate change within the coachee. As mentioned previously, these techniques constitute part of what we call 'soft learning' and are useful in preparing the coachee for action learning.

Relaxation

Coaching literature is surprisingly lacking in any detailed information on relaxation techniques. At first glance it may appear that relaxation is diametrically opposed to the core impetus of coaching which is towards change, action and forward movement. Relaxation can conjure up feelings of inaction and stasis, and may ultimately be seen as a waste of valuable time. Yet coaching involves the body and mind, and relaxation is a crucial technique to prepare the coachee, both mentally and physically, for moving into action.

S. B. is a competent, smart, highly-stressed executive. His department had recently undergone major expansion and his ability to cope was under scrutiny by a doubting management. Previously S. B. had been 'in control' of information and strategic planning but the changes now demanded that he share information with his colleagues and delegate some of his work. S. B. arrived at the coaching sessions flurried and stressed and in no state to take in information. Although delegation was the nominated 'topic' for coaching, the initial focus of the coaching sessions was on relaxation techniques. S. B. needed time and space to lower his level of physiological arousal, to calm his racing thoughts and to prepare his body and mind for taking action. Therefore, the first four coaching sessions were spent practising relaxation exercises. S. B. was encouraged to use these techniques as an integral part of his daily life and work. Only when these practices were being integrated into S. B.'s life did the coaching intervention address the issue of delegation.

In Chapter 2 we mentioned various sources of personal and organisational stress. These included role overload, role ambiguity, co-worker stress and a lack of balance between work and life. Such stressors manifest in the physiological, emotional and cognitive realms. For example, stress can result in increased blood pressure, stomach upsets and a tightness, even pain, in the neck, shoulders and back. Emotional responses to stress include edginess, nervousness, anger, and feelings of powerlessness. Importantly, and this fact is frequently overlooked in the literature on stress, when we are under pressure our cognitive abilities can be impaired. We fail to think clearly, tend to make poor decisions, have a shortened concentration span, have mental blocks and are generally unreceptive to new or creative ideas. Clearly, a coachee who is experiencing high levels of stress is in no position to immediately move into action. New information will not be absorbed, coaching may be viewed as just another pressure to cope with and real behavioural change is highly unlikely to occur.

Relaxation techniques deserve to be considered seriously by the coach as a necessary prelude to goal setting and action-planning in some coaching situations. The coach may need to assume the role of educator and inform the coachee about stress, its deleterious effects on performance and how relaxation and meditation can help to offset these. The coach also adopts the role of instructor by teaching and demonstrating the various techniques to the coachee.

What is relaxation?

We all have our personal idea of what relaxation is and how we achieve it. For some it can be going to the movies, zonking out in front of the television, watching videos or having a few drinks. Yet relaxation should not be confused with 'time out for ourselves' or hobbies and recreation. It is possible that some individuals may be relaxed during these activities but this is not necessarily true. When we refer to relaxation in this chapter we are talking about techniques that aim to relieve and release tension in the body. Meditation techniques, on the other hand, are specifically designed to calm the mind.

Relaxation techniques can vary in their complexity and the amount of time required to practise them. The coach has to adapt the suggested techniques to the individual coachee. For instance research (and our experience) suggests that it is useless to 'teach' a relaxation or meditation technique to a coachee and then expect him or her to practise it for twenty minutes twice a day even though this is the recommended time frame to achieve optimal results. First, it is difficult, if not impossible, for many busy individuals to find forty minutes a day to rehearse any new technique, least of all one where the benefits may not be immediately obvious. Second, it may be an absolute impossibility for a stressed, time-pressured person to sit and relax for twenty minutes. Five minutes a day may be a more reasonable starting point.

Apart from time constraints, the nature of the relaxation exercise has to be tailored to suit the individual coachee's life style and image. We have conducted relaxation sessions with executives who have drawn the office blinds so that colleagues could not see them engaging in an activity that clearly did not fit with their image. Sitting at their desk doing ten rounds of abdominal breathing may be all that certain individuals are prepared to do. Others may find a quiet space, usually at home, and will allot a longer period to practise relaxation or meditation. Finally, these exercises can be associated with New Age or religious practices and this can be disconcerting for some individuals. Relaxation and meditation techniques therefore have to be individualised and tailored to meet the coachee's time frame, beliefs, lifestyle and availability to practise.

Relaxation techniques

The following techniques are neither mandatory nor definitive. Many coaches may have their own relaxation scenarios that they are comfortable with and that have proven effective. These guidelines are for coaches who are not familiar with relaxation techniques or are looking for a brief, structured exercise to use with their clients. Many coachees have their own particular techniques that work for them. In such cases, the role of the coach may simply be to build the technique into the coaching sessions, to determine ways in which coachees can 'cue' themselves to carry out the techniques (how, when and where) and set goals so that coachees are committed to performing the techniques on a regular, ongoing basis.

Some guidelines for the coach

1 There is a phenomenon called relaxation induced anxiety (RIA). As its name implies, RIA describes a state of anxiety some individuals may experience when practising relaxation.

The reasons for RIA remain obscure but there are methods the coach can use to lessen the likelihood of it occurring or to weaken its effects:

➤ First, ask the coachee about previous attempts at relaxation. What technique(s) did they use? What happened? What were the benefits? Were there any side effects?

➤ Closing their eyes may cause some individuals to feel uncomfortable. When suggesting that the individual closes his or her eyes (as described below), always add 'if you are comfortable with that. Otherwise, it is fine to leave your eyes open'.

➤ Try to refrain from using the phrase 'letting go'. It can imply or signal loss of control to some individuals and may cause anxiety. Rather than talking about 'letting go' of tension, the coach can employ words such as 'let the tension fade away' or 'feel the tension melting away'.

2 The coach has to ensure that the coachee is aware that relaxation is not a quick fix. Of course, once the technique has been mastered it can be a powerful and fast method of relieving stress and tension. However, learning and practising relaxation techniques takes time, effort and perseverance. The 'pay-off' might not be immediate, and impatient, driven individuals may find this frustrating and give up prematurely. Practising in the coaching sessions and developing goals and action plans to ensure the practice continues outside the sessions is critical if any real benefits are to be gained.

3 When working with the coachee on any relaxation technique, it is crucial that the coach matches the coachee's pace. We have probably all experienced the frustration of listening to guided relaxation tapes where the speaker proceeds either too fast, too slow or unevenly. In a face-to-face session the coach can match the coachee's breathing and can provide instructions or guidance that synchronise with the coachee's breathing rhythms and observed levels of comfort or discomfort.

A how-to-breathe technique

Prior to the commencement of any relaxation exercise, it is imperative that the coach spends some time with the coachee on breathing. For any relaxation technique to be truly effective breathing has to be done through the nose. The abdomen rather than the chest should rise and fall with each breath.

 Checklist

How to use:

✔ as an exercise the coach and coachee practise together at the beginning of each coaching session until the coachee has mastered the exercise.

When to use:

✔ when the coachee appears stressed and is breathing incorrectly.

Why use:

✔ to prepare the coachee for further relaxation and meditation exercises

✔ to develop the skill of abdominal breathing—the coachee can transfer this skill to all aspects of his or her life.

Step one Explain the importance of breathing through the nose and into the abdomen rather than the chest. Inform the coachee that although the technique appears simple, abdominal breathing can take time to master and that it is not uncommon to lose one's count during the 10-breath cycle. Recommend that the coachee simply return to 'one' and begin the cycle over again if this does occur.

Step two Ask the coachee to place a hand on his or her abdomen.

Step three Ask the coachee to breathe in and out three times through the nose. Observe whether the abdomen rises and falls. It is unlikely that the coachee will perfect this technique without a reasonable amount of practice.

Step four Review the procedure. What difficulties did the coachee have in breathing as suggested?

Step five Guide the coachee through a cycle of ten breaths whereby the coach counts aloud from one to ten on each 'out' breath.

Step six Ask the coachee to repeat the procedure alone, counting silently from one to ten on each out breath.

Step seven Ask the coachee to do another cycle (ten breaths) counting the breaths silently.

Step eight Review the procedure and address any difficulties the coachee may be experiencing. Usually, it is simply that the individual is not accustomed to abdominal breathing. Reassure the coachee that this exercise takes time to perfect.

Step nine Repeat Step six until the coachee has done at least ten cycles of the breathing exercise.

Step ten Establish a goal which involves the coachee practising a cycle of breathing at least three times a day. Determine with the coachee *when* he or she will do the exercise (on waking, at midday and before going to sleep are common choices) and *how* the coachee will cue himself or herself to do the exercise. In a busy routine it is easy to forget to do even the simplest of assignments, regardless of how committed the individual is. Together the coach

Exercise

and coachee have to determine possible obstacles that might stop the coachee practising the breathing routine and create solutions to overcome these barriers.

Step eleven   Gradually increase the number of breathing cycles the coachee does at the nominated times.

A general relaxation technique

Checklist

How to use:

✔ as a relaxation script to be 'read' to the coachee during the coaching session

✔ as an audio tape that the coachee can use outside the coaching sessions—the coach can tape the first relaxation session.

When to use:

✔ after the coachee feels he or she is fairly competent using the how-to-breathe technique

✔ at the commencement of each coaching session for the entire coaching cycle if the coachee is particularly stressed or anxious.

Why use:

✔ to release and relieve stress and tension so the coachee is better prepared to take on new learning and new actions

✔ to provide the coachee with a relaxation technique that he or she can continue to use on an ongoing basis.·

Exercise

Step one   Ask the coachee how relaxed he or she feels on a scale of 1 (not very relaxed) to 10 (very relaxed). Encourage the coachee to get comfortable. This may involve loosening a tie, taking off shoes and moving to a more comfortable chair.

Step two   Read the following script (approximately 10 minutes) taking care to match the coachee's breathing and pace yourself accordingly:

Sitting comfortably, with your eyes closed if you wish, breathing quietly through your nose. You are beginning to relax. Slowly focus your attention on your breathing—slowly breathing in and out through your nose. Feel your abdomen rise and fall with each breath.

Let any sounds just come and go. The same with your thoughts—don't try to get rid of them, just let them be. When you become aware that you're thinking, just slowly and gently bring your attention back to your breathing, in, out, in, out—good. You are feeling more and more relaxed. Feel free to adjust your position if that makes you more comfortable

Now I would like you to bring your attention to your head. Feel any tension or tightness in the head region, feel the tension drain away. Notice any tension or tightness in your forehead and face—let the tightness fade away. Feel the muscles in your whole face loosen and relax, any tension is just draining away. You are feeling more and more relaxed, calm and peaceful.

Now gently bring your attention to your neck and shoulders. Is there any tension there? Focus on any tightness in the muscles and let them relax. Feel the tightness melt away as you feel more and more relaxed. Notice if there is any tension in your arms and chest, let the muscles go loose, good—more and more relaxed.

Now bring your attention to your chest and abdomen. As you breathe slowly through your nose feel if there is any tightness in your abdomen and stomach area. Often we hold in our emotions by contracting the abdomen—just breathe slowly and feel any tension melt away. Breathe fully, with each breath your body is becoming more and more relaxed. Any thoughts that come to you, just let them be. Bring your attention back to your breathing.

Now focus your attention on the muscles in your legs and feet. Let the muscles hang loose. Feel any tightness and let it dissolve as you become more and more at ease, as the tension drains from your entire body. Just breathing quietly, being aware of the rise and fall of your abdomen—feel the tension and tightness and any pain drift away as you feel relaxed and calm. Good, breathing calmly and evenly.

Now just bring your attention to the top of your head again. Imagine a white light, clear and warm pervading your whole body. As the light moves through your body all negativity, tensions and stress just flow out through your toes. Feel the white light pervade your entire body leaving you feeling light and clear, calm and relaxed—good.

Now I am going to count backwards from five to one—when I get to one, I would like you to open your eyes and stretch. Counting now: 5   4   3   2   1.

Step three   Review the relaxation procedure with the coachee. Ask:

➤ How relaxed does the person feel on a scale of 1 (low) to 10 (high)?

➤ Did the coachee have any difficulties with any of the instructions?

Exercise

> Would the coachee benefit from having a tape of the exercise? (This would obviously facilitate practice.)

Step four Establish a goal that involves the coachee listening to the tape twice a day until the next session. Ideally, the coachee will integrate this exercise into his or her life and will continue to use it after the coaching sessions have ended.

Meditation techniques

To some individuals, the notion of meditation still conjures up images of incense, saffron-robed monks and Eastern religions or cults. Meditation has traditionally been associated with religion and the attempt to attain enlightenment or nirvana. For our purposes, we are discussing meditation from a secular point of view. It is true that some religious devotees claim that meditation without the ultimate goal of enlightenment is useless. However, we suggest that meditation techniques can be useful to help clear the mind of its constant chattering and clutter and subsequently increase mental alertness and enhance work performance.

There are various kinds of meditation. Some involve reciting a mantra, others highlight the importance of focusing on an image while some simply involve concentrating on the breath. The meditation guidelines listed below focus chiefly on the latter. As will be evident from the following techniques, meditation and relaxation are closely related. The breathing techniques in relaxation are virtually the same as those used in meditation. In meditation, however, the emphasis is on clearing the mind, rather than relaxing the body.

Meditation is about breathing. According to many meditation teachers, to master our breath is to control our bodies and minds. Breathing is a tool and breathing properly is said to build up lung capacity and revitalise all body organs. Meditation is about mindfulness, and learning techniques to gain control when one feels upset or scattered. It is a means by which we can increase our self-awareness. The following simple techniques are guidelines for the coach who wishes to add meditation to his or her toolkit of coaching techniques.

A centring technique

Checklist

How to use:

✔ as a script that can be read to the coachee

✔ as a technique that can be learnt in the coaching sessions and applied in any situation.

Checklist

When to use:

✔ when the coach considers the coachee to be 'scattered' or preoccupied and not fully attending to the coaching sessions

✔ when the coachee complains of problems with concentration or of 'losing it'.

Why use:

✔ to increase the coachee's mindfulness, focus and self-awareness

✔ to assist the coachee to 'be' in the present and not confuse what has happened with what is happening now.

Exercise

Step one   Encourage the coachee to get comfortable.

Step two   Do at least three rounds of the 10-breath breathing cycle, breathing in and out through the nose, and being aware of the rise and fall of the abdomen.

Step three   Read or recite the following script to the coachee:

Sitting comfortably, if you wish to close your eyes, do so now. Feeling relaxed, being only in the present, you have nothing to do but be present. Focus your attention outside of yourself, you don't have to think about being present, just be aware of what is happening around you.

Notice the space you are in, the size and shape of the chair, your feet on the floor. What sounds are there in the room? What can you hear? Feel the temperature in the room. You are alert but relaxed—if thoughts enter your mind just let them fade away. Focus on the external world. Are there patterns of light you can see? Just sit, being in the present, hearing my voice. If you move or yawn, simply notice that and gradually bring your attention back to just being in the present. Now slowly open your eyes.

Step four   Debrief. Ask the coachee:

➤ How do you feel now?

➤ What was the easiest part of the exercise?

➤ What was the most difficult part?

Step five   Ask the coachee to repeat the exercise without your guidance.

Step six   Debrief as in Step four. Depending on how competent the coachee feels about doing the exercise alone, either repeat again with your guidance or set a homework assignment for the coachee to practise the technique daily until the following session.

Exercise

Step seven Depending on how well the coachee has practised and mastered the technique, it is now time to increase the difficulty of the task. Usually, the coachee wishes to remain centred while dealing with other people or performing a task. This second stage of the exercise introduces another person (i.e. the coach). The coach and coachee are to sit down in front of each other and look at each without doing or saying anything. The coachee may initially feel uncomfortable, tired, and fidgety, and at times his or her eyes may water. However, the coach and coachee are to continue to look at each other and the coachee is to practise the centring technique as previously learned. The procedure can be repeated several times until the coachee feels centred.

Step eight Once the coachee is able to remain centred in the presence of another person (the coach), the next step is to use the technique in the company of a colleague or in the workplace. It is particularly beneficial if the coachee can use this technique in a situation that is difficult or stressful. A homework exercise, or goal of the session, might be to practise this technique in a typically stressful situation where the coachee does not have to do anything.

Step nine The final step in mastering the centring technique is for the coachee to use the skill while performing a task. The coach and coachee should role-play this in the session and the homework assignment could be to perform the technique at least five times during the following week. Monitoring, reviewing and adjusting goals if necessary should continue until the coachee feels competent in using centring even in highly demanding, challenging situations.

A simple meditation breathing technique

This technique is based on an ancient Buddhist exercise for clearing the mind or 'channels'.

Checklist

How to use:

✔ as a technique to be learnt during the coaching sessions.

When to use:

✔ when the coachee is not interested in more detailed or involved meditation techniques.

Why use:

✔ to settle the mind and to improve concentration and focus.

Exercise

Step one Make sure that the coachee is comfortable.

Step two Ask the coachee to gently place the second finger of his or her right hand on the right nostril. Breathe in through the left nostril and (placing the second finger of the left hand on the left nostril) uncover the right nostril and breathe out.

Step three Repeat this step three times.

Step four Ask the coachee to gently place the second finger of his or her left hand on the left nostril. Then, breathe in through the right nostril and (placing the second finger of the right hand on the right nostril) uncover the left nostril and breathe out through it.

Step five Repeat this step three times.

Step six Ask the coachee to breathe in through both nostrils and out through both nostrils.

Step seven Repeat this step three times.

Once coachees have practised the skill they will be able to do the breathing exercise without having to place their fingers on their nostrils.

Counting the breath meditation

Checklist

How to use:

✔ as a method to be taught in the coaching sessions.

When to use:

✔ when the coachee wants to learn a simple meditation technique.

Why use:

✔ to equip the coachee with a simple meditation procedure to clear the mind

✔ as a foundational practice the coachee can build upon and develop.

Exercise

Step one Ensure the coachee is in a comfortable, relaxed position, either sitting in a chair or on the floor.

Step two Ask the coachee to sit up straight, hands placed comfortably on the lap, palms up with the right palm placed over the left. The coachee is to focus only on his or her breath.

Step three   Once the coachee has established a regular breathing pattern, count aloud on each 'out' breath from one to ten. Repeat the process of counting from one to ten for five cycles (50 breaths).

Step four   Ask the coachee to mentally count his or her out breaths from one to ten. Continue this procedure for ten minutes.

Some guidelines to give the coachee:

1   When commencing a meditation session, always ensure there are no distractions, such as telephones, family, etc.

2   Where possible, meditate in the same place and try to keep that space free for meditation only.

3   If the coachee loses count, return to 'one' and begin the cycle again.

4   Allow any noises and thoughts to come and go. Do not attempt to get rid of them.

5   When the coachee realises he or she is thinking, simply say 'thinking' and return to counting the breaths.

6   If the coachee is not accustomed to meditation, use an alarm clock to signal the end of the agreed upon session time. Although, as mentioned previously, twenty minutes is the recommended time period, five to ten minutes can be adequate for beginners. Over time, the period can be extended.

7   The coachee might initially experience more mental 'turbulence' and mind chattering than usual. However, this is not caused by meditation. The meditation process simply allows us to recognise just how scattered and 'busy' our minds are. The mind does settle down, although the time frame for this varies with the individual.

8   Persistence is important for any real results to occur. The coachee has to realise that the process can be difficult, and sometimes boring and frustrating with minimal obvious benefits, particularly at the beginning. However, the long-term benefits are enormous and the technique can be a powerful life- and work-enhancing tool.

Visualisation techniques

Visualisation techniques or imagery are discussed frequently in self-help literature. While many of the techniques are undeniably useful and practical, the promises made are sometimes unrealistic. Simply visualising what one wants unfortunately does not mean that one gets it.

Visualisation techniques alone are rarely effective. They usually have to be combined with learning relaxation skills, exploring values, challenging self-limiting beliefs and behaviours, and setting achievable and realistic goals and action plans.

Furthermore, visualisation techniques require persistent effort and practice. The need to persevere with these techniques cannot be overemphasised.

Research from sport psychology indicates that even highly driven elite athletes frequently fail to place sufficient emphasis on the importance of visualisation and don't practise it regularly. Some of the more powerful, tried and proven visualisation techniques can be found in sport psychology literature and therapy literature. Although sport psychologists scorned the use of visualisation techniques for many years, research now shows that they can be highly effective in enhancing an athlete's confidence and skill performance. Visualisation is also referred to as 'mental rehearsal'. Visualisation techniques are also successfully employed in therapy, for example in desensitising individuals with phobic anxieties and fears. These techniques tend to work most effectively when they are accompanied by relaxation procedures that increase the individual's ability to absorb new information.

So what is visualisation? Imagery or visualisation is similar to our everyday sensory experiences of hearing, feeling and seeing. However visualisation occurs in the mind in the absence of any external stimuli. Imagining oneself in a particular situation and imagining the feelings associated with it can have an almost identical effect on the central nervous system as experiencing the actual experience. Some general benefits of visualisation are as follows:

➤ It can provide a mental picture or a blueprint of how to act.

➤ It aids in the practice of old and new skills.

➤ It increases self-awareness.

➤ It improves concentration and focus.

➤ It enhances confidence and feelings of control.

Visualising new behaviours

Individuals have varying abilities to visualise. Some coachees report rich, detailed imagery while others find the process difficult and frustrating. The exercises mentioned below are more effective with coachees who demonstrate superior powers of visualisation.

 Checklist

How to use:

✔ as a skill to be taught and practised in the coaching session

✔ as a homework assignment for the coachee to do on a daily basis.

When to use:

- ✔ when a coachee reports a visually rich account of a situation he or she wishes to change

- ✔ after self-limiting beliefs about the situation have been confronted

- ✔ when a coachee appears to have mastered a relaxation technique.

Why use:

- ✔ to replace negative mental images with positive, efficacious ones.

Exercise

Step one   Ensure the coachee is relaxed.

Step two   In order to assess the coachee's ability to visualise, ask him or her to recall and vividly describe some known specific space or location such as a room or garden. The details are to be as vivid as possible and the coachee is to employ all his or her senses when describing the place.

Step three   Ask the coachee to describe the current 'unwanted' situation in as much detail as possible—what he or she is thinking at the time, what feelings are present, where the tension is and what the coachee is doing.

Step four   Establish the coachee's expectations regarding the outcome of the visualisation exercise. If these are unrealistic the coach needs to spend some time discussing the likely outcome and the amount of work involved in practising the skill.

Step five   Ask the coachee to visualise the situation as he or she would like it to be. This might include the following: looking and feeling confident during a presentation, the context and content of what he or she will say, the response of others and the ease with which the task is completed.

Step six   Ask the coachee to practise visualising the scene on a daily basis until the next coaching session.

Step seven   The next step is to translate the imagined scene in to reality. Ask the coachee to use the new 'imagined' behaviour in a real life situation, such as making a presentation.

Step eight   Monitor, evaluate, reassess and continue practising the technique until the coachee has incorporated the new behaviour into his or her repertoire.

M. Q. is a 37-year-old manager in a large financial services organisation. She reported having difficulties expressing anger at work. When her assistant made errors in a report M. Q. would become furious, scribble in red over the offending piece of work, literally throw it on her assistant's desk and storm off without saying a word. Such behaviour was creating difficulties with her staff and senior management was concerned about her ability to manage. During the coaching sessions, M. Q. and the coach first explored the self-limiting beliefs that underpinned her behaviour and practised various assertion techniques. M. Q. then employed visualisation techniques to imagine herself behaving differently. For example, she imagined herself feeling calm and assertive, placing the report calmly on the assistant's desk, giving clear and precise directions and making certain her instructions were understood. Over time, M. Q. was able to generalise the visualisation technique to other work situations such as behaving calmly and effectively at team meetings and management meetings.

The SWITCH technique

The SWITCH pattern is a visualisation technique that involves individuals mentally replacing a scenario they do not want (e.g. feeling anxious and giving a poor presentation) with one they desire (e.g. feeling confident and making a successful presentation). The individual visualises two pictures—one of the unwanted scenario (the cue picture) and one of the desired picture (the outcome picture) and then repeatedly switches from one to the other. The cue picture (the undesirable state) should be seen from the coachee's own eyes. The outcome or desired picture should be dissociated, in that the coachee sees himself or herself from a distance. Although the technique is not a replacement for dealing with underlying issues, it can be useful in overcoming negative or self-defeating expectations.

How to use:

✔ in conjunction with challenging self-limiting beliefs

✔ as a technique to be practised in other situations.

When to use:

✔ when the coachee has images or expectations of failure

✔ when the coachee has an unwanted habit, for example procrastination.

Why use:

✔ to alter negative self-fulfilling prophecies

✔ to decrease anxiety and heighten confidence

✔ to develop positive habits.

Exercise

Step one   Ask the coachee to keep his or her eyes open and mentally develop a picture on a movie screen of the current situation, for example feeling anxious and observing the audience looking bored and unimpressed.

Step two   Ask the coachee to develop a picture of the desired outcome, for example feeling confident and observing the audience looking engrossed in the presentation.

Step three   Ask the coachee to imagine the unwanted or cue picture as being big and bright and filling the screen. This might involve imagining his or her sweating palms and the faces of the bored audience.

Step four   Ask the coachee to mentally place a small dark image of the desired or outcome picture in the lower corner of the cue picture.

Step five   Now ask the coachee to *zoom* the small, desired image onto the screen so that it quickly grows brighter and larger and completely covers the first image which then vanishes. It is essential that this process is *very rapid*, taking a couple of seconds at most.

Step six   Ask the coachee to repeat the switch (Steps two, three, four and five) at least five times.

Step seven   Continue to practise the technique until the coachee feels confident and competent that he or she can use it without the coach's guidance.

Step eight   Test the effectiveness of the technique. Ask the coachee to try to imagine the original cue picture. The coachee should find it difficult to do this without the desired picture quickly zooming into place.

Trance states

The subject of trance states such as hypnosis has always been plagued by controversy. Issues such as who is competent and accredited to practise hypnosis as well as the effectiveness of the technique remain the subject of debate and vehement disagreements. Recently, the use of hypnosis in recovering repressed memories, and accessing and attempting to integrate multiple personalities, gained a great deal of attention within psychological literature. Much of it was critical and dismissive.

There is not even a consensus on what hypnosis is, how it works and whether there are qualitative differences between it and relaxation. Unfortunately, a detailed discussion on the subject is well beyond the scope of this book.

For our purposes, we have chosen to view hypnosis on a continuum, with light relaxation at one end and deep hypnotic trance at the other. While only qualified and accredited professionals can practise deep hypnosis or hypnotherapy, we suggest that light trance can be safely practised by coaches who have been trained and supervised by a psychologist. If coaches wish to learn hypnosis they must ensure that they undertake a recognised and accredited course on the subject.

Hypnosis and visualisation are frequently used in psychotherapy to overcome phobias. Essentially, the client unlearns the connection between anxiety and a feared situation. The general procedure is for the individual to learn a relaxation response, then draw up a hierarchy of phobic anxieties. These are ranked from mild anxiety-provoking situations (e.g. thinking about entering the conference room) to high anxiety-provoking situations (e.g. delivering the presentation). The client then visualises gradually entering the feared situations in a relaxed state. Once the client has mastered his or her fears in the imagined situation, he or she confronts the feared situation in real life.

We are certainly not encouraging coaches to practise the technique discussed below with phobic or even severely anxious individuals who should immediately be referred on to a clinical psychologist.

Case Study   G. A. is a 'creative' executive in an advertising company. She experienced considerable anxiety when presenting to prospective clients. She had practised self-hypnosis in the past but had forgotten the technique and wanted to resume using it. Several coaching sessions were devoted to practising the light trance sessions described below and G. A. listened to a tape of the sessions on a daily basis. At the end of the coaching intervention, G. A. reported feeling more confident, and better prepared for making presentations. A three-month follow-up indicated that G. A. was not only receiving positive feedback on her presentations but her performance was a factor in the agency gaining more business.

Inducing a light trance state

Checklist

How to use:

✔ as a learning exercise in the coaching sessions

✔ as an audio tape for the coachee to practise with outside the sessions.

When to use:

✔ when a coachee expresses a wish to learn self-hypnosis

✔ when a coachee presents with some form of performance anxiety that he or she cannot 'work on' in real life.

Why use:

✔ to enhance self-confidence

✔ to enhance concentration

✔ to decrease anxiety

✔ to enhance a skill performance.

Exercise

Step one   Ask the coachee to relax and visualise a peaceful scene—somewhere he or she would feel calm, relaxed and safe.

Step two   Ask the coachee about the visualisation:

➤ How easy was it to visualise?

➤ Did the coachee visualise in colour?

➤ Could he or she hear sounds?

➤ Did the coachee feel 'present' at the scene?

➤ How 'real' was the experience?

➤ Did the coachee experience any difficulty visualising?

Depending on the coachee's responses, further practice at visualisation might be necessary. Otherwise, proceed to Step three.

Step three   Together with the coachee work out a hierarchy of anxiety-provoking situations. For example: (1) giving a talk to a close friend; (2) presenting in front of three

Exercise

friends; (3) presenting to four people on the team; (4) presenting in front of the team and a stranger; and finally (5) presenting in front of the team and five strangers. The trance sessions should begin with the setting that comes first on the hierarchy. Once the coachee feels comfortable with this situation, the next coaching session will involve the scenario listed second on the hierarchy and so on until the last and most anxiety-provoking scenario.

Step four Encourage the coachee to get comfortable. Do three rounds of a breathing technique as described above (e.g. a simple meditation breathing exercise) or a technique the coachee is familiar with and finds effective.

Step five Read the following script to the coachee:

Close your eyes if you feel comfortable doing so. Feel yourself starting to relax—with each breath you are feeling more and more relaxed. You are going deeper and deeper into relaxation, feeling calm, all the worries are floating away. You are feeling more and more relaxed.

Notice there is some lightness in your arm, your arm is feeling lighter and lighter. You are more and more relaxed, deeper and deeper. Your arm is feeling light—as though there is something lifting it up, lighter and lighter. Feel your arm move upwards off the chair— all the time you are feeling more and more relaxed.

Now let your arm move gently back into its original position. You are feeling calm, perfectly relaxed, tranquil and peaceful. While you are in this relaxed state see yourself in the conference room where you give your presentations. Notice how you are standing, your posture is erect, you are feeling and looking confident and calm. Feel the calmness, feel the confidence. Notice your friend sitting at the table, he is interested and absorbed in what you are saying. Hear yourself clearly introducing the product. You sound confident and relaxed. You are interesting. You are enthusiastic and calm. You are in the flow zone—your performance is smooth and effortless. You are alert but relaxed. Notice how impressed your friend is, you are calm and confident. You proceed to present your information in a clear, logical and interesting way. Your presentation is successful. You are calm and confident.

You are now at the end of the presentation. Listen to your friend enthusiastically applauding your performance—you are proud and confident.

I am going to count backwards from five to one. When I reach one I would like you to open your eyes and stretch   5   4   3   2   1.

Step six Provide the coachee with an audio tape of the session. Ask the coachee to commit to listening to the hypnosis tape daily until the next coaching session.

Exercise

Step seven If the coachee carries out the action plan and feels confident about presenting to a friend, move on to the next item on the hierarchy (i.e. presenting in front of three friends) and adjust the script accordingly. Continue on through the hierarchy until the coachee feels confident about presenting to prospective clients.

Summary Relaxation, meditation, visualisation and trance states can have a powerful effect on coachees. We suggest that coaches build a brief relaxation or meditation period into every session regardless of the coaching topic. As well as allowing the individual coachee a respite from the stress of work, it generates an atmosphere of alert calmness that can facilitate learning. Although coaches require training, supervision and practice with a clinician in the effective use of all the techniques discussed above, they have to be particularly alert to the ramifications of using trance techniques or any techniques which induce an altered state in the individual.

Problem-solving techniques

Problem solving is an integral part of coaching. Throughout the coaching sessions coaches listen and ask questions. This process guides the coachee in solving problems, exploring options, making choices and developing strategies to enhance work performance or life quality.

Problem solving in coaching can be carried out either formally or informally. The purpose of this chapter is to outline several examples of formal problem-solving models such as: a generic model for problem solving, a costs–benefits analysis, a force-field analysis, a SWOT analysis, brainstorming, an options model, and the IDEAL model.

A generic model for problem solving

The following model outlines the stages of problem solving in the context of a typical coaching intervention. The process offers the coach a structure within which to clarify the coaching issue, establish goals and determine strategies to reach these goals.

Exercise

Step one   Together with the coachee, explore the coachee's current situation as it relates to the purpose of the coaching sessions.

Step two   Work with the coachee to define the problem or issue to be addressed— preferably in one sentence.

Step three   Together, review all the coachee's possible options.

Step four   Clarify and prioritise the coachee's values.

Step five   Explore the coach's and coachee's feelings, hunches and intuitions.

Step six   Establish a hierarchy of possible goals.

Step seven   Analyse the risks, alternatives and consequences of setting and achieving these goals.

Step eight   Ask the coachee to nominate the first goal to be achieved.

Step nine   Together, list all the possible obstacles to goal achievement.

Step ten   Brainstorm solutions to these obstacles.

Step eleven   Implement the action plan.

Step twelve   Review the outcomes of the action plan and continue the process until all the nominated goals are met.

A costs–benefits analysis

Often, in a particular work or life situation, a coachee is faced with two alternatives. The individual may feel ambivalent about making a choice and can oscillate between the two alternatives, feeling more and more confused and losing sight of the available options. Or maybe, after endlessly weighing up the options, the individual may be inclined to make an impulsive, emotional decision that he or she later regrets. The coach's role can be to work with the coachee to clarify the available alternatives and make a rational choice or decision. As the following case scenario demonstrates, a costs–benefits analysis is a simple yet effective formula for working with alternatives and choices.

Case Study

S. N. is a 49-year-old accountant and long-time senior partner of a large accounting firm. He is dissatisfied with his position, and feels there is no room for advancement and that the work increasingly lacks interest and challenge. S. N. has always dreamed of setting up his own accountancy practice but the prospect of financial uncertainty, working on his own and having to market his services to a new client base is daunting. The ongoing state of indecision and restlessness was producing constant tension in S. N. who decided to work with his personal, external coach in order to bring some resolution and relief to his predicament. The coach and S. N. employed the costs–benefits analysis model to analyse his dilemma.

Exercise

Step one   The coach asked S. N. to nominate the two available alternatives, for example remaining an employee (alternative 1) or starting his own accounting practice (alternative 2).

Step two   The coach asked S. N. to list the costs and benefits of alternative 1 (remaining an employee). For example:

Costs	Benefits
Lack of challenge	Financial security
Brick wall—no room for advancement	Co-worker support
Boredom	Established client base

Step three   The coach asked S. N. to list the costs and benefits of alternative 2 (setting up his accounting practice). For example:

Costs	Benefits
Unstable income	Challenge, excitement
Lack of social and professional support	Flexible time schedule
Marketing and establishing a client base	Increased self-worth

Step four   Together, the coach and S. N. examined which of S. N.'s core values were at stake. For example: financial security (value 1) *versus* autonomy (value 2).

Step five   The coach suggested to S. N. that he had to choose between the two values or accept that he was unwilling or unable to make a choice.

Step six   S. N. chose financial security as being more critically important to him at this stage of his life. Together the coach and S. N. worked together to better manage the 'costs' of remaining in the work situation. For example:

➤ How could S. N. make the work situation more challenging?

➤ Could he make a lateral move in the company?

➤ Could he introduce a project he could manage?

➤ Was there a mentoring role for S. N. in the company?

➤ Could S. N. change how he thinks or feels about work?

If the coachee had chosen autonomy and consulting, the coach and coachee would work together to manage the 'costs' of leaving stable employment. For example:

➤ How can the coachee budget to allow for the initial loss of income? Would it be practical to remain in the current position on a part-time basis until the consultancy business is built up? How could the coachee cut down on current living costs?

➤ How could the coachee exploit his or her current network?

➤ What skills does the coachee lack to be a successful consultant?

➤ How could these skills best be acquired?

➤ What strengths does the coachee have that can be exploited?

A force-field analysis

Based on Kurt Lewin's 'field theory', force-field analysis describes the field of forces or pressures acting on a particular event at any given time. In essence, the theory suggests that forces that act to change a situation are balanced by forces that act to resist the change. Force-field analysis is a method for listing, discussing and working with the forces that will positively or negatively affect a coaching intervention, or change itself. The analysis allows both the coach and coachee (or the organisation) to recognise and work with the forces that can assist or impede the proposed changes.

Positive forces that assist in effecting change are called 'driving forces' while those impeding or obstructing change are called 'restraining forces'. Through brainstorming, exploring, analysing and charting these forces the coach and coachee can:

➤ establish what kind of obstacles are likely to be encountered

➤ determine what forces might be marshalled and strengthened to promote the desired changes

➤ identify what resources and ongoing support structures might be necessary

➤ develop an action plan to weaken the opposing forces

➤ develop a method of monitoring and evaluating the shifting forces.

 Case Study   J. H. is a coach in a medium- to large-sized financial organisation. He has been coaching several individuals for over a year. During this time the company has been restructured. As a result, staff with technical expertise have been promoted to managerial positions for which they lack managerial and interpersonal skills. The organisation's training program is not adequate to meet the employees' needs, staff morale is low and customer complaints are escalating. Two of the senior managers being coached by J. H. firmly believe, as does J. H., that a coaching program will produce significant positive changes in the company.

However, there is considerable opposition to the idea from several senior managers. The major objections are that there is not sufficient staff to take on a coaching role, external coaches won't be familiar with the culture of the organisation and the training budget has been cut. Finally, there is a belief among some managers that change would be more disruptive than beneficial and also a 'we've always done it this way' mentality. J. H. arranged a meeting with the CEO, the management team and HR personnel to discuss the introduction of a coaching program. Because of the known forces pushing for change, as well as those forces resisting change, J. H. chose to use the force-field analysis model to explore the issue.

Exercise

Step one On a whiteboard, J. H. drew the following diagram which summarised the forces working for change (driving forces) and those working against change (the restraining forces).

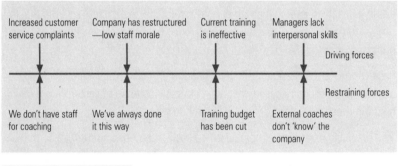

Figure 14.1 Driving and restraining forces in introducing a coaching program

Step two J. H. requested that all attendees worked together to reach a consensus on the impact (high (H), medium (M) or low (L)) of each of these forces. Figure 14.2 illustrates the results of this collaboration.

Step three It is generally agreed that when working with a force-field analysis, change is more likely to be produced by weakening the restraining forces. Therefore, J. H.'s strategy was to work with the organisation on the following restraining forces that could hinder the introduction of the coaching program.

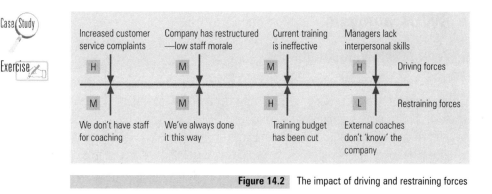

Increased customer service complaints	Company has restructured —low staff morale	Current training is ineffective	Managers lack interpersonal skills	
H	M	M	H	Driving forces
M	M	H	L	Restraining forces
We don't have staff for coaching	We've always done it this way	Training budget has been cut	External coaches don't 'know' the company	

Figure 14.2   The impact of driving and restraining forces

1   The training budget has been cut (H)

➤ How can we rationalise the training budget to derive most benefit?

➤ Can coaching replace any current, expensive training programs?

➤ Can coaching be added on to any training program to ensure transfer of skills?

2   We don't have the staff for coaching (M) and external coaches don't know the company (L)

➤ Can we train existing staff so they can carry out a coaching program?

➤ What skills do coaches need?

➤ How can these be best acquired? What training programs are available for coaches?

3   We've always done it this way (M)

➤ How has maintaining the status quo benefited the company?

➤ What are the disadvantages of not changing?

➤ What can be gained from introducing coaching?

➤ How do these benefits meet the challenges facing the company?

➤ What will happen if change does not occur?

Through discussion, brainstorming and, importantly, collaboration, the forces and questions raised by J. H. were clarified and analysed in ongoing meetings. Eventually, a successful coaching program for all senior managers and managers was introduced in the organisation.

A SWOT analysis

1 With an individual coachee

A SWOT analysis involves analysing and working with the strengths, weaknesses, options and threats pertinent to a particular situation. Strengths and weaknesses are internal forces at play, whereas opportunities and threats refer to external forces impacting on the situation. The coach can employ this method of problem solving with an individual coachee when, for instance, the coachee is deciding upon a career move or when working with small businesses or organisations.

Case Study — P. T. is a successful lawyer in a public organisation. For various reasons, such as limited opportunities for promotion and difficult colleagues, she applied for a position with a prestigious private law firm. However, when she was offered the position P. T. became anxious and ambivalent. Her coach suggested they conduct a SWOT analysis to analyse and explore P. T.'s career situation. Together, P. T. and the coach constructed the following analysis.

Strengths:

➤ relevant specialist knowledge of law

➤ diligent, learns quickly

➤ experienced team worker and team leader.

Weaknesses:

➤ fear of failure

➤ lack of experience working in the private sector

➤ moderate presentation skills.

Opportunities:

➤ greater chance for promotion

➤ experience working with a prestigious law firm

➤ possibilities of working internationally.

Threats:

➤ limited job security in a very competitive arena

➤ burnout due to the 'notorious' demands the law firm imposed on new recruits.

Through the use of the SWOT analysis, the coach and P. T. were able to isolate the strengths that could be enhanced and the weaknesses that P. T. would need to overcome. Action plans were put in place to produce these changes, and P. T. developed contingency plans to deal with the perceived threat in terms of job security. Stress management techniques and strategies to sustain a life/work balance were introduced in order to offset the potential for burnout.

2 A SWOT analysis in organisations

As the following case study illustrates, a SWOT analysis is also a useful tool for analysing the coaching needs of an organisation.

Case Study

W. W. is an executive coach who was approached by the training manager of a medium- to large-sized bank to discuss the possible introduction of a coaching program for the senior staff. The training manager was convinced of the benefits of coaching but was uncertain as to how a coaching program would 'fit' with the bank's culture, and learning and development needs. W. W. decided to apply a SWOT analysis in order to determine the bank's needs and the ways in which a coaching program could successfully meet these.

A SWOT questionnaire was distributed to all senior executives and their staff. The results of the survey established the following view of the organisation with regard to staff relations.

Strengths:

➤ There are good relations between top and middle management.

➤ Staff are optimistic.

➤ Staff are respectful of each other and each other's job demands.

Weaknesses:

➤ Staff are not willing to discuss difficult issues.

➤ Creativity is stifled by conformity.

➤ Staff do not stretch or challenge themselves.

Opportunities:

➤ Key managers are well placed to support a coaching program.

➤ The CEO and senior managers value development of individual staff.

➤ A new appraisal system has been introduced.

Threats:

➤ The company does not have internal staff who are trained to develop and implement the coaching program.

➤ Some managers view coaching as 'too soft'.

While it is beyond the scope of this chapter to detail the entire SWOT analysis carried out in the organisation, other areas which the analysis was applied to included:

➤ Leadership

➤ Interpersonal skills of managers

➤ Staff training and development

➤ Team relations

➤ Evaluation of current learning and development programs

Having completed the analysis, W.W. was able to present a proposal to the training manager that outlined specific needs that the coaching program could address. The process of completing the questionnaires also served to align staff to the introduction of coaching.

Brainstorming

Brainstorming can be employed with a team or an individual coachee. Research suggests however that when two or more people brainstorm together they do not generate as many ideas as individuals would if they were constructing a separate list. The phenomenon is known as 'production blocking' and it occurs when individuals are too polite to spontaneously announce their ideas in a group situation, especially when others are talking.

Similarly, when an individual coachee is brainstorming with a coach, he or she may be intimidated by the coach's suggestions and feel inhibited about expressing his or her own ideas. It could be useful then if the coach suggests that each individual first draws up his or her own list of ideas and then offers them up for discussion.

1 Brainstorming in team coaching

Case Study J. M. is coaching a group of managers in a large retail company. One of the issues that has arisen during the course of the coaching sessions is the need for a more effective appraisal system that will allow goals and action plans to be individually developed for all staff. As the current appraisal system is haphazard, and essentially just a formality, J. M. decided the most effective way to solve the problem was to conduct a group brainstorming session.

Exercise **Step one** Guidelines for the brainstorming session were clarified with the team. These included the following:

1 Spontaneity was encouraged. Evaluation would occur later in the process.

2 All ideas were to be considered.

3 All ideas were to be given equal weight.

4 Negative comments were discouraged.

5 Combining ideas or 'piggy-backing' of ideas was encouraged to develop concepts.

6 Quantity was considered more important than quality.

Step two Team members were allocated time to generate ideas individually.

Step three W. W. called for ideas from the group and listed them on a whiteboard.

Step four Impossible or impractical ideas were discarded.

Step five Through consensus, the best three ideas were chosen.

Step six The group conducted a SWOT analysis of these three ideas.

Step seven The best idea was selected.

Step eight Goals were established to realise the idea.

Step nine The coach and team developed an action plan and established monitoring and evaluation methods to track the goals.

Step ten The goals were reviewed and evaluated on an ongoing basis.

2 Brainstorming with an individual coachee

Case Study M. N. is a 40-year-old senior manager, recently promoted to an executive position that required her to relocate to another city. She had no friends or support network in the new city. M. N. saw her social isolation as embarrassing. She was extremely independent and the coach suspected that she was somewhat hesitant about discussing personal aspects of her life. In order to make the exploration and analysis less threatening the coach decided to use brainstorming as a means of generating ways in which M. N. could develop a social network.

Exercise **Step one** The coach and M. N. discussed the goal of the brainstorming session:

➤ What problem or issue does M. N. wish to solve?

➤ What does M. N. wish to gain by solving this problem?

➤ How will the situation look when the problem has been solved?

➤ What is the single, most important thing M. N. wants to gain?

➤ What might M. N. lose?

➤ What is M. N. prepared to trade-off?

Step two The coach encouraged M. N. to be spontaneous and to generate as many ideas as possible.

Step three The coach and M. N. individually generated their own ideas.

Step four M. N. listed all the ideas on a whiteboard.

Step five M. N. chose the three best ideas.

Step six The coach and M. N. conducted a SWOT analysis of these ideas.

Step seven Together M. N. and the coach established goals to realise the ideas.

Step eight The coach and M. N. developed an action plan, and established monitoring and evaluation strategies.

Step nine The action plan was reviewed and evaluated.

An options model for problem solving

Sometimes a coachee is faced with a situation that requires a choice between changing the situation, changing his or her attitude towards the situation, tolerating the situation or leaving it.

The following model is a simple yet effective method of working with the coachee to recognise his or her options in a specific situation.

Case Study

T. E. is a 30-year-old technician working with a very difficult, demanding and aggressive colleague. He has reached the stage where he dreads going to work. Not only is his constant state of tension impacting on his work performance but his home life is also suffering. Family arguments are escalating, he is emotionally unavailable to his wife and children and his health is being adversely affected. T. E. is unable or unwilling to take any effective steps to change the situation and is feeling overwhelmed and virtually powerless. The coach decided that the options model of problem solving would be particularly appropriate for T. E.

Option one   Changing the situation

➤ Can T. E. approach the demanding colleague and discuss the difficulties he is experiencing working with him or her?

➤ Can T. E. approach the CEO and ask to work on another project?

Option two   Change one's self

➤ Can T. E. change his beliefs about the colleague?

➤ Can T. E. change the way he feels about the colleague?

➤ Can T. E. change his expectations about the colleague's behaviour?

➤ Can T. E. be more assertive? less defensive?

Option three   Tolerate the situation

➤ Can T. E. choose to ignore the colleague's rudeness?

➤ Can T. E. be more light-hearted about the situation?

➤ Can T. E. see any humour in the situation?

➤ Does the colleague have strengths and knowledge that T. E. can focus on and benefit from?

Option four   Leave the situation

If the situation cannot be changed, and T. E. is unwilling or unable to change his attitude or tolerate the existing state of affairs, the only option may be to leave the job. The coach and T. E. would explore this final option.

➤ What would be the financial repercussions of leaving?

➤ Are other jobs readily available?

➤ What competencies does T. E. need to develop or acquire for a new position?

➤ How will his decision impact on his family? his colleagues?

➤ How can the coach best assist T. E.?

The IDEAL model for problem solving

The IDEAL model (identifying, defining, exploring, acting and looking back) has been adapted from the work of Newell and Simon who applied information-processing theory to human problem solving. The IDEAL model is especially useful in coaching for skills. Together, the coach and coachee can assess the skills deficit and design an appropriate action plan to develop new skills or enhance existing skills.

Case Study

K. L. is a senior manager who presented a rather conflicting picture of his work situation to the coach. According to K. L., he was fulfilling his role as a team leader with considerable skill and success. Yet his colleagues complained of K. L.'s poor interpersonal skills and his seeming indifference to their work pressures and deadlines. K. L. was mystified about (and rather angry at) his colleagues' appraisal of him. He was challenging and slightly hostile to the coach, demanding to know what approach the coach would use to 'fix' the situation. After discussing the role of the coach and K. L.'s expectations of the coaching sessions, the coach determined that the IDEAL model—because of its simplicity and clear structure—would answer K. L.'s concerns and best facilitate change.

Stage one Identifying

➤ What is the problem?

➤ What is causing the difficulty?

➤ What is maintaining the problem?

➤ What skills are missing?

Stage two Defining

➤ What are the major features of the problem?

➤ What is the core element of the problem?

➤ How can we best define the problem?

Case Study

Stage three   Exploring

➤ What aspects of the problem can be worked with?

➤ What specific new skills are necessary?

➤ What existing skills can be enhanced?

Stage four   Acting

➤ What actions have to be taken?

➤ How can the skills best be learned?

➤ How can the skills best be transferred to the workplace?

Stage five   Looking back

➤ How is K. L. performing?

➤ How is K. L.'s behaviour different?

➤ In what ways has K. L.'s new skills impacted on his work performance?

Summary

Problem solving underscores most coaching interventions. As with most other techniques, not all problem-solving methods are appropriate for all coachees or all problems. Frequently, the coachee has his or her own tried and true procedure for working through an issue. In such cases the coach should discuss why the coachee has chosen a particular method and whether it is the most effective and appropriate for the problem at hand. The coach can then introduce a wider selection of problem-solving techniques from which the coachee can choose.

Role-playing

Role-playing is a well documented and frequently used method of learning. After several years of working with executives we have found it to be a powerful and valuable coaching tool. Role-playing can be performed by a single individual protagonist or with help from other individuals such as the coach.

Dramatic role-playing—adopting a persona

In order to challenge our attitudes and behaviour it may be necessary to understand and internalise another person's point of view or way of being in the world. Acting out a 'character role' gives the coachee the unique opportunity to realise and understand another individual's outlook.

Dramatic role-playing requires that the individual temporarily assume the persona of another or act out a role that is diametrically opposed to his or her usual behaviour. Rather than having to work through emotions and self-limiting beliefs, a role-play can engender understanding and empathy for the other. For instance, the coachee may role-play a colleague with whom he or she is having difficulties. Acting the role of the colleague may enable the coachee to experience and better understand the colleague's emotions and attitudes. It can provide the coachee with the opportunity to recognise and accept the internal logic of the colleague's previously incomprehensible or frustrating behaviour. The coachee is then able to script and role-play his or her own new behaviour in the light of the acquired insight and empathy.

Case Study F. E. is a 36-year-old male who was referred for coaching by the CEO in relation to ongoing interpersonal difficulties with a recently promoted senior manager. F. E. had been opposed to the promotion from the beginning and considered the new manager to be incompetent and dictatorial. The coach asked F. E. to role-play the senior manager while the coach acted out F. E.'s habitual style of relating to him. By adopting the senior manager's role, F. E. began to understand some of the difficulties the senior manager was facing. F. E. began to appreciate that the senior manager's behaviour was a function of insecurity and a perceived lack of support from above. As a result, F. E. was able to soften his approach and take a more collaborative rather than combative stance towards his colleague.

Role-playing for attitude change

A second, less dramatic role-play method involves the coachee adopting a position or point of view that differs greatly from his or her own perspective. Research from social psychology suggests that individuals tend to ignore evidence that is contrary to their beliefs. We employ defence mechanisms and often do not even remember contrary or challenging facts. However, research indicates that when an individual is asked to present an argument that is opposed to his or her usual viewpoint there is a shift in the direction of the espoused beliefs. That is, we change our attitudes to the position we are advocating and become receptive to information supporting this view.

Role-playing for attitude change can be a useful vehicle for the coach. It can be especially effective when the coach is encouraging the coachee to alter his or her attitude towards an event or an individual because the attitude is preventing the coachee from changing and growing.

Case Study J. J. is a 45-year-old senior manager working with a coach to enhance her presentation skills. Although she has been to several workshops on presenting and appeared to have a sound knowledge of what a successful presentation involved, she was reluctant to put these skills into practice. Through talking with J. J., the coach determined that the fundamental barrier to J. J.'s progress was her belief that assertiveness (which she equated with aggressiveness) was antithetical to her personal beliefs and the company's mission. The coach requested that J. J. make a presentation in the coaching session on the advantages of being assertive, and how adopting an assertive role would benefit her and the organisation. After the presentation, the coach challenged J. J. to defend her stated position. As expected, J. J. was able to look at the issue of assertion in a more positive and objective light. Together, the coach and J. J. went on to establish goals and strategies to enhance J. J.'s presentation skills.

The 'as if' technique

The 'as if' technique can be viewed as a type of role-playing. It involves trying out a new lifestyle or way of behaving. For instance, an individual may act 'as if' he or she is organised, calm or confident for a period of two weeks. It is not a technique for learning new skills as such but rather a means of changing how one thinks about and experiences self, others and the world in general. George Kelly, who developed this technique, suggested that individuals should think of their old personality as being on vacation during these two weeks.

The purpose of the 'as if' technique is to:

➤ find more satisfying ways of behaving, thinking, and interacting with the world

➤ test different styles of behaviour in real life situations to see how they work

➤ improve self-concept.

As the following case study demonstrates, the 'as if' technique can be particularly useful in coaching when the coach and coachee do not wish to explore emotional states or ways of behaving. Instead, the coaching intervention is aimed towards changing the behaviour first, and then exploring what has been learned and which of the new behaviours the coachee wishes to keep.

Case Study

D. M. is a 36-year-old librarian who tended to be overemotional and prone to episodes of stress and discomfort which were affecting her work relationships. The coach and D. M. agreed that D. M.'s issues did not warrant a referral for therapy and that together they could work on the situation. The coach decided that as well as working with D. M. on relaxation strategies, she would employ the 'as if' technique whereby D. M. agreed to act 'as if' she were calm and relaxed for two weeks.

Exercise

Step one The coach asked D. M. to write a description of her current life style and ways of behaving. D. M.'s description of herself was as follows:

I am essentially good-natured and empathic but respond to the problems of others by becoming overly involved and upset. I take everything personally and seriously and often respond intensely to minor provocation. Although intelligent, my emotions often take precedence over my rational mind and I am not using my intelligence effectively to solve problems.

Step two   The coach then asked D. M. to write a description of her new behaviour and life style.

D. M. wrote that she would not seek out people with problems. Although she would remain compassionate, she would distance herself and not 'own' other people's emotions or problems. She would practise relaxation and would be lighthearted and calm even in the face of difficulties. She would enjoy life more and be fun to be with.

Step three   The coach and D. M. agreed that D. M. would inform significant others of the changes in her lifestyle and that she would act in the new way for the following two weeks. During this period D. M. would keep a diary of her experiences.

Step four   After the two-week interval the coach and D. M. devoted three sessions to discussing what D. M. had learned about herself in the experiment and which aspects of the new lifestyle she wished to keep.

Step five   Together, D. M. and the coach worked on strategies to ensure that the chosen new behaviours would become fully integrated and sustained.

Of course, the 'as if' technique is not suitable for all coachees. If the individual's problems are serious enough to warrant therapy the coach should not continue on with the coaching relationship, even if the coachee may be disinclined to take the therapy route. However, if the coachee is psychologically and emotionally intact then using the 'as if' technique can circumvent an exploration of emotions and beliefs by working directly and immediately to change the individual's habitual behaviour.

Role-playing for skills acquisition

We have found role-playing to be particularly useful when coaching individuals for interpersonal skills or dealing effectively with clients and customers. Some specific areas of coaching where role-playing produces powerful results include:

➤ assertion skills (e.g. practising specific assertion statements)

➤ anger management skills (e.g. controlling anger outbursts at work)

➤ client presentation skills (e.g. presenting to prospective clients)

➤ sales skills (e.g. closing a deal)

> people skills (e.g. dealing with clients)

> feedback skills (e.g. conducting performance appraisals)

> conflict-management skills (e.g. dealing with a difficult colleague).

In essence, role-playing for skills acquisition involves the coach and coachee in playing out a script. It is a cost-effective and efficient method of learning new skills and enhancing current skills. However, no matter how realistic the simulation, skills can only be thoroughly learned by being exercised in a natural setting. Role-playing is therefore always a prelude to the coachee applying the skills in a real-life situation.

Training often involves role-playing. However, individuals may be guarded, competitive and anxious when performing in front of a group. The one-on-one nature of coaching provides the individual with privacy and immediate feedback. The coach can also supply ongoing support and reassurance to the coachee. Finally, the role-play can be specifically tailored to the individual's needs and situation.

Some role-playing techniques

1   The coach and coachee can script the role-play, videotape it and then critique it together.

2   The coach and coachee can role-play the specific situation, stopping at particular points so that the coach can review and critique what has just occurred. The coachee can then repeat the episode incorporating the coach's suggestions or move on to the next stage of the script.

A dramatic role-play for acquiring or enhancing skills

Some coaches may be familiar with role-playing and may have developed their own techniques to suit their particular style. There are no hard and fast rules about role-playing. However we have found the following model and guidelines to be useful.

Checklist

How to use:

✔   within the coaching session

✔   as a homework/practice exercise.

When to use:

✔   when coaching for interpersonal skills

✔   when coaching for customer and sales skills.

Why use:

✔ to practise and rehearse new skills in a safe environment

✔ to gain confidence

✔ to learn from immediate feedback

✔ to prepare for difficult situations in the future.

Step one   Explain the purpose and benefits of the role-play to the coachee.

Step two   Agree on whether the role-play will be videotaped or not.

Step three   Ask the coachee to clearly nominate the target skills, for example managing anger.

Step four   Ask the coachee to describe, in detail, a previous incident where he or she has responded inappropriately (e.g. with anger). Determine what the coachee was thinking and feeling at the time. Ask the coachee to describe, in detail, the behaviour of the other person(s) involved in the incident.

Step five   The coach and coachee then role-play this situation. The coachee plays himself or herself and the coach role-plays the 'other'.

Step six   Together the coach and coachee devise a script around a potential conflict situation.

Step seven   The coachee is directed to role-play the opposite position to the one he or she would normally take, for example a non-aggressive, polite role.

Step eight   The coach and coachee continue to devise scripts and practise the coachee's new behaviour, varying the potential conflict situations.

Step nine   The coach creates 'surprise' scenarios that the coachee might encounter. The coachee has to role-play his or her new responses in order to rehearse potentially difficult situations so he or she feels more comfortable when they arise.

A generic role-play model for acquiring and enhancing skills

Step one   Explain the purpose and benefits of the role-play to the coachee.

Step two   Agree on whether the role-play will be videotaped or not.

Step three   Ask the coachee to clearly nominate the target skills, for example making effective sales calls to prospective clients.

Exercise

Step four   The coach and coachee have to agree on the coach's role:

➤ Will the coach play a hostile prospect? A talkative customer? A demanding supervisor?

➤ Will the coach intervene during the presentation or when it is over?

➤ Will the coach model the desired behaviours?

Step five   Ask the coachee to role-play the target behaviour or skills.

Step six   Give feedback to the coachee either during the role-play or at the end, as agreed previously. (See below for details on giving feedback.)

Step seven   Ask the coachee to re-enact the scenario from beginning to end.

Step eight   Request that the coachee practise the behaviours in front of a mirror, or (preferably) in front of a friend or family members.

Step nine   Encourage the coachee to practise the skill in a real-life setting.

Step ten   Review and practise the skill until the coachee achieves the desired level of performance.

Giving feedback

After a role-play the coach should:

➤ ask the coachee to critique his or her own performance

➤ ensure that the coachee discusses both his or her strengths and weaknesses

➤ ask the coachee what he or she has learned

➤ ask what the coachee would like to change about his or her performance

➤ ask the coachee how easy it will be to transfer the new behaviour/skills to the real world

➤ draw up an action plan and ensure the coachee is committed to practising the skill

➤ establish review and feedback procedures.

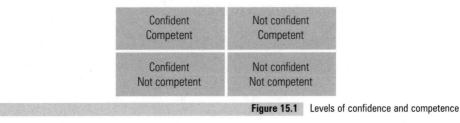

Figure 15.1   Levels of confidence and competence

As practising coaches, we have found the following model, adapted from Buckley and Caple (1996), to be a useful guide when giving feedback to the coachee on his or her performance in a role-play. As shown in Figure 15.1, the model has four levels.

Confident and competent While this level is clearly the one both the coach and coachee desire, there is always something the coachee can learn. We view this situation as an opportunity for the coach to 'stretch' the coachee and role-play a more difficult or challenging situation.

Not confident and competent The coach may have to assure the coachee that he or she has reached the requisite standards. Lack of confidence may be related to the coachee's self-limiting beliefs or unrealistic standards of perfection. If so, the coach should explore these. The coach might also encourage the coachee to enact the role-play in front of others in order to get corroborative feedback that he or she is performing well.

Confident and not competent The coach can be in a difficult situation when the coachee incorrectly believes that he or she is competent at a task. We suggest it may be useful to videotape the coachee's performance so that there is 'hard evidence' to the contrary. Furthermore, the coach can encourage the coachee to seek independent feedback about his or her performance.

Not confident and not competent If the coachee evidently lacks the requisite skills, the coach may recommend technical skills training. Providing the coachee with videos, tapes or books to enhance performance can be helpful. If motivation appears to be an issue, the coach should explore the coachee's values and motivators. Conflicts may have to be resolved before the coachee can move forwards.

Summary Role-playing, as with all the techniques discussed in this book, has to be used judiciously. If the client suggests that simulation is too artificial and unrelated to the real situation, then the chances are that he or she will not benefit from the exercise. However, the coach should spend extra time explaining the rationale of role-playing to the coachee, emphasising the opportunity it presents for rehearsing skills in a safe, learning environment. The coach also has to appreciate the value of the technique and feel comfortable and competent in playing his or her role realistically and without any signs of self-consciousness or unease.

Journalling and mind-mapping

Although journalling and mind-mapping are both written exercises, they are distinct techniques and should be thought of as such. Journalling is a written record, in various forms, that enables the coachee to monitor, reflect upon and record different aspects of the coaching experience. Mind-mapping, although it too can stimulate creative thinking, is essentially a visual means of organising information.

Journalling

Journalling involves keeping a personal record containing observations and reflections about our thoughts, feelings and actions. Our lives are an ongoing process of organising and structuring our experiences. Writing can open up new possibilities for making meaning out of our lives. Keeping a personal journal, regardless of its format, can be a means of creating the self and increasing self-knowledge. As Anaïs Nin states, it can link the content of a dream to our actions so that they become harmonious and interactive (cited in Rainer 1978). Our writings, observations and musings also reveal the extent to which we have control over, and responsibility for, how we perceive the world. Journal writing also provides access to our inner self. It can tap into our intuition and reveal aspects of ourselves that may otherwise remain hidden. It is generally agreed that writing taps into a deeper level of creativity, self-discovery and self-awareness than the spoken word. Writing helps us to crystallise our thoughts and makes action more likely.

There are various forms of journalling. It can involve keeping a personal diary, life-mapping, writing a book of one's life, making lists, and asking and answering questions. Importantly, keeping a diary or journal can allow the coachee to monitor his or her own thoughts, feelings and behaviours, particularly in the context of learning a new skill.

Through journalling, the coachee can:

➤ access questions and solutions more easily

➤ develop new and broader perspectives on self and others

➤ clarify, track and actualise goals

➤ monitor new skills and behaviours

➤ develop awareness of self-limiting beliefs

➤ understand how he or she learns best

➤ integrate life experiences.

Some guidelines for journal writing

1 Journal writing can take time and requires patience and self-discipline on the part of the coachee.

2 Writing about oneself is sometimes viewed as 'adolescent self-absorption'. It is crucial that the coach emphasises to the coachee that journalling is essentially a learning experience.

3 As Jung noted, it is important that self-exploration be balanced with a strong basis in day-to-day reality.

4 Diaries are generally considered to be private and confidential memoirs. The coachee must have the choice as to whether to share its contents with the coach or not.

The coach can suggest the following journalling techniques at various stages of the coaching intervention. Usually the coachee brings the journal or observations to each session for further discussion and feedback from the coach.

Journalling techniques

Diaries

1 A coaching diary

A coaching diary is an efficient and relatively simple technique through which a coachee can document his or her development during the various stages of the coaching intervention. It provides the coachee with a way to review and evaluate the progress of the sessions.

Checklist

How to use:

✔ as a special book or journal that the coachee can make regular entries in—these will be discussed at specified coaching sessions.

When to use:

✔ when coachees are monitoring self-limiting beliefs and dealing with emotions

✔ at the beginning of the coaching intervention.

Why use:

✔ to evaluate the outcome of the coaching sessions

✔ to enhance self-monitoring skills

✔ to generate further topics for discussion.

There is no one prescribed method for maintaining a coaching diary. The coachee may choose to write in free-form—jotting down reflections, ideas, feelings and intuitions about the coaching alliance. It is critical though that the coachee's entries be made on a regular, ongoing basis.

Coachees may also choose to use a more structured form of diary writing. Such a diary could include the following questions:

➤ What have I learned in this coaching session?

➤ How will that assist me?

➤ Where can I use what I have learned?

➤ How has what I have learned so far impacted on my usual behaviour?

➤ How do I feel about the coach?

➤ How has my attitude toward the coach, and coaching, changed since the last entry?

➤ Are my expectations about coaching being met?

➤ Do I have any needs that are not being met through coaching?

➤ Am I progressing at a rate that I find satisfactory?

➤ In what way(s) have I benefited most from the coaching sessions?

2 A self-awareness diary

As we have already noted, self-awareness is a critical competency for a coach and a necessary condition for change on the part of the coachee.

Checklist

How to use:

✔ as an exercise for the coachee to carry out on a daily basis for at least three weeks—the coachee can choose to either share or not share his or her reflections with the coach.

When to use:

✔ when a coachee appears to be reacting to, rather than directing, his or her own life

✔ when a coachee seems to lack self-awareness.

Why use:

✔ to enhance self-awareness

✔ to help recognise patterns

✔ to encourage responsibility for behaviour.

Exercise

Step one   Prepare the following list of questions for the coachee and ask him or her to answer them on a daily basis for at least three weeks.

➤ What themes occupied my mind today?

➤ What life situations were particularly significant?

➤ What life situations were particularly difficult or burdensome?

➤ What made me feel good?

➤ What made me feel bad?

➤ What strategies did I use to manage my thoughts?

➤ How effective were these strategies?

➤ How well did I manage my feelings?

➤ Did I try anything new?

➤ What did I enjoy most today?

➤ What did I learn today?

➤ What will I do differently tomorrow?

Step two   If the coachee agrees to share the journal, discuss its contents—either during or after the three weeks.

3 A situational diary

A particularly effective journalling technique is one in which the coachee makes regular diary entries relating to the topic or issue being addressed in the coaching sessions, such as dealing with a difficult colleague.

Checklist

How to use:

✔ as a technique whereby the coachee makes three or four entries per week over the entire coaching period.

When to use:

✔ when the coachee seems to lack an awareness of the thoughts and feelings surrounding a specific skill.

Why use:

✔ to enhance the awareness of thoughts and feelings that are impacting on performance

✔ to generate strategies to change undesired behaviours.

Step one   Draw the following charts for the coachee.

Situation	Reactions
1 Describe what happened.	1 What were my feelings? 2 What was I thinking? 3 What did I do?

1 How do I feel about my feelings?

2 How do I feel about my thoughts?

3 How do I feel about my actions?

4 What did I learn from the situation?

1 What might I change about:

- my feelings?

- my thoughts?

- my actions?

2 What three goals might bring about these changes?

✎

✎

✎

Step two Ask the coachee to complete the charts immediately after the relevant incident(s). The coach and coachee discuss the coachee's diary entries together in the following coaching sessions.

4 A self-monitoring diary

Self-monitoring, as mentioned previously, is a means of bringing about changes in behaviour. It is useful to supply the coachee with a structure to help conduct the procedure.

Checklist

How to use:

✔ as an ongoing assignment throughout the coaching program.

When to use:

✔ when a coachee is developing or enhancing a specific skill such as assertiveness.

Why use:

✔ to monitor the frequency of the desired behaviour

✔ to chart the progress of the coaching program

✔ to encourage self-monitoring and journalling in the acquisition of future skills.

Exercise **Step one**   The coach and coachee should select the specific skill for development or enhancement.

Step two   Provide the coachee with the following list of questions to be answered at the end of each day:

➤ How many times did I engage in the behaviour?

➤ How many times did I not engage in the behaviour when I could have?

➤ Why did I engage in the behaviour?

➤ Why did I avoid the behaviour?

Step three   At each coaching session ask the coachee:

➤ Was keeping a journal useful for you?

➤ In what way was it useful?

➤ What changes did it help bring about?

Step four   Review the journal entries and give feedback to the coachee.

5 A structured-question diary

One method for structuring the coachee's observations, reflections and comments is to list a series of questions and ask the coachee to keep an account of these on a regular basis. A structured-question diary can be especially useful when the coachee is exploring values, anger responses, time-management issues or the development of interpersonal skills.

A values diary

➤ Is my life purpose clear to me?

➤ What gives me the greatest happiness in my life?

➤ What three values are most important to me now?

➤ Which of these values is my top priority right now?

➤ What do I have to do to realise the three values?

➤ In what ways do I express my values in my everyday life?

➤ What do I have to do to express my values more clearly?

An anger diary

➤ What situation(s) made me angry?

➤ What happened? When? Where?

➤ What was I thinking?

- ➤ What was I feeling?
- ➤ What irritated me the most?
- ➤ What did I do?
- ➤ What do I think about what I did?
- ➤ How do I feel about what I did?
- ➤ What could I do differently next time?

A time-management diary

- ➤ Where can I be more efficient in my life?
- ➤ What are my 'time wasters'?
- ➤ What are three things I should be doing but am currently avoiding?
- ➤ What excuses do I use to procrastinate?
- ➤ What goal(s) can I establish to manage my time better?
- ➤ What is the first action I must take to reach this goal?

An interpersonal-skills diary

- ➤ What interpersonal skill do I most need to develop?
- ➤ How can I enhance this skill?
- ➤ What beliefs are getting in my way?
- ➤ What feelings are preventing me from changing and developing?
- ➤ How and where can I practise the new skill?
- ➤ How do I feel when I try out the new behaviour?

A book of one's life

Writing a book of one's life is another variant of journalling. The coachee does not of course have to write an entire autobiography—he or she simply writes a title for the book, a table of contents and details of one chapter.

Checklist

How to use:

- ✔ as an exercise the coachee can do throughout the coaching sessions, and after he or she has finished.

When to use:

- ✔ when the coachee appears to lack direction or identity
- ✔ when the coachee's life seems to lack coherence.

Why use:

- ✔ to recognise patterns in one's life

- ✔ to highlight peak experiences

- ✔ to better understand any unresolved experiences from the past.

The coach should give the coachee the following instructions:

1   Write a *book title* that best captures the essence or flavour of your life.

2   Write a *table of contents* for the book—the contents should highlight the key points or experiences of your life.

3   *Choose one chapter heading* that is especially significant to you and list five experiences you would talk about in this chapter. How have these experiences impacted on your life?

4   Revise the title and chapter headings of your book. What are they?

Life-mapping

It is generally accepted that each of us has a unique life map or path encompassing all our individual routes and journeys. Our life map reveals our values and goals, our successes and failures, and the choices we have made that have determined our destiny. Life-mapping is a valuable technique to help the coachee clarify his or her life path.

How to use:

- ✔ as an exercise for the coachee to carry out early on in the coaching intervention.

When to use:

- ✔ when the coachee is experiencing a conflict of values

- ✔ when the coach recognises life patterns which the coachee may not be aware of.

Why use:

- ✔ to empower a coachee who may feel that life has just 'happened' to him or her

- ✔ to clarify values

- ✔ to map a future path

- ✔ to provide coherence to a life that may seem 'scattered'.

Exercise

Step one   Provide the coachee with the following instructions:

1   Obtain a large piece of paper and a pencil.

2   Record your birth on the left edge of the paper.

3   Draw a continuous line mapping your life from the past into the future—map the high points with peaks and the low points with valleys. Write what your age was when the events occurred.

4   Using a colour pen, draw in the following periods:

➤ when you took risks

➤ when obstacles got in your way

➤ when you made the best decisions

➤ when you made the worst decisions.

5   Ask the coachee: Do you recognise any patterns?

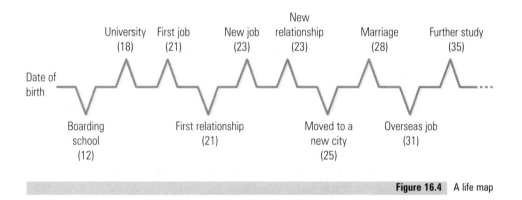

Figure 16.4   A life map

Step two   Review the life map and discuss the following questions with the coachee:

➤ If the life map belonged to someone else how would you perceive that person?

➤ What values are reflected in the important events?

➤ Was there a conflict of values?

➤ How did you overcome obstacles?

➤ Why were the best decisions the best for you?

➤ Why were the worst decisions the worst for you?

➤ What would you change about your life map?

➤ What regrets do you have?

Exercise

➤ Are you holding on to the past in any way?

➤ Where are you going in the future?

➤ How can coaching help you get there?

Step three   Develop goals and strategies to help the coachee clarify and move towards his or her life plan.

Self-characterisation

Self-characterisation, or writing a character sketch about oneself, is a journalling technique developed by George Kelly. Essentially, it involves the coachee writing about himself or herself in the third person.

 Checklist

How to use:

✔ as an exercise to be completed in the session

✔ as a homework assignment at the beginning and end of the coaching intervention.

When to use:

✔ when the coach is unable to get a clear picture of how the coachee sees himself or herself.

Why use:

✔ to allow the coach and coachee to gain insight into the coachee's perception of himself or herself and his or her life

✔ to monitor any changes in the coachee's perceptions and self-construct.

 Exercise

Step one   Ask the coachee to write a brief character sketch of himself or herself—as if he or she were in a play. The sketch is to be written by 'a friend' who knows the coachee intimately. It is to be written in the third person, for example, 'Bill is a generous...'

Step two   Together with the coachee, review the character sketch in the following coaching session.

Step three   Repeat Steps one and two in the second last coaching session.

Writing lists

Marion Milner, a psychoanalyst, practised an interesting form of journalling. She kept an ongoing list of everything she desired and everything she observed that made her happy. Milner claims that writing lists in this way taught her about her own happiness and how she could achieve it.

Writing lists clearly has a place in coaching. For instance, the coach can encourage the coachee to write lists on the following topics:

➤ What I want to achieve

➤ What makes me happy

➤ What makes me angry

➤ What I am prepared to tolerate

➤ What I am willing to trade-off

➤ What I am good at

➤ What areas of my life I can improve

Mind-mapping

Mind-mapping, developed by Tony Buzan in the 1970s, is an effective method of organising information and improving thinking skills. Mind-mapping allows us to see the big picture and the details. It enhances the free association of ideas, generates creativity, and integrates logic and imagination. Mind-mapping has a virtually unlimited number of uses within coaching. Some areas in which the coach and coachee can employ mind-mapping techniques include:

➤ Presentation skills

➤ Report writing

➤ Brainstorming

➤ Sales calls

➤ Goal setting

➤ Action planning

➤ Personal growth

➤ Time management

➤ Life/work balance

Mind-mapping techniques can vary in complexity. They can include the use of colours, symbols, images, even music. The purpose of this chapter is to review the basic elements of mind-mapping and provide several examples of its use in coaching.

1 A simple mind-mapping exercise

Exercise

Step one   Ask the coachee to draw a rectangle or a circle in the centre of the page.

Step two   Ask the coachee to write the topic that he or she wants to 'map' in the rectangle or circle.

Step three   As each idea or theme comes to mind, ask the coachee to draw a line radiating out from the rectangle or circle.

Step four   As each idea emerges, the coachee is to assess whether it is an extension of an existing idea. If it is, then he or she should continue the line. If the idea is a variation of an existing idea, then ask the coachee to draw a branch off the central line and label it. If the idea is a new one, then the coachee is to draw a new line from the rectangle or circle. The following figure illustrates the features of a basic mind map.

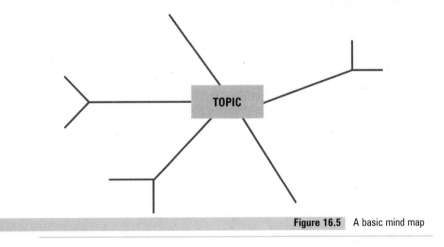

Figure 16.5   A basic mind map

2 Mind-mapping for life/work balance

It can be extremely useful for a coachee to use mind-mapping to establish a visual representation of all the major aspects of his or her life. Simply isolating the various areas of one's life can make it appear more manageable. The coachee can then focus on each life area, elaborate on it, and nominate features of it which are especially rewarding or in need of rebalance.

H. G. is the senior manager with a large accounting firm. While his career was on track, H. G. felt that he was not meeting his needs in other areas of his life. He was generally dissatisfied but found it difficult to pinpoint the specific areas of his life that lacked fulfilment. The coach encouraged H. G. to mind-map all the major areas of his life and the aspects of each area that he could explore in his search for a more balanced lifestyle. H. G. was asked to number, in terms of importance, those aspects of his life he felt were most in need of attention. Once H. G. was able to prioritise the areas of his life he most wanted to change, he and the coach set goals and strategies to create the desired changes.

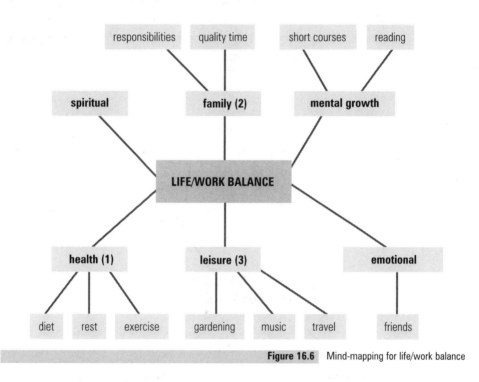

Figure 16.6   Mind-mapping for life/work balance

3 Mind-mapping for presentation skills

Coaches are frequently asked to work with coachees on their presentation skills. The coachee may be making formal presentations to prospective clients or simply presenting his or her views at a committee meeting. Mind-mapping makes presenting easier and more effective. It also helps the coachee deliver the message with more confidence and authority.

L. R. is a sales representative recently promoted to a position that involves making regular presentations to prospective and existing clients. Although his knowledge of the product is exceptional, L. R. regularly fails to present his knowledge and expertise in a satisfactory or engaging manner. The general manager referred L. R. to the in-house coach for work on his presentation skills. After the initial assessment and discussions it became clear to the coach that L. R. was actually skilled in the various aspects of presenting (he had enrolled in several workshops on presentation skills as preparation for his promotion). However, in the heat of the moment he became anxious and was unable to recall what he had learned. L. R. was interested in mind-mapping but did not have the requisite knowledge to use it effectively. The coach and coachee brainstormed the various critical elements of presenting and L. R. devised a mind map of these as a memory aid to use during his presentations.

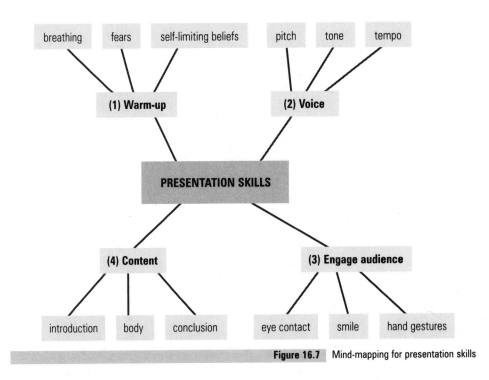

Figure 16.7 Mind-mapping for presentation skills

4 Mind-mapping for sales calling

A mind map can be particularly useful as a visual 'script' for individuals working in sales. It can be employed to isolate and prioritise the critical features of a product. Furthermore, a mind map can efficiently highlight and summarise the essential ingredients of a successful sales call.

Case Study   B. B. is employed as a coach in a large call centre. Part of her brief is to coach team leaders to work with new staff members. B. B. recognised that although the recruits generally were given adequate information and skills training, the information was presented in such a way as to appear confusing and, at times, overwhelming. B. B. worked with the team leaders to develop a simple mind map that could guide the recruits through the various stages of calling.

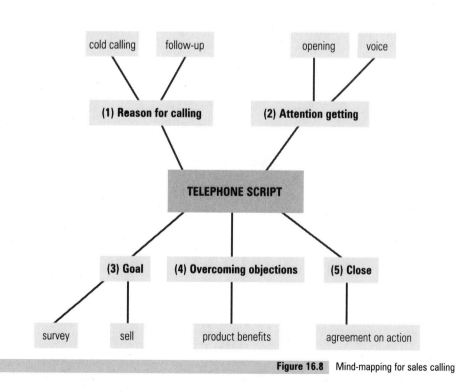

Figure 16.8   Mind-mapping for sales calling

Summary

The journalling techniques described in this chapter are suggestions rather than prescriptions. Some coachees may not appreciate the purpose or the value of journalling. Indeed, it may not appeal to all coaches as a useful technique. However, if used thoughtfully and creatively journalling can tap into realms that go beyond traditional forms of assessment and homework assignments. Mind-mapping can be employed in a variety of coaching interventions. However, individuals who absorb and process information visually may be particularly attracted to this technique, and creative coachees will frequently develop their own elaborate style of mind-mapping.

Evaluation

It is critical that coaches recognise the importance of evaluating coaching outcomes. As mentioned, coaching is an emerging profession and there is a lack of empirical studies testifying to its effectiveness. We can no longer afford to simply sing the praises of coaching. If coaching is to develop and attain true professional status it is imperative that coaches produce evidence to show it is effective and useful. Otherwise, it may be coopted by other professions.

In our coach training workshops we are frequently asked about evaluation issues and methods. Coaches who do not have a background in research are especially concerned about the role of evaluation in coaching and the requisite skills needed. The purpose of this chapter is to highlight some of the major issues in evaluation and to offer some general guidelines for coaches.

Some benefits of evaluating coaching programs

There are numerous reasons why evaluating coaching outcomes is essential. Some of the benefits of evaluation include the following:

➤ It allows the coach to prove to the client how and why coaching is effective. Also, the coach can offer prospective clients information that demonstrates a return on investment.

➤ It allows the coach to justify the advantages of coaching over traditional training methods which usually are not evaluated, or certainly not on any long-term basis.

- The coach can evaluate the effectiveness of what the organisation is currently doing and provide a rationale for how coaching can fill the gaps.

- Outcome studies provide coaches with information on how and why coaching works. They present opportunities to develop and update our knowledge, skills and abilities. Overall, we can build on the evaluation data to improve the efficiency of our coaching services.

Of course, we are not suggesting that coaches necessarily conduct complex statistical analyses of coaching outcomes. However, it is important that we are aware of the issues surrounding evaluation, that we appreciate its role in the coaching process and that we can develop our own methods of evaluation.

Responsive evaluation

Responsive evaluation involves recognising and responding to the interests and expectations of the sponsors and stakeholders indirectly involved in the coaching intervention. The coach has to select the level of evaluation required by the organisation. This will depend on the scope of the coaching enterprise. As mentioned, the interests of sponsors and stakeholders have to be considered and the evaluation conducted accordingly. In order to establish the needs of the organisation the coach could consider the following questions:

- What are the organisation's strategic plans for the future?

- What are the day-to-day operational needs?

- What personal mastery skills are necessary?

- Are the organisation's needs currently being met? If so, to what extent?

- How will coaching fit in with the current learning and development programs?

- What specific areas should the coaching program target?

- What gaps will the coaching program fill?

- What are the current methods of evaluation?

- What is the line of reporting—who reports to whom and what is the chain of command?

What are we evaluating?

The exact nature of what is being evaluated depends on the needs of the organisation, the issues addressed in the coaching intervention and the coach's own particular model or framework for evaluation.

An extremely useful method for evaluating coaching programs is to calculate a return on investment (ROI). The ROI is a measure of the monetary benefits obtained by an organisation over a specified time period in return for a given investment in a coaching program. That is, the ROI is the extent to which the benefits (outputs) of coaching exceed the costs (inputs). The ROI can be employed to justify a planned investment and to evaluate the extent to which the desired return was achieved.

Some costs (inputs) to be considered in calculating a ROI include:

➤ design and development costs

➤ administration costs

➤ facilitator or coach costs in the program delivery

➤ facility costs

➤ the coachee's costs (i.e. travel and coaching that is undertaken in work time).

The following is a list of some of the items that should be measured in relation to a specific coaching intervention. These benefits (outputs) include:

➤ level of knowledge acquired

➤ level of skills acquired

➤ changes in attitudes and behaviour

➤ changes in levels of effectiveness

➤ coachees' career progress

➤ program satisfaction

➤ program weaknesses

➤ employee retention

➤ business goals achieved.

However, as well as the above hard measures, coaches should also measure the following coaching outcomes in order to determine if they have been enhanced:

➤ ability to perform at optimal levels

➤ quality of relationship skills

➤ level of personal power

➤ ability to handle work pressure

➤ ability to handle personal pressure

- ability to handle life events

- ability to handle change

- emotional wellbeing

- level of creativity

- level of resilience

- strength of character

- ability to problem solve

- quality of work and home life

- state of health.

Operationalising

Once the coach has decided which variable(s) he or she intends to measure, it is necessary to operationalise this. That is, we have to specify what we are going to measure in relation to each of the variables. However, it is easier to operationalise, or measure, some variables than others. Measuring a coachee's career progress for instance can be relatively simple. It can be evaluated in terms of promotions, raises or career decisions. On the other hand, it may be difficult to measure the coachee's level of effectiveness in the organisation because it involves various managerial competencies. One way to deal with this is to measure the coachee's self-confidence or self-efficacy in relation to various tasks. Self-efficacy, as noted earlier in this book, is a person's perception of how capable they are of successfully carrying through a required course of action. The coachee can rate his or her self-efficacy in relation to management tasks such as evaluating staff, delegating, and making decisions.

Sources of data

Once the coach has decided which variables to measure in the evaluation process, and what elements of each individual variable to measure, he or she has to decide which sources of data to employ. Some questions to consider include:

- Will I use self-assessments? Which ones will I use? At which stages of the coaching process will these be utilised?

- Will I contact the coachee's senior manager or CEO?

- Will I approach the coachee's colleagues?

- Will I have access to and analyse performance appraisals and other records relating to the coachee such as 360-degree appraisals?

Measurement tools for evaluating outcomes

The following tools are standard forms of measurement employed in evaluating outcomes. We have adapted these from Cone (2001) and have applied them to the coaching process.

1   *Interviews*   As discussed in our chapter on assessment issues and profiles (see Chapter 4), one of the most common measurement tools in coaching is the interview or discussion. This can be structured or unstructured. An effective method of evaluation is to use the interview as a pre- and post-intervention measure. Coaches can interview the coachee, colleagues, managers and clients at the beginning of the coaching intervention, towards the end of the intervention, and three or six months later as a measure of the long-term effects of coaching.

2   *Self-reports*   As discussed in detail in Chapter 4, self-report methodology is an invaluable tool for the coach. Of course, with all self-reports there is the likelihood of self-presentation bias. Most of us are not completely objective when talking about ourselves. Therefore, obtaining information from a third party can be extremely useful.

3   *Ratings by others*   Most coaches are familiar with the 360-degree performance appraisals conducted by many organisations. While there are some problems with this type of measurement (namely bias) it is recommended that the coach obtain as much information about the coachee as possible. Ideally, information could be gathered from friends, family, colleagues and clients. In Chapter 4 we provide a competence feedback profile which we administer to the coachee's colleagues at the beginning of the coaching cycle, midway through the sessions and at the conclusion of the intervention. We have found that this relatively simple form of assessment provides useful 'diagnostic' information as well as evaluation data.

4   *Self-monitoring*   As discussed previously, self-monitoring or self-observation involves asking the coachee to observe his or her behaviour and record its occurrence. As well as providing baseline data at the beginning of the coaching cycle, self-monitoring can be used to track the progress of the coaching intervention. However, there is always the question of how accurately we can record our own behaviour.

5   *Direct observation*   It is generally agreed that some of the best data derives from direct observation. Shadowing, in which the coach follows, observes and critiques the coachee while he or she is performing specific tasks, is a typical example of direct observation.

When designing an evaluation process involving direct observation the coach has to nominate the following:

➤   What will I observe?

➤   Am I observing qualitative or quantitative changes?

➤   How frequently will I observe these behaviours?

- How will these observations be recorded?

- Will I score the frequency of certain behaviours?

- Will I use a narrative description? That is, will responses be written, or spoken into a tape recorder?

Reporting to the organisation

At the conclusion of the coaching intervention the coach should write a brief report to the major stakeholders about the evaluation process. The report should include:

- a summary of the personal and operational skills the coach is or has been working on, and how these have impacted on the coachees' performance

- the methods of data collection

- a summary of the findings

- a description of the benefits of the coaching program to the individual coachee(s) and the organisation

- conclusions and recommendations, such as the need for further coaching or training.

External evaluation

It may be useful to establish an external source of evaluation depending on the scope of the coaching intervention. Our experience suggests that participants in a coaching program are more likely to give objective and detailed information to an external source. There is a higher degree of confidentiality and participants are more open and honest in their feedback. When evaluating coaching programs we have found it necessary to work closely with the providers of the coaching service in terms of their objectives, the data they require and the procedures to be followed.

Ongoing session evaluation

Evaluation should not just be relegated to the end of the coaching intervention. To a certain extent the coach is always, at least informally, evaluating what is working, what is not working and what progress the coachee is making. As we have mentioned previously, evaluation should be built into the coaching process—perhaps even into the contract. Each coaching session should begin with an evaluation of the coachee's progress since the last meeting, for instance:

➤ How has the coachee transferred the skills learnt in the coaching session to the workplace?

➤ What obstacles were encountered?

➤ What gains were made?

➤ What victories has the coachee achieved?

➤ What habitual behaviour or self-limiting beliefs has the coachee become aware of?

➤ How has this affected his or her actions?

➤ What issues need to be further explored?

➤ Does the coachee require more direction in certain areas?

➤ Does the coachee require more support and encouragement in certain areas?

Our students have found the following guidelines, adapted from Mary Beth O'Neill (2000), to be especially useful in evaluating coaching on an ongoing basis. She too highlights the importance and usefulness of evaluation periods in the coaching sessions.

1 Ask the coachee to assess his or her own effectiveness in terms of the coaching goals, for example:
   ➤ the strengths he or she has recognised
   ➤ the challenges, if any, he or she has experienced
   ➤ the extent to which the business goal(s) has been achieved.

2 Give your feedback:
   ➤ Identify the extent to which you think the coachee has achieved his or her goal.
   ➤ Identify any challenges the coachee still has to face.
   ➤ Highlight the coachee's achievements. As mentioned throughout our book, it is unlikely that any true changes will occur in the absence of an appreciation and recognition of the coachee's achievements. The coachee has to be aware of his or her strengths in order to leverage them when facing other challenges.
   ➤ Ask the coachee to recognise any habitual patterns that he or she may have started, or avoided. For example, any negative self-talk, self-limiting beliefs or conditioned emotional responses should be explored. The coach and coachee can then discuss any triggers or cues that the coachee can be made aware of in order to avoid these responses in future situations.

3 Plan the next action to achieve the set goals, or reconsider and establish new goals.

Summary Evaluating coaching services is a complex and sometimes time-consuming task. We have attempted to outline some of the major issues that coaches need to address. We have also offered some guidelines which should simplify and streamline the process. However, it is ultimately the coach's responsibility to design his or her own evaluation procedures that are appropriate and acceptable to the individual coachee and the particular organisation the coach is working with at any given time.

PART THREE

Practice management and future trends

Establishing and marketing a coaching practice

Although coaches may be confident and competent using the various tools and techniques we have discussed, this is of little value if they do not have the skills to establish and market their coaching practice. While this chapter does not attempt to provide a detailed guide on how to set up and market a coaching practice, it does offer a brief overview of some of the marketing principles related to this exercise.

Many coaches invest an enormous amount of time building up their coaching knowledge, skills and abilities. Yet they fail to focus on marketing, selling, and building their practice. A considerable number of coaches are in transition, for example from psychology, consulting and training where many have been employees in the public and private sectors. It is more difficult for these individuals to establish a coaching market compared to coaches who already have a client base. However coaches, like other professionals, must market their services. Whether coaches are establishing their own practice and marketing themselves to the public or are in-house providing coaching services to the organisation, coaching interventions have to be promoted and 'sold'.

We have divided the chapter into two sections: guidelines for establishing and marketing a coaching practice as an external coach, and promoting coaching within an organisation.

Establishing a coaching practice

Develop a marketing plan

Many coaches hire a marketing consultant to work on a plan for their business. However, this can be expensive and unnecessary. There are numerous excellent marketing texts the coach can access, or short marketing courses they can attend. If the coach decides to develop his or her own marketing plan the following guidelines are useful.

1 *Prepare a capability statement*

The capability statement can provide the basis for your advertising brochure. It should contain:

➤ a brief description of your credentials—academic background, experience, qualifications

➤ a description of the areas of coaching you specialise in such as life skills coaching, executive coaching or business coaching

➤ a definition of coaching

➤ an explanation of why coaching works

➤ a description of the assessment tools and techniques you use to assess needs, accelerate learning and evaluate outcomes

➤ a brief description of the coaching process you employ

➤ a statement about the results the client can expect

➤ a history of your experience—the types of individuals/organisations you have worked with

➤ a definition of your role as a coach

➤ an explanation of your coaching philosophy

➤ a description of the coachee's role

➤ a list of the specific interventions/services you offer

➤ a statement about what differentiates you from your competitors. For example, you could provide details on what your 'banner' is and what value you add to the organisation.

2 *Establish your personal vision statement and your mission statement*

A personal vision statement propels and inspires you in both your professional and everyday life. It helps you control and direct your life. To develop a vision statement the coach can consider the following questions:

➤ What do I want to create in my life and the world around me?

➤ What do I really enjoy doing?

➤ What brings me happiness and fulfilment?

➤ What is important to me?

➤ What are the main values in my professional life?

> ➤ What are the main values in my personal life?

> ➤ What am I good at?

A mission statement essentially describes who you are, your core skills and what you stand for. Developing a mission statement can take time. It can be helpful to list ten to twelve words that describe your services in a way that is representative of you and your vision. After you have done this try and incorporate these words into one or two sentences that sum up what your coaching services represent.

3   *Identify your market*

As coaching becomes increasingly specialised, it is important that coaches nominate their area or areas of expertise. While this is not intended to limit the coach's services in any way, it allows the coach to target his or her markets. The following are some questions to ask when trying to choose your market niche:

1   Who do I want to work with?

2   What knowledge, special skills, and abilities do I have?

3   Can I describe my ideal clients?

4   Do I understand their needs?

5   How can I research their needs?

6   Can I provide the services to match their needs? How can I adapt my existing services?

7   Which clients do I most like working with?

8   Which clients do I least like working with?

9   What issues/topics do I work best with?

10 What specific products can I offer?

11 What are the demographics of my target group (e.g. particular industries, organisations, etc.)? How will I prioritise these?

12 Do I wish to offer short- or long-term interventions or both?

13 Will I travel to see clients? If so, how far am I prepared to travel?

14 What am I prepared to sacrifice? For example:

> ➤ How often will I travel?

> ➤ Am I prepared to relocate if necessary?

> ➤ Will I work longer hours? how many? for how long?

Develop a business plan

1   *Consider your life/work balance*

> ➤ How much time am I prepared to allocate to developing the business?

> ➤ How much time can elapse before I have my first paying client?

➤ What will be the cost of working longer hours—to personal relationships, to family, to my health and to my personal time?

➤ What rewards am I seeking, for example wealth, prestige, better life/work balance, fame, recognition, self-fulfilment?

2 *Determine your budget*

➤ What is the financial cost of setting up or developing my coaching business?

➤ What are the specific costs—new computer systems, stationery, business cards, advertising, etc.?

➤ How will that impact on other financial areas of my life?

➤ What development period can I afford before I get my first paying client?

➤ How much money do I need to cover the initial drop in income?

➤ Do I have a financial contingency plan?

➤ Is offering tried and true services (e.g. training, therapy) on a part-time basis and gradually moving to full-time coaching sensible? If so, what is the time frame for this transition?

3 *Establish your goals*

➤ Where do I want to be in three months time?

➤ How many clients do I want to be working with?

➤ What is my desired or projected income?

➤ What services will I provide?

➤ Where do I want to be in six months? two years? five years?

4 *Carry out a SWOT analysis of your goals* (see Chapter 14)

5 *Develop an action plan*

What do I need to do to reach these goals, for example:

➤ develop marketing literature—brochures, business cards, etc.

➤ carry out cold calling, mail-outs, etc.

➤ undertake further professional development courses

➤ acquire advanced business skills

➤ acquire a coach or mentor

➤ network with 'resource' professionals in other areas

➤ further develop products/services

➤ further develop a business system—client database, filing, general administration tasks/skills.

6 *Prioritise goals*

➤ How will I operationalise each goal?

> What will be my first step, second step and so on?

> How will I measure the success of each goal?

Some tips for marketing your practice

Networking

> Join relevant clubs and associations such as chambers of commerce, coaching associations and small business groups.

> Attend coaching conferences and workshops.

> Join or initiate discussion groups or meetings with practising coaches in your area.

Presentations

Coaching is a personalised service. In many respects the client is buying you. One very effective method of advertising and marketing your services is to give presentations on the topic of coaching, particularly your specialty area.

An external coach can offer to give a seminar to the organisation that has shown interest in his or her coaching services. Similarly, it is an effective method for an in-house coach to use to align others in the organisation with the planned coaching program. Ideally, the seminar should be attended by the decision makers in the organisation, and those individuals who will be either directly or indirectly involved in the coaching program such as managers, line managers and HR personnel. It is critical to incorporate a question-and-answer period into the seminar so that the coach can (1) conduct an informal coaching needs analysis; (2) demonstrate how coaching can meet these specific needs; and (3) address any questions from the individual attendees.

The following headings are guidelines the coach may use when preparing a presentation to an organisation or indeed any group of prospective clients.

Outline for a seminar on coaching:

1 What is coaching?

2 The history of coaching

3 Types of coaching relevant to the organisation

4 Specific, planned coaching interventions

5 The benefits of coaching—general, and specific to the organisation (e.g. how coaching will benefit the company financially, customer benefits, etc.)

continued...

The external coach can provide a free introductory seminar, using the above format, to a specific target group such as small business owners in the local area. It is advisable to provide participants with a handout that briefly explains:

➤   what coaching is and what it is not

➤   the specific benefits of coaching to the target group

➤   the specific coaching services the coach will provide

➤   the coach's contact details.

Speaking at business breakfasts, lunches and other business functions is also a recommended marketing technique. As with all presentations, it is crucial to establish the audience's level of knowledge about coaching and adapt the content accordingly. Presenting a paper at coaching conferences is another way for the coach to network and establish his or her credentials as an expert in a specific coaching area.

Direct marketing

Perhaps the greatest hurdle the external coach has to overcome is actually meeting and speaking with prospective clients. This involves direct marketing techniques such as cold calling. In our experience, many coaches would benefit from paying more attention to, and gaining skills in, the use of direct marketing strategies and techniques. There are many texts and courses available on how to successfully employ direct marketing tactics to enhance one's profile and attract new clients.

Coaches often run the risk of not developing a telephone marketing campaign because they are too busy focusing their attention on the following tasks:

➤   Spending a lot of time building a web site that will not attract customers. Once the coach has developed his or her practice, a web site is useful for current and prospective clients to visit and view the range of services. However, clients do not usually go to web sites to seek out prospective coaches.

➤   Developing and refining products and systems until they are 'perfect'.

➤   Mailing brochures to companies without any preliminary contact to establish whether they are interested in the coaching services.

Marketing in-house coaching programs

As mentioned above, the in-house coach frequently has to sell a coaching program to senior management and the individuals who will participate as coachees. The following steps are recommended to facilitate the introduction of a coaching program in an organisation.

1 *Step one* involves researching and gathering quantitative and qualitative data to support the efficacy of coaching in organisations.

2 *Step two* involves conducting a coaching needs analysis (see Chapter 3) of all levels of the organisation.

3 *Step three* involves choosing one section of the organisation, such as a particular department, in which to pilot the coaching program.

4 *Step four* involves developing interventions to match the specific needs of this department.

5 *Step five* involves establishing a strategic plan to expand the program into other sections of the organisation.

6 *Step six* involves introducing the coaching program at a seminar as discussed above.

The purpose of the seminar is to align the key stakeholders in the organisation with the coaching program. The in-house coach is clearly advantaged in that he or she knows the organisation well and can speak in specifics rather than generalisations. For instance, the in-house coach can highlight the needs of specific business units and the particular coaching interventions that would be tailored to these needs. An in-house coach is more aware of and able to tap into available resources in the organisation. He or she can conduct a costs–benefits analysis in real rather than hypothetical figures.

Summary This chapter provides only a brief overview of some of the central issues involved in establishing and marketing a coaching service. The extent of the planned intervention, the culture of the organisation, the position of the coach in the organisation and the specific needs of the organisation all impact on how the coach markets his or her services. Finally, paramount in the success of any coaching program is the coach's competencies and training in the use of the necessary coaching tools and techniques. Research suggests that many coaching programs flounder because the coach lacks the requisite training in the coaching skills and abilities necessary to implement the coaching program once he or she has succeeded in marketing it to the organisation.

Future trends and issues in coaching

Research suggests that more organisations and businesses will struggle with the changes inherent in shifting markets and a more diverse, sophisticated workforce. Power no longer remains the privilege of a few at the top. Individuals are becoming more empowered to make decisions, to innovate, and to manage risks in ways that affect the success of the business. Yet with these new responsibilities come new challenges and demands. Coaching will increasingly become recognised as the vehicle to assist individuals in dealing with these demands and realising their full potential.

We agree with those who claim that the twenty-first century demands that we move towards a world of individuals and collectives who are self-organising, self-directing and self-sufficient. Self-awareness, the ability to reflect and learn, and a sense of self-efficacy are essential survival competencies. Coaching plays a critical role in developing and enhancing these qualities in individuals, teams, groups and organisations.

Coaching is a voluntary partnership. It reaches its true potential in a trusting and committed environment. Today, some organisations are beginning to develop a more open and honest approach to coaching. Attitudes towards coaching are changing. It is no longer seen as a 'sign' that an individual is underperforming or that a person nominated for coaching is receiving preferential treatment. Coaching is becoming increasingly recognised, across all organisational levels, as critical to business growth and success.

Credentialling

Credentialling remains a vexed topic in the coaching industry. There are no internationally recognised organisations or regulations to monitor the credentials of coaches. Virtually anyone can claim to be a coach. Coaches hail from a variety of backgrounds including management, human resources, consulting, psychology and education. Some individuals leverage their personal experience as former managers or CEOs to sell their coaching services. It is this diversity of professions that contributes to some of the difficulties inherent in the accreditation of coaches and the establishment of credentials. Yet, if coaching is to maintain and develop its standing as a profession it requires industry regulations and minimum standards for coaching qualifications and competencies. The coaching industry has to be seen as a self-regulating and distinctive profession.

As we mentioned in Chapter 1, the issue of coaching as a stand-alone practice will become increasingly topical as more and more consultants are being trained as coaches. Consultant groups have their own client base, and knowledge and experience in selling coaching services to clients. Coaches in private practice may not have these advantages. The trend is that consulting groups are retraining and reskilling their in-house consultants to become coaches and are hiring external coaches on a contractual basis. With their widespread industry experience, consulting groups will further drive the coaching profession.

Certified coaches from various training institutions will, in future, collaborate and work together to develop the following: (1) training and academic standards; (2) specialty coaching niches and the accompanying competencies; (3) a code of ethics; and (4) the requirements for continuing professional learning and development. Defining the standards and requirements for coaching may become the province of national or state licensing boards, as in the case of psychologists, lawyers, doctors and other professionals. However, we may be several years away from reaching that point.

Even today though, life skills coaches in Canada require training, supervision and registration. Furthermore, some states in the United States have proposed regulations governing life skills coaching. As it becomes more accepted that coaching is a psychology-based process, life skills coaches everywhere will require training, supervision and registration like counsellors and therapists. It may be more difficult to regulate executive and business coaching.

Territorial struggles, professional rivalry, and hegemony can only detract from the recognition and status of coaching as a true profession. Coaches within the profession have to consult with each other and generate their own definitions and boundaries. Some issues pertinent to the establishment of credentials include:

➤ What is coaching?

➤ What are the specific types of coaching?

➤ What are the requisite competencies for each type of coaching?

➤ Which models of coaching are empirically based and validated?

➤ What basic academic qualifications are necessary?

➤ What is the minimum amount of training required and from which training institutes?

Ethics and coaching

Confidentiality

Coaching, as frequently stated, is a relationship built and maintained through trust. When a third party is involved, the issue of coachee confidentiality can be particularly important. The coaching profession has to clearly nominate the terms and conditions of confidentiality that bind all coaches. It is generally accepted that the coach does not divulge any information about the coachee without permission. Similarly, any data collected from the coachee or others in the organisation should be anonymous. However, does the coach have a duty to inform the organisation if the coachee is sabotaging the organisation or behaving in an unethical manner? Is there a question of the greater good? Guidelines for such situations have to be established so that the coach, coachee and sponsor are aware of the coach's ethical responsibilities.

Closely linked to the issue of confidentiality is the status of the communication between the coach and the coachee. Such communication is not 'privileged' as in the case of a lawyer and client. Coaching records can be subpoenaed. Likewise, coaches can be liable for giving misleading or irresponsible advice. The law of professional responsibility limits the freedom of the individual to give advice and keep client confidences. Coaches require some knowledge of the legal principles surrounding the coaching role. Standardised guidelines have to be provided for all coaches.

Psychological harm

The risk of the coaching intervention causing physical harm to the coachee, or to others as a result of the coachee's actions is, admittedly, minimal. However, a coachee may be at risk due to psychological harm including embarrassment, anxiety or discomfort. These states are more likely to occur when the coach is dealing with issues of personal mastery rather than operational or technical skills. Major change may mean that the coachee experiences some of these states. However, it is essential that the coach fully explain to the coachee that he or she may experience certain uncomfortable feelings during the course of the sessions. The coach has to obtain 'informed consent' from the coachee on this matter at the beginning of the coaching intervention. Coaches require ethical guidelines for managing psychological harm.

Limitations of competency

All professions recognise their areas of competency and their limitations. Until there are established standards and credentials, coaches have no external criteria against which to measure their levels of competency. We have to be aware of what we know and what we do not know. Closely related to this is the need for all coaches to recognise and tell the coachee when they are offering well-founded advice, or merely offering an opinion.

Coaches have to continue their professional learning and development. As we have mentioned throughout this book, this includes being trained, skilled and supervised by a clinician in the use and practice of the tools and techniques associated with coaching.

Coaching involves the continuous pursuit of the latest validated learning and change technologies. It is critical that coaches are familiar with, and trained in the use of, the tools and techniques of behavioural analysis which is based in the science of psychology. It was to meet this need that our coach training school was established. At this stage of its evolution, coaching is also beginning to draw from and apply knowledge from other behavioural sciences such as sociology and anthropology, as well as technology and economics.

Coaches require a standard against which to judge our limitations. Equally, we have to be clear on the differences between coaching and other, related professions such as therapy, consulting and workplace counselling. As we discussed in Chapter 1, each role has different underlying assumptions. We have to clarify these with ourselves and with the coachee. We are not suggesting that coaches who are also trained in a specific profession, such as therapy or consulting, cannot adopt this role in the coaching intervention. We do however have to clarify when we are moving into these roles, what it means in terms of the techniques and skills we employ, and what impact it is having on the coachee and the coaching outcome. Research, and standardised guidelines as to the definitions and limitations of each role, will help to clarify these issues.

Rules for terminating an assignment

There has to be agreement on the rules for terminating a coaching relationship, and the financial implications of this. For example, is a coach allowed to refuse to work with a coachee because he or she does not like the coachee? When there are time and financial constraints on a coaching relationship, can the coach terminate the relationship even though this may impact negatively on the coachee?

Relationships with coachees

All the usual rules regarding the sexual, personal and financial exploitation of others apply to coaching. Clear guidelines have to be established to delineate the boundaries of the coach's relationship with coachees and organisations. For instance, some coaches forfeit part of their initial fee for a percentage of the financial gains made by the coachee as a result of coaching. Others choose to be paid in stock options. While there is certainly nothing illegal or unethical about these transactions, they do raise the issue of the coach's objectivity and agenda. For example, the coachee's personal agenda and concerns may take second place if the coach is solely committed to raising revenue.

Guidelines for practice evaluation

As the demand for coaching interventions that impact on the bottom line increases, it is crucial that coaches adhere to certain standards of evaluation, particularly in an organisational change program. Some of the guidelines suggested by The American Evaluation Association (AEA) translate into the coaching arena. These are as follows:

1 The evaluation should be carried out in a systematic fashion and be based on data.

2 The evaluation process should be conducted in such a manner as to ensure integrity and honesty in the process.

3 All stakeholders are to be treated with respect, dignity and worth.

4 Evaluations should contain diverse perspectives and cater to public welfare as well as to the specific organisation or stakeholders.

Spirituality in organisations

There has been an increasing interest in spirituality in business recently. The trend is likely to continue. One explanation for this movement is that as people in developed countries experience more economic prosperity and stability, their basic needs for survival and security are being met. According to Maslow's hierarchy of needs, once these lower needs are met individuals move towards satisfying their needs for self-esteem and self-actualisation. Spiritual development is a facet of self-actualisation.

As work absorbs more and more of our time, individuals are demanding that it satisfy more than their financial needs. Personal and spiritual growth cannot be separated from the workplace. We are no longer prepared to 'forfeit' so many hours of a day in a work environment that does not contribute to our spiritual development as we define it. At the foundation of a spiritual culture is the assumption that individuals need to belong to a community, and make contributions towards building a better world. The globalisation of the economy and the advances in communication technologies suggest that collaboration rather than competition may be necessary for survival.

Some organisations are already attempting to induce a spiritual corporate culture, and 'spiritual intelligence' is highlighted as a management or leadership competency. Some of the recognised key elements of a spiritual culture include:

➤ honesty with self

➤ mutual trust and honesty with others

➤ commitment to quality

➤ commitment to serve

➤ commitment to employment

➤ a recognition of the importance of values

➤ a focus on optimal development

➤ the art of transcendence (i.e. being able to rise above ego and beyond the material world)

➤ an acknowledgment of ancient and modern spiritual psychologies and philosophies.

Interestingly, with the exception of the final two items, the critical role of each of these qualities in coaching was discussed in relation to trust and commitment in Chapter 6. Coaching interventions and organisations that fail to honour these aspects of human relatedness may become increasingly outmoded. Understanding an organisation's spiritual profile may become as important for a coach as knowing about an organisation's strategic position.

Leadership and physical fitness

There is a growing body of research that suggests that physical fitness is a contributing factor in successful leadership. Fitness contributes to stamina, mental clarity, and coping skills and these contribute to a leader's effectiveness. Coaching will increasingly focus on this aspect of the executive's life—even classifying fitness as a competency for leaders and managers. Of course, this does not imply that the executive or business coach will have to adopt the role of fitness trainer. There is already a growing niche area for physical fitness coaches. However, coaches generally will be required to:

➤ Be aware of the research attesting to the relationship between leadership and physical fitness.

➤ Be able to provide the executive with a basic exercise and diet plan if he or she does not wish to consult with a fitness trainer.

➤ Be able to devise adequate evaluation methods to measure the results of the fitness program.

➤ Be a role model.

Coaching temporary employees

There is a growing trend to employ more and more temporary workers. However, most coaching programs in organisations tend to focus on permanent rather than temporary staff. This is partly because it is often assumed that temporary staff focus more on the economic elements of their contract whereas permanent employees are more involved with and committed to the organisation. Yet current research suggests the opposite—temporary employees have higher rather than lower levels of job commitment and satisfaction in the organisation when compared with permanent staff. These results suggest that coaching temporary employees is worth the investment. Increasingly, coaching programs are focusing on maintaining and developing skills, as well as building and enhancing loyalty and commitment.

Future areas of research

As mentioned previously, there has not been a great deal of research into the effectiveness of coaching with individuals or organisations. Yet, as coaches, it is incumbent upon us to ensure that the profession is not absorbed by other professions or by the prevailing culture of control and command. Coaching is a distinctive profession and we must articulate this distinctiveness. We have to define what we are doing, what our processes involve and the underlying assumptions of our work. With this in mind, we suggest the following areas for future research:

1   The approaches and styles of coaching that comfortably accommodate race, age and gender issues.

2   The durability of the behavioural changes associated with coaching.

3   The relationship between coaching and the long-term effects on an organisation.

4   The aspects of the coaching process that most contribute to a successful outcome (e.g. the personality characteristics of the coach, the length of the coaching intervention, the quality of dialogue, goal setting, feedback, etc.).

5   The features of the manager as coach's role that most contribute to successful business outcomes.

6   The benefits and limitations of telecoaching and coaching via e-mail. How different are the outcomes compared to face-to-face coaching sessions? Are certain coaching issues best dealt with via e-mail, telecoaching or face-to-face?

7   The personal characteristics of the coach that contribute most to a successful coaching outcome.

8   The differences between various models of coaching such as the appreciative inquiry approach, the reflective style and the behavioural change models. Are certain approaches more effective for particular coaching issues?

9   The approaches and techniques that engender the greatest self-efficacy and self-confidence in coachees.

10 The characteristics of effective leadership.

11 The personality characteristics of a coachee that lend themselves to coaching. For example, are we able to empirically define patterns of resistance in coachees?

12 The ways in which leaders develop vision and align others with it.

Benchmarking

Most organisations recognise that their success and even survival are tied increasingly to human capital or the collected skills, talents and knowledge of their personnel. Yet investments in human development are difficult to measure and evaluate. At the moment there is a lack of solid, consistent data on how coaching affects an organisation's bottom-line profits. There is also a lack of data comparing and benchmarking the results of one coaching program against another. Without this evidence, many organisations will continue to be reluctant about investing large sums of money in coaching programs. Future studies have to examine factors such as coaching expenditures, outsourcing practices, coaching content, methods of learning and evaluation practices. Core evaluation questions have to be designed to be 'benchmarkable' across organisational type, coaching models employed and coaching interventions used. Emerging industry associations could sponsor these studies which would be conducted by specialist research bodies.

Coaching and business goals

Throughout this book we have noted the increasing demand for coaching programs to be linked to business goals and business success. Coaching has to nominate the measurable outcomes of a coaching intervention. These may include the number of increased sales, the levels of absenteeism, staff morale, the number of new clients and customer satisfaction.

However, while it is true that coaching should and must show a return on investment, this is not as straightforward as it may appear to be. For example, a coach may be working with an individual on self-mastery skills that include increased self-awareness and increased self-responsibility for thoughts, feelings and actions. The process may involve the coachee undergoing significant internal changes long before these changes manifest in perceivable external changes. If a coach is driven solely by the return on investment factor, he or she is at risk of reverting to a traditional training model that provides the necessary skills training in a short time frame. The collaborative, trusting partnership where both coach and coachee are engaged in learning may be undermined.

Organisations need to develop other methods of measuring the progress and success of coaching programs apart from the traditional bottom-line outcomes. Even now, some consulting and coaching organisations are going beyond measuring typical ROI outcomes. In the future, outcome measures will have to include the level of the individual's wellbeing, creativity, clarity of thought and enhanced relationships with others. If these improve so will productivity and the quality of the individual's work and working life.

In order to employ and retain top staff, tomorrow's leaders in industry will focus on enhancing the quality of employees' work and working life through appropriate learning and development programs. This holistic approach to the individual's wellbeing will provide organisations with bottom-line results, longevity and more sustainable, profitable business outcomes. However, a new way of thinking is necessary if organisations are to develop their people in this manner. Coaching is the perfect vehicle for this.

Summary We believe that coaching will continue to flourish and gain increased status as a profession. Yet, as coaches, we cannot risk complacency. We have to establish, from within the profession, standards and criteria against which we can judge ourselves as competent coaches. We also have to ensure that the marketplace is provided with criteria by which to judge and evaluate our performance. Furthermore, we have to engage in ongoing research into the variables at play within the coaching process. Finally, we have to be models of lifelong learning by updating and enhancing our coaching knowledge, skills and abilities.

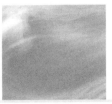

Glossary

anchoring A technique whereby the individual associates an internal response (e.g. feeling confident) with an external trigger (e.g. touching his or her arm) so that the internal state can be immediately accessed.

'as if' A technique whereby the individual pretends or acts as though a desired state, such as being organised or feeling assertive, has already occurred.

benchmarking for coaching programs A process whereby a business systematically measures itself against other businesses in terms of its coaching processes and procedures. It entails an in-depth analysis and data gathering to track each process and detect any weaknesses. It allows businesses to compare themselves with best or better practice coaching standards.

business coaching Generally, this refers to external coaches who work with individuals or organisations on operational mastery skills, such as organisational restructuring, developing change initiatives and working with groups in transition. Business coaches also work with start-up businesses, entrepreneurs and other businesses to grow and expand their services.

business practice coaching The methodology the business coach employs when working with individuals to establish and develop a business. The business model is applicable to start-up companies, entrepreneurs and other professionals wishing to establish a business. Different coaches employ different blueprints for their practice model.

clarification   A dialoguing technique whereby the coach invites the coachee to expand upon and further understand his or her own thoughts and feelings. It brings to the surface any 'blind spots' or discrepancies and paves the way for the coachee to become clear about the coaching issues, what is working and what is not.

coaching culture   The climate within an organisation that embraces learning and development in a context of coaching competencies and an attitude or philosophy of coaching.

coaching intervention   Any partnership between a trained coach and an individual, group or team to facilitate the purposeful achievement of goals within the context of constructive, honest and authentic dialogue.

coaching needs analysis   A method to determine an organisation's specific coaching needs by reviewing tasks, identifying job performance criteria, assessing gaps in learning and development programs, establishing organisational goals and objectives and defining potential coaching areas.

commitment   The mutual obligations of the coach and the coachee in the coaching partnership. It involves the coach making and keeping promises to support, guide and challenge the coachee. In turn, the coachee promises to learn, to persevere and to change.

confrontation   A means of inviting the coachee to become aware of discrepancies between verbal and non-verbal expressions, feelings and thoughts, feelings and actions and commitments to goals and subsequent actions.

Constructionism   An epistemology that underpins coaching. It states that we can only access meaning through social interaction and that it is through conversation and language that we create knowledge. No one person or school of thought has access to more truth than another. In the coaching partnership, the coach does not hold a privileged position in terms of knowledge and power.

containment   In coaching this refers to the coach's ability to 'hold onto' the coachee's feelings of anger or anxiety. By not responding in a defensive or judgmental manner the coach allows the coachee to more easily accept his or her feelings and express them in a more appropriate or helpful fashion.

counters   A term coined by McMullen that refers to statements an individual makes to counteract negative or self-limiting comments made by the individual's own inner, critical voice.

depth psychology   A generic term that covers any psychological system that assumes that the explanations of behaviour are found in the unconscious. Self psychology and Freudian and Jungian psychoanalysis are examples of depth psychology.

dialoguing Broadly refers to various conversational techniques, such as listening and questioning with intent and purpose. Dialoguing underpins the coaching relationship and serves to establish rapport, commitment and trust as well as to diagnose issues, solve problems and forward the action.

emotion An affective state with distinctive cognitive appraisals and a tendency towards action.

emotional intelligence Refers to the individual's capacity to perceive emotion, to integrate it with thought, to understand it and to manage or regulate it. Also known as emotional effectiveness.

executive coaching A one-on-one relationship between a coach and a leader or executive to help develop and enhance the individual's professional effectiveness and work performance. It can involve coaching for skills, coaching for performance, coaching for development and coaching for the executive's agenda.

Existential psychotherapy Derives from the philosophy of Existentialism. It focuses on the individual's immediate and subjective experiences in and of the world. It highlights the individual's free will and necessity for choice and action.

Existentialism A twentieth century philosophical movement which emphasises personal decisions and choices that have to be made in a world that is without reason and without purpose.

feedback Occurs when a coach, coachee, colleagues or group report back honestly and objectively regarding an incident, a situation or behaviours relevant to the progress of a coaching intervention.

fixed idea Any idea or conclusion the individual has reached at some stage of his or her life that has set up an automatic way of reacting or dealing with life without having to examine specific situations. Individuals with fixed ideas are unable to rationalise their beliefs and may be illogical or dogmatic when discussing them.

Gestalt therapy This type of therapy is associated with Fritz Perls. It focuses on broadening the individual's self-awareness in the present by drawing on past experiences, memories, emotional states and bodily sensations.

group or team coaching This type of coaching usually entails working with clients in a series of workshop-type sessions over a period of several weeks or months. Group coaching focuses on a group of individuals who share a common issue. Team coaches work with individuals who are part of a team, such as a project team or a brand team.

hard skills   Technical, operational or position skills. These can include delegation skills, negotiation skills, strategic planning skills and introducing organisational change. Hard skills frequently contain a component of soft skills.

Humanism   A movement, usually non-religious, that espouses a belief in man's capacity for self-growth, self-determination and autonomy. Man is not simply a pawn in a game but can make a difference to the world.

intrapersonal   The thoughts, desires and conflicts that occur within a person's mind.

life skills or personal coaching   This type of coaching focuses on personal growth and development issues. The life coach works with individuals to improve their lives, to work through transitions and to find fulfilment and balance. Some of the major areas of life coaching include: vision and purpose, health, spirituality, emotional growth, career choices, leisure and life/work balance.

mentoring   Sometimes confused with coaching. Mentors tend to be recognised experts within a particular field or industry, they assist the individual on the career ladder, advise and draw heavily upon their own experiences and tend to represent the standards, values and vision of the organisation.

Morita psychotherapy   Developed by Morita Shoma this type of therapy blends Buddhist thought and Western psychotherapies. The goal of the therapy is to immerse the patient in the needs of the moment so that he or she loses awareness of neurotic symptoms. It entails being in the present, not clinging to happiness and being responsible for our actions, regardless of our emotional states.

narcissistic injury   A psychoanalytic term that broadly refers to a blow to or an attack on an individual's sense of self and self-esteem.

observational coaching   Involves observing and collecting data on the individual's performance (phase one). In phase two, data is analysed in order to clarify the coaching issue and goals. In the third phase, strategies and action plans are constructed and put in place to achieve the stated goals.

operational mastery   Effectiveness in and control over those leadership or management skills associated with the technical or operational side of a business or organisation.

pacing   A method of establishing rapport whereby the individual matches certain aspects of his or her behaviour, such as tone of voice or hand gestures to those of the person with whom he or she is communicating.

path   A route or structured journey with established guideposts that a coachee has set out to follow with a coach.

peer coaching   Involves either one person with expertise giving another support, alternatives and suggestions (expert coaching) or two individuals of similar abilities giving feedback and support to each other so that both individuals learn (reciprocal coaching).

personal mastery   A form of 'self-overcoming'. It includes our capacity for self-observation, for facing reality and choosing a life that is in synchrony with our vision. It entails self-awareness regarding our thinking, our self-limiting beliefs and our conditioned emotional responses and the power to regulate these.

possibilities   The openings and opportunities that the coach and coachee generate together in the coaching partnership.

principles   The rules of procedure that are generally accepted in coaching. Currently these are subject to much variation and a lack of consensus. However, as coaching becomes increasingly professionalised, all coaches will recognise certain principles that inform the coaching relationship.

rational emotive therapy (RET)   Developed by Albert Ellis, this is a directive form of psychotherapy that focuses on the rational, problem-solving aspects of emotional and behavioural responses.

readiness for coaching   The coachee's current desire and capacity for coaching. The coach has to appreciate that it is the coachee's readiness that will determine the success of the coaching intervention. Coaching has to focus on the individual's readiness rather than that of the coach or the organisation.

reality therapy   Developed by William Glasser, this therapy proposes that we choose our behaviour and that we are therefore responsible for what we think, feel and do. The overall aim of reality therapy is to help individuals to find more effective methods of meeting their needs for belonging, power, freedom and fun.

reflecting   A dialoguing technique to show understanding of the coachee's thoughts and feelings. Reflection involves the coach repeating or rephrasing a coachee's statements, including an explicit identification of the coachee's feelings.

reflective coaching   Involves working with and encouraging coachees to reflect on their own issues rather than helping fix them. Through a process of questioning, listening and challenging, the coach facilitates the coachee to access the information, strengths and resources that he or she already possesses.

reframing   A dialoguing skill that gives another meaning to words or statements. Through changing a conceptual or emotional viewpoint to another frame that still fits the facts, the coach offers the coachee an alternative, more helpful perspective. Putting a positive spin on things, externalising and changing tenses are versions of reframing.

resistance in coaching   Refers to the coachee's opposition to or reluctance to instigate the changes that the coaching intervention demands. It can be conscious or unconscious and may be viewed as a natural part of the change process.

scaling   A simple rating technique whereby the coach can measure or evaluate the coachee's subjective psychological or physiological experience using numbers rather than words.

self-actualisation   The final level of development that individuals can achieve according to Abraham Maslow's theory of personality. Some qualities associated with this stage include independence, autonomy, few but deep friendships, a philosophical sense of humour and a resistance to outside pressures.

self-limiting beliefs   Any assumptions, perspectives or convictions that are holding an individual back from reaching his or her full potential. They can also include 'fixed ideas' where a thought functions as a 'truth' that the person automatically acts upon.

shadowing   A form of direct observation whereby the coach follows, observes and critiques the coachee while he or she is engaged in particular tasks. Feedback from the coach can be given on the spot (live coaching) or after the shadowing period.

slippage   The process whereby an individual reverts to earlier, unwanted behaviours that had been addressed and modified in the coaching intervention. It can involve beliefs, feelings, assumptions as well as actions.

soft skills   Includes a broad range of personal skills or behaviours such as self-awareness, emotional effectiveness, interpersonal competencies, insight and creativity.

solution-focused therapy   A type of brief therapy that emerged in the United States in the 1980s. It adheres to the principle of minimal intervention, it is solution rather than problem focused, it emphasises the present and future rather than the past and is most effective when there is a clear issue or central focus to the work.

systems coaching   Involves recognising, aligning, and working with the concerns and goals of key stakeholders, key business units or departments in a public or private organisation. A systems approach demands that an executive coach understands the executive's role in the system as well as the coach's own place in it.

technique   The 'art' and form by which coaches employ coaching tools such as assessment, managing emotions and overcoming resistance.

trance states   Altered states of consciousness wherein the individual focuses on minimal stimuli. Trance states can range from relaxation to deep hypnosis.

transactional analysis (TA)   Developed by Eric Berne, TA is a type of psychotherapy that focuses on what people say and do to themselves and to each other. It assumes that we make current decisions based on past premises that may no longer be valid. Our life scripts or personal life plans, which include parental injunctions are made early in life. However, individuals can transcend their early programming by understanding past decisions and making new choices.

workplace counselling   Sometimes mislabelled as coaching, this type of counselling follows a remedial model which emphasises deficits and gaps in performance. It is needs based and occasional and does not cater to the individual's development needs.

Bibliography

Apter, M. J. (ed.) 2001, *Motivational Styles in Everyday Life: A Guide to Reversal Theory*, American Psychological Association, Washington, DC.

Argyris, C. 1991, 'Teaching Smart People How to Learn', *Harvard Business Review*, May/June, pp. 99–109.

Beckhard, R. & Pritchard, W. 1992, *Changing the Essence: The Art of Creating and Leading Change in Organizations*, Jossey-Bass, San Francisco, CA.

Bee, F. & Bee, R. 1998, *Facilitation Skills*, Institute of Personnel and Development, London.

Beer, M. & Nohria, N. 2000, *Breaking the Code of Change*, Harvard Business School Press, n.p.

Boak, G. & Thompson, D. 1998, *Mental Models for Managers: Frameworks for Practical Thinking*, Century Business Books, London.

Bramley, P. 1996. *Evaluating Training Effectiveness*, Second Edition, McGraw-Hill International, UK.

Branden, N. 1994, *The Six Pillars of Self-Esteem*, Bantam Books, New York.

——1999, *The Psychology of Self-Esteem*, Bantam Books, New York.

Buckley, R. & Caple, J. P. 1996, *One-to-One Training and Coaching Skills*, Kogan Page, London.

Buzan, T. 1974, *Use Both Sides of Your Brain*, E. P. Dutton, Inc., New York.

Carr, A. 1999, 'The Psychodynamics of Organizational Change: Identity and the "Reading" of Emotion and Emotionality in the Process of Change', *Journal of Managerial Psychology*, Vol. 4, No. 14(7/8), pp. 573–85.

Carroll, M. 1996, *Workplace Counselling*, Sage Publications, London.

Champoux, J. E. 2000, *Organizational Behaviour: Essential Tenets for a New Millenium*, South Western College Publishing, n.p.

Childre, D. 1998, *Freeze Frame*, Planetary Books, Boulder Creek.

Clarkson, P. 1992, *Transactional Analysis Psychotherapy: An Integrated Approach*, Routledge, London.

Cone, J. D. 2001, *Evaluating Outcomes: Empirical Tools for Effective Practice*, American Psychological Association, Washington, DC.

Cooperrider, D. 1995, 'Introduction to Appreciative Inquiry', *Organizational Development*, Fifth Edition, Prentice Hall, New York.

Covey, S. R. 1998, *The 7 Habits of Highly Effective People*, The Business Library, Australia.

Divine, L. & Flaherty, J. 1998, 'Coaching Essential Competencies For Leaders', in Proceedings of the 1998 Leadership Conference, *The Art and Practice of Coaching Leaders*, UMUC: National Leadership Institute, pp. 95–104.

Dryden, W., Neenan, M. & Yankura, J. 1999, *Counselling Individuals: A Rational Emotive Behavioural Handbook*, Third Edition, Whurr Publishers, London.

Edmonson, A. 1999, 'Psychological Safety and Learning Behaviour in Work Teams', *Administrative Science Quarterly*, June, pp. 1–17.

Ellis, A. 1962, *Reason and Emotion in Psychotherapy*, Citadel Press, Secausus, NJ.

Erickson, E. 1963, *Childhood and Society*, Norton, New York.

Evered, R. D. & Selman, J. C. 1989, 'Coaching and the Art of Management', *Organizational Dynamics*, Vol. 18, pp. 16–32.

Fernandez, E. & Turk, D. C. 1995, 'Clinical Review: The Scope and Significance of Anger in Pain', *Pain*, Vol. 61, pp. 165–75.

Flaherty, J. 1998, *Coaching: Evoking Excellence in Others*, Butterworth, Woburn, MA.

Fransella, F. & Dalton, P. 2000, *Personal Construct Counselling in Action*, Second Edition, Sage Publications, London.

Fridja, N. H. 1988, 'The Laws of Emotion', *American Psychologist*, Vol. 43, pp. 349–58.

Friend, F. 2000, 'Coaching at the Executive Level', www.coachingandmentoring.com

Fritz, R. 1989, *The Path of Least Resistance*, Fawcett Columbine, New York.

Fromm, E. 1960, *Psychoanalysis and Zen Buddhism*, Unwin Paperbacks, London.

Gegner, C. 1997, *Summary of Executive Coaching Research Project*, www.coachingnetwork.org.uk

Gerber, M. J. 1995, *Thinking for a Change: Discovering the Power to Create, Communicate, and Lead*, Arum Books, London.

Goldberg, M. L. 1999, *The 9 Ways of Working: How to Use the Enneagram to Discover Your Natural Strengths and Work More Effectively*, Marlowe & Company, New York.

Goldsmith, M., Lyons, L. & Freas, A. 2000, *Coaching for Leadership:How the World's Greatest Coaches Help Leaders Learn*, Jossey-Bass/Pfeiffer, San Francisco.

Goleman, D. 1996, *Emotional Intelligence: Why it Can Matter More Than IQ*, Bloomsbury, London.

Hill, C. E. & O'Brien, K. M. 1999, *Helping Skills: Facilitating Exploration, Insight and Action*, American Psychological Association, Washington, DC.

Honey, P. & Mumford, A. 1987, *A Manual of Learning Styles*, P. Honey Publications, Maidenhead, UK.

Hudson, F. M. 1999, *The Handbook of Coaching: A Comprehensive Resource Guide for Managers, Executives, Consultants and Human Resource Professionals*, Jossey-Bass, San Francisco.

Hurley, K. V. & Dobson, T. E. 1991, *What's My Type? Using the Enneagram System of Nine Personality Types to Discover Your Best Self*, Harper Collins, San Francisco.

Kelly, G. A. 1991, *The Psychology of Personal Constructs*, Routledge, London.

Kilburg, R. 2000, *Executive Coaching: Developing Managerial Wisdom in a World of Chaos*, American Psychological Association, Washington, DC.

Kiser, G. A. 1998, *Masterful Facilitation: Becoming a Catalyst for Change*, AMACOM, New York.

Kouzes, J. M. & Posner, B. Z. 2000, 'When Leaders are Coaches', in *Coaching for Leadership: How the World's Greatest Coaches Help leaders Learn*, Jossey-Bass/Pfeiffer, San Francisco.

McGovern, J., Lindemann, M., Vergara, M., Murphy, S., Baker, L. & Warrenfeltz, R. 2001, 'Maximizing the Impact of Executive Coaching: Behavioral Change, Organizational Outcomes, and Return on Investment', *The Manchester Review*, Vol. 6, No. 1, pp. 1–10.

McMullin, R. 1986, *Handbook of Cognitive Therapy Techniques*, Norton, New York.

Magruder-Watkins, J. & Mohr, B. J. 2001, *Appreciative Inquiry: Change at the Speed of Imagination*, Jossey-Bass/Pfeiffer, San Francisco.

Mahoney, M. J. 1991, *Human Change Processes: The Scientific Foundation of Psychotherapy*, Basic Books, New York.

Maister, D. H., Green, C. H. & Galford, R. M. 2000, *The Trusted Advisor*, The Free Press, New York.

Mermelstein, J. 2000, 'Easy Listening, Prolonged Empathic Immersion, and the Selfobject Needs of the Analyst', in A. Goldberg (ed.), *How Responsive Should We Be?: Progress in Self Psychology*, Vol. 16, pp. 175–89, The Analytic Press, Hillsdale, NJ.

O'Connell, B. 1998, *Solution-Focussed Therapy*, Sage Publications, London.

O'Connor, J. & Seymour, J. 1994, *Training With NLP Skills for Managers, Trainers and Communicators*, Thorsons, London.

O'Hanlon, B. & Beadle, S. 1997, *A Guide to Possibility Land*, W.W. Norton & Co, New York.

O'Neill, M. B. 2000, *Executive Coaching with Backbone and Heart*, Jossey-Bass Publishers, San Francisco.

Priest, S., Gass, M. & Gillis, L. 2000, *The Essential Elements of Facilitation*, Kendall/Hunt, Iowa.

Prochaska, J. O., Norcross, J. C. & DiClemente, C.C. 1994, *Changing for Good*, Avon Books, New York.

Rainer, T. 1978, *The New Diary: How to use a journal for self guidance and expanded creativity*, Angus & Robertson, London.

Reich, R. 2001, 'Your Job is Change', www.learningfastcompany.com

Reinsmith, W. A. 2000, 'Archetypal Forms in Teaching: A Continuum', www.archive.uwaterloo.com

Reynolds, D. K. 1982, *The Quiet Therapies: Japanese Pathways to Personal Growth*, The University of Hawaii Press, Honolulu.

Riso, D. R. 1995, *Discovering Your personality Type: The New Enneagram Questionnaire*, Houghton Mifflin Company, New York.

Rogers, C. R. 1961, *On Becoming a Person: A Therapist's View of Psychotherapy*, Houghton Mifflin Co, Boston.

Schabracq, M. J. & Cooper, G. L. 2000, 'The Changing Nature of Work and Stress', *Journal of Managerial Psychology*, Vol. 15, No. 3, pp. 1–13.

Schein, E. H. 2001, 'Coaching and Consultation: Are They the Same', in M. Goldsmith, L. Lyons & A. Freas (eds.), *Coaching for Leadership: How the World's Greatest Coaches Help Leaders Learn*, Jossey-Bass/Pfeiffer, San Francisco, pp. 65–73.

Senge, P., Kleiner, A., Roberts, C., Ross, R., Roth, G., & Smith, B. 1999, *The Dance of Change: The Challenge of Sustaining Momentum in Learning Organizations*, Nicholas Brealey Publishing, London.

Skiffington, S., Fernandez, E. & McFarland, K. 1998, 'Towards a Validation of Multiple Features in the Assessment of Emotions', *European Journal of Psychological Assessment*, Vol. 14, No. 3, pp. 202–10.

Solomon, R. C. & Flores, F. 2001, *Building Trust in Business, Politics, Relationships and Life*, Oxford Press, New York.

Sperry, L. 1996, *Corporate Therapy and Consulting*, Brunner-Mazel, New York.

Stephenson, P. 2000, *Executive Coaching*, Prentice Hall, Australia.

Stowell, S. J. & Starcevich, M. M. 1998, *The Coach: Creating Partnerships for a Competitive Edge*, Centre for Management and Organization Effectiveness, Utah.

Wahl, C. & Williams, L. 1998, 'The Use of Metaphor in Coaching', in Proceedings of the 1998 Leadership Conference, *The Art and Practice of Coaching Leaders*, UMUC: National Leadership Institute, pp. 283–9.

Watkins, J. M. & Mohr, B. J. 2001, *Appreciative Inquiry*, Jossey-Bass/Pfeiffer, San Francisco.

Weaver, R. G. & Farrell, J. D. 1999, *Managers as Facilitators: A Practical Guide to Getting Work Done in the Workplace*, Berrett, San Francisco.

Webber, A. 2001, 'Learning for a Change', www.learning.fastcompany.com

Weick, K. E. 1999, 'Organizational Change and Development', *Annual Review of Psychology*, pp. 301–15.

Whitworth, L., Hinsey-House, H. & Sandahl, P. 1998, *Co-Active Coaching: New Skills for Coaching People Towards Success in Work and Life*, Davies-Black Publishing, California.

Witherspoon, R. 2001, 'Starting Smart: Clarifying Coaching Goals and Roles', in M. Goldsmith, L. Lyons & A. Freas (eds.), *Coaching for Leadership: How the World's Greatest Coaches Help Leaders Learn*, Jossey-Bass Pfeiffer, San Francisco, pp. 165–85.

Wycoff, J. 1991, *Mindmapping: Your Personal Guide to Exploring Creativity and Problem-Solving*, Berkley Books, New York.

Young, M. E. 2001, *Learning the Art of Helping: Building Blocks and Techniques*, Second Edition, Merrill Prentice Hall, Columbus, Ohio.

Zaccaro, S. J. 2001, *The Nature of Executive Leadership: A Conceptual and Empirical Analysis of Success*, The American Psychological Association, Washington, DC.

Zeus, P. & Skiffington, S. 2000, *The Complete Guide to Coaching at Work*, McGraw-Hill Australia, Sydney.

continuous change, 50–1
Cooperrider, D., 19
coping style, 209–10
cost benefits analysis
  of a fixed belief, 190–1
  and problem solving, 257–9
Covey, S. R., 125, 164
credentialling of coaches, 312–13

Darwin, Charles, 201
deletions in questioning, 170–1
Dell University, 48
dialoguing
  listening skills, 162–8
  open, 158–60
  questioning skills, 168–74
  reframing, 174–5
  and solutions, 178
  using metaphors, 175–8
Divine, L., 8, 9, 22, 30
Dostoyevsky, F., 19

eastern influences, 9
Edmonson, A., 47
ego states, 153
Ellis, A., 180, 181, 182
emotional intelligence, 196
emotions, 195–223 *see also* feelings
  accepting responsibility for, 212–14
  and anchoring, 221
  classifying, 199–201
  and coaching, 201–7
  definition of, 198
  guidelines for exploring, 203–5
  labelling, 215–6
  managing, 214–20
  negative, 198–9
  recognising, 208–13
  response delay, 219–20
  self-disclosure by coaches, 202–3
  stability of, 199
  techniques for working with, 207–23
  thought and feelings, 198
empathy in coaches, 124–6, 184
Enneagram, 112, 113, 114
Epicetus, 180
episodic change, 51
Erickson, E., 139
evaluation, 79–80

of coaching programs, 295–6
  external, 300
  measurement tools for, 299–300
  ongoing session, 300–1
  responsive, 296
Evered, R. D., 42
executive coaching, 14–16
existentialism, 8–9
expert coaching, 20
external coaches, 27–9

Fast Company magazine, 37
fears, as a barrier, 135–8
feedback, 14, 20, 32
  from coach, 77, 301
  from coachee, 75
  competency feedback profile, 104–5
  from management, 75
  after role-playing, 276–7
  and self-limiting beliefs, 183
feelings *see also* emotions; fear
  creating positive, 222–3
  ownership of, 147–8
Fernandez, E., 198
FIRO-B (Fundamental Interpersonal Relations
      Orientation-Behaviour), 112, 113, 114
fixed beliefs (ideas), 189–93
Flaherty, J., 8, 9
flexibility in coaches, 127
Flores, F., 138, 159
follow-up sessions, 81
force-field analysis, 259–61
four stage model of personal change, 32–3
Frankfurt School, 122
freeze-frame technique, 222–3
freeze-theory of emotions, 220
Freud, S., 225, 231, 232
Frijda, N. H., 199
Friend, F., 40
Fritz, R., 150
Fundamental Interpersonal Relations Orientation-
      Behaviour (FIRO-B) *see* FIRO-B

games, 153, 155–7
Gegner, C., 3
Gestalt therapy, 145, 151
Golberg, M. J., 113
Goldsmith, M., 8
Goleman, M., 125, 143

group coaching, 20
guidelines
    for coaching process, 59–81
    for exploring emotions, 203–5
    for introducing a coaching program, 52–3
    for listening skills, 163–4
Gurdjieff, G., 113

Harvard School of Business, 8
Hesse, H, 199
Hill, C. E., 125, 206
Honey, P., 111
Horney, K., 182–3
Hudson Institute, The, 8
humanism, 8, 38
Hurley, K. V., 113
hypnosis, 251
hypnotherapy, 221

IDEAL model for problem solving, 268–9
imagery *see* visualisation techniques
individual in the organisation model of change,
    36–7
individual profiles, 92–4
in-house coaches, 27–9
injunctions, 154–5
internal critic/inner voice, 191–3
interventions, for executive coaching, 14, 15

job analysis profile, 102–3
journalling
    book of one's life, 285–6
    definition of, 278
    diaries, 280–5
    guidelines for, 279
    life-mapping, 286–8
    self-characterisation, 288
    techniques for, 280–6
    writing lists, 289

Kelly, G., 272, 288
Kilburg, R., 8, 25, 143, 176

language *see also* dialoguing
    definition of, 158
    use of, 148–9
Law of Habituation, 199
leaders
    competencies of, 38
    and physical fitness, 316

leadership competencies wheel, 106
leadership profiles, 105–10
learning models, 22
learning organisations, 46–9
learning styles, assessment of, 110–12
learning styles questionnaire (LSQ), 111
Levinger, B., 52
Lewin, Kurt, 32, 259
life balance profile, 93
life skills coaching, 7, 18–19
life/work balance
    business owners' profile, 96–7
    for coaches, 306–7
    mind-mapping for, 290–1
life-mapping, 286–8
listening skills, 162–8

Mahoney, M. J., 85, 225
management, reporting to, 75–6
managers as coaches, 37, 42
Manchester Consulting Inc., 3
Maslow, A., 8, 21, 315
MBTI (Myers-Briggs Type Inventory), 112, 113, 114
McGregor's Theory X, 195
McMullen, R., 191
meditation, 243–7
mentor, definition of, 12
Mermelstein, J., 163
metaphor, use of, 175–8
Milner, M., 289
mind-mapping, 289–93
models
    of coaching, 19–20
    of learning, 22
    of organisational change, 49–52
    of personal change, 32–7
Montaigne, M., 181
Morita psychotherapy, 212
motivational model of change, 33–4
Mumford, A., 111
Myers-Briggs Type Inventory (MBTI) *see* MBTI

neurolinguistic programming (NLP), 221, 232
Newell and Simon, 268
niche coaching practice areas, 14–19
Nietzsche, F. W., 122, 181, 185, 199, 231
Nin, A., 278
Nohria, N., 51, 52
non-verbal communication, 231–5

slippage, prevention of, 79–80
small business profiles, 95–8
Socrates, 168
Solomon, R. C., 138
solution-focused therapy (SFT), 11
Sperry, L., 56
stakeholders, 64
Start-ups magazine, 12
stress, 17, 43–6
structured-question diary, 284–5
SWITCH visualisation technique, 250–1
SWOT analysis, 262–4, 307
systems coaching, 20, 25–9

team coaching, 20
  and brainstorming, 265
team members, profile for, 115–16
Theory E (economic value-driven change), 51–2
Theory O (organisational capability-driven change), 51–2
trance states, 251–5
transactional analysis (TA), 153
transactional dialogue, 160

transformational dialogue, 160
trust
  developing and growing, 138–9
  displaying, 140
  importance of, 138
  lack of, 141–2
  self, 139–40
Turk, D.C., 198

unconditional acceptance, 8

values profile, 93–4
vision/mission statement, 95–6, 305–6
visualisation, 247–51

Wahl, C., 176
Williams, L., 176
Witherspoon, Robert, 8, 16
work performance profile, 98–100
Working with Emotional Intelligence, 125
workplace counselling, 5–6

Young, M., 125